MISOGYNY, CULTURAL NIHILISM, AND OPPOSITIONAL POLITICS

Contemporary Chinese Experimental Fiction

Misogyny, Cultural Nihilism, & Oppositional Politics

•‿

CONTEMPORARY CHINESE EXPERIMENTAL FICTION

LU TONGLIN

•‿

STANFORD UNIVERSITY PRESS

Stanford, California 1995

Stanford University Press
Stanford, California

© 1995 by the Board of Trustees of the
Leland Stanford Junior University

Printed in the United States of America

CIP data are at the end of the book

Stanford University Press publications are distributed exclusively by
Stanford University Press within the United States, Canada, and Mexico;
they are distributed exclusively by Cambridge University Press
throughout the rest of the world.

Acknowledgments

I express my gratitude to both the Harvard Mellon Program and the Center for Chinese Studies at the University of California at Berkeley for one-year writing grants as well as to the University of Iowa for summer and travel grants. My special thanks go to my friends Rey Chow, Maureen Robertson, Mihai Spariosu, and Yue Ming-bao, whose support and contributions cannot be described simply by words. I also thank Can Xue, Chen Yu-shih, Hugh Clark, South Coblin, Marguerite Decker, Marina Perez De Mendiora, Yi-Tsi Feuerwerker, Thomas Gold, Lionel Gossman, Marie-Claire Huot, Kao Yu-kung, Wendy Larson, Gregory Lee, Liu Kang, Philip Lutgendorf, Susan Mann, Adriana Mendez, Norindr Panivong, Tim Reiss, David Stern, Eugene Vance, Fred Wakeman, Wang Zheng, Stephen West, and Mitsuhiro Yoshimoto, for discussions or/and suggestions. I am grateful to the two anonymous readers for Stanford University Press for their constructive criticisms. This project started with a seminar, and I thank my students at the University of Iowa as well as at Harvard University, especially Wang Ban, Zhong Xueping, and Zhu Ling. Ruth Weil did a wonderful job of editing the first draft. I am also thankful for support from my friends He Li, Yasumi Kuriya, Li Shu, and Qian Haiyan as well as from my family members Lu Tongxin, Lu Tongyan, and Lu Yuanyuan. Last but not least I thank John Ziemer of Stanford University Press for being such a terrific editor.

An earlier version of Chapter 2 appeared in *Politics, Ideology and Literary Discourse in Modern China*, edited by Kang Liu and Xiaobing Tang; reprinted by permission of Duke University Press © 1993. An earlier version of Chapter 3 was published in a volume edited by me, *Gender and Sexuality in Twentieth-Century Chinese Literature and Society*; reprinted by permission of the State University of New York Press © 1993.

L. T-l.

Contents

Preface

Four years ago as I was reading Chinese literary journals in the Library of Congress in preparation for a seminar on contemporary Chinese fiction at the University of Iowa in Spring 1990, I was both fascinated and shocked by what I was reading. Fascinated because a large number of works had broken away from the rigid conventions of socialist realism that had dominated Chinese literature for decades. Shocked because most works contained conspicuously misogynistic elements.

Since then, I have been asking myself Why has the subversion of Communist ideology been accompanied by a misogynistic discourse? Why has the emancipation of women under the Communist party not only failed to change women's inferior status but also provided excuses for current misogynistic tendencies? What is the relationship between different perceptions of the gender hierarchy and cultural nihilism, which has prevailed among several generations of modern Chinese radical intellectuals? What roles do women play in oppositional politics, the source of numerous revolutions in modern Chinese history?

The present book is the outcome of my attempt to answer these questions. I have used texts written by six Chinese writers as test cases for a cultural and ideological study of modern China. Except for Lu Xun, the writings of the other five—Mo Yan, Can

Xue, Zhaxi Dawa, Su Tong, and Yu Hua—belong to the category of a contemporary Chinese literary form I call experimental fiction (*shiyan xiaoshuo*), to borrow a vaguely defined term from contemporary literary criticism in mainland China. This form can be perceived as one of the most successful attempts to subvert conventions of socialist realism in Chinese literature.

The chapter on Lu Xun, the only noncontemporary in this book, can be justified by his influence on his descendants. The famous May Fourth radical has had a great impact on subsequent generations of Chinese intellectuals, especially these experimental writers. As products of an iconoclastic intellectual who was nevertheless tied to traditional Chinese society, Lu Xun's works serve as a bridge between traditional culture and post-socialist China. The other chapters of the book are devoted to contemporary works that illustrate the ambiguous relationship between subversion and misogyny from various perspectives. As a generation of intellectuals who are trying to subvert their fathers' subversion, can these writers avoid falling into their fathers' trap of oppositional politics by implicitly having recourse to their grandfathers' ideology (in this case misogyny)? Can they break away from the apparently endless circle of violence and vacillation that has dominated modern Chinese history? Does the gender hierarchy they are trying to preserve in their writings contribute to consolidating the basis of this vicious circle, namely, the traditional patriarchy?

MISOGYNY, CULTURAL NIHILISM, AND OPPOSITIONAL POLITICS

*Contemporary Chinese
Experimental Fiction*

Introduction

The June 1989 crackdown on the student demonstrations in Tian'anmen Square marked the symbolic death of communism in China; violence had become the only means to legitimize a discredited regime. Similarly, after more than eighty years of Communist domination, the declarations of independence by Russia, the Ukraine, and Belorussia in December 1991 led to the disintegration of the Soviet Union. These events resulted in the disappearance of Communist superpowers. Although the death of a Communist regime can take various forms, the problems faced by post-socialist countries in their transition to a free-market economy are similar. The party, as the authority figure, has gradually been replaced by money, which decentralizes any transcendent signifier, be it political, religious, or cultural. Although the Communist party still controls China, radical economic changes have undermined its political power. The transition from a centralized economy to a market economy and the collapse of communism have left an ideological vacuum.

To a large extent, the death of communism has provided those who live in post-socialist countries a degree of freedom. They no longer need follow the party line. Freedom, however, does not amount to democracy. The latter requires a balance between particularity and universality, individual and society, identity and difference, whereas the former, without being carefully contextualized, may simply mean an open identity or a floating signifier. In order to articulate a new identity, the apparently freed subject in post-socialist countries often chooses to construct a racial, cultural, or gendered Other against which she or he redefines her or his subject position.

In the post-socialist ideological vacuum, minorities, be they ethnic, racial, regional, religious, national, or gendered, serve as the convenient Other(s). The marginalized Other can be used as a scapegoat onto which one can project any existing social problem. The presence of the Other negatively proves the existence of a possible solution to problems, as if the elimination of this largely imagined Other is a means of restoring the good old order.[1] Since a clear-cut ideological division no longer exists in the contemporary world, a clearly defined external enemy has disappeared from the horizon of post-socialist countries. This external enemy may be interpreted as Western imperialism for the Communist party at the international level, or as the Communist power itself for some dissident intellectuals at the national level. In the past, this enemy was used to justify socialist society, which was held together by the party against the enemy. The trend in post-socialist countries seems to be to repeat the old logic of the Communist party—namely, to look for an Other to replace the disappearing enemy, in order to regain a "normal" social order, which justifies itself against the Other. The construction of a racial, gendered, or religious Other in post-socialist countries aims to fill the void left by the collapse of communism. To this extent, it may *prima facie* appear to be subversive of certain aspects of communism, such as a strictly regulated gender policy in the case of most contemporary Chinese experimental fiction. At the same time, the scapegoat policy allows the establishment of a new hierarchy in which the victimizers will sooner or later become victims, since the inherent slave-master logic of the old regime has not changed. Moreover, because the Communist party has already occupied the space of minority discourse by using the oppressed class, gender, and race as representations of its political stances, those who construct the Other in opposition to communism risk reoccupying the ideological position of traditional oppressors, which has already been subverted by this ideology.[2]

The construction of the Other in a post-ideological society also provides the lacking subject with a sense of identity as being different from the Other and the world of confusion with a sense of order, which is defined as the opposite of the common enemy. As long as the construction of the Other offers the basis of a possible difference, it may take the form of nationalism, racism, sexism, religious fanaticism, or homophobia. The difference, as a symptom, serves as the basis for a symbolization, to borrow Žižek's expression, endows the world of ideological vacuum with a meaningful appearance.[3] As illustrated by the cases of anti-Semitism in Eastern Europe, where the Jewish population is insignificant, and of xenophobia in the region of former East Germany, where foreigners are difficult to find, the difference may well be created by the subject in search of an identity on the basis of a fantasy. The construction of the Other, which does not depend on any substantial difference of the object, is in the final analysis a display of the subject's power over that Other. As a result, because of its fantasized nature, the difference needs to be sustained and reasserted even more by power and violence.

Gil Delannoi explains nationalism in terms of "two principal characteristics":

> The first characteristic is an inferiority complex expressed by a feeling of weakness, a desire for revenge, and an impression of losing identity. The second, which results from the first, consists of a fear of the Other, or a desire to exclude that Other. This may be transformed into a propaganda effort, in conjunction with a will to political and state power, which responds to the feeling of weakness.[4]

Because it is "such a flexible, if not empty, ideology,"[5] nationalism in various forms has been used to rearticulate the anger of Eastern European peoples in their world of ideological vacuum and economic failures. We need to remember, however, that nationalism is only one of the forms a post-socialist society may use to try to articulate a collective identity defined by a largely imagined Other. The search for an imaginary Other both as a negative definition of the subject's identity and as a scapegoat for a dead-end situation can take a number of different forms. Even in other forms, Delannoi's statement on nationalism remains valid: this search is often expressed by paranoia as the motivation for the will to power.

Women as the Most Significant Minority

In China, the Communist party still wields power. Although the Chinese people have already pronounced its death sentence, the regime still exercises control over people's lives largely by means of military force.[6] Economic reform, which has gone much further in China than in most East European countries, has brought not only Western investment and technology but also Western ideology, which serves as a counter-reference to the already shaken Communist ideology. Nevertheless, the bloody crackdown in June 1989, which marked the symbolic death of Communist ideology, also reasserted the party's political power by means of military force. In other words, like most East European countries, China confronts an ideological vacuum. But unlike the peoples of most East European countries, the Chinese people have not fully explored their differences, which are superficially repressed by the party.

In China the search for a marginalized and demeaned Other has essentially taken the form of misogyny, for several reasons. First, in comparison with other large countries, such as the United States and the former Soviet Union, China is ethnically a relatively homogeneous society. China's ethnic minorities, who live mostly in border regions, are diverse and occupy a relatively small proportion of the entire population. Due to the relatively insignificant roles played by ethnic minorities and the central power's tight control of them, nationalism still is not widespread in China. Furthermore, because of its transitional stage as well as its concentration of military force, the Chinese government, regardless of world opinion, has by and large succeeded in silencing its ethnic minorities such as the Tibetans by means of violence. Second, because Chinese leaders often came from the laboring class, there is a certain continuity between the past slaves and the current rulers.[7] Due to this continuity, political leaders have felt somewhat reluctant to use the laboring class as a simple representation of their political stance, since the representee and the means of representation would then become indistinguishable.

For these reasons, women were chosen as the most convenient component of minority discourse for the Communist party. Perceived as the equivalents of inferior men in the Confucian tradition,[8] women have indeed been the largest minority in Chinese civilization in the sense of powerlessness. Because of their numbers and irreducible differences from the leaders, women can be saved repeatedly and glamorously without being confused with their saviors. As the major components of minority discourse, women have been appropriated by the Communist party. This official representation of women by no means encourages a genuine formulation of them as subjects or an independent gender identity. By claiming to be the ultimate spokesman of the people—especially the oppressed people—the Chinese Communist party has articulated Chinese women's "objective interests." These interests are roughly summarized by Mao Zedong's famous slogan "What men can do, women can also do." In other words, in traditional China, a woman could speak only through the voice of her husband, who assigned her the honorable social function as mother of his male descendants. Ironically, in socialist China, the emancipated second sex also remains largely silenced. This time, women must speak through the voice of the new patriarchal order, the Communist party. Their "objective interests" are no longer limited to the reproduction of copies of their sexual partner (although this is still an important factor), since they themselves must become copies of men by imitating them in the public sphere. In other words, according to these two patriarchal voices, women desire either to be carriers of men's images or to become their images. In both cases, women's objective interests are the interests of their spokesmen, who have turned them into objects of men's self-interests instead of subjects of their own desires.

By the same logic, women cannot be truly equal to their masculine models in the workplace, since copies cannot emulate their originals. To this extent, the use of women to represent the party's political stance has objectified women's oppression; it is as if the power of their spokesman, the party, had naturally empowered them by eliminating any possible oppression of women in the present tense. According to the party's logic, women's oppression belongs to an evil past, and its disappearance glorifies their savior, the present regime. Consequently, women's emancipation, as a gift from the benevolent party, has paradoxically silenced any voice that deals specifically with gender issues, unless this can be attributed, or traced back, to an evil past. A spurious identification of women's objective interests with those of the Communist party has eliminated any possible "constitution of the duality of mythical space and social imaginary."[9] As a result, women cannot truly resist the current patriarchal order, since the party supposedly not only knows where women's best interests lie but also directly represents these interests. Any woman who attempts to articulate a subject position risks becoming the enemy of the party, and thus, the enemy of her own interests.[10] Nevertheless, women's massive participation in production has indeed changed their economic status and theoretically bestowed financial independence on them.

As Luce Irigaray points out: "Equality between men and women cannot be realized without *considering gender as sexual* and without rewriting the rights and duties of each sex in terms of *the differences* in their social rights and duties."[11] The apparent equality between men and women, largely based on the masculine standard of Mao Zedong's slogan "What men can do, women can also do" is insufficient, because it not only fails to address the problem of women's oppression efficiently but also contributes to complicating the problem.[12]

Women's emancipation, when limited to the socioeconomic level, cannot fundamentally change traditional patriarchal values. Contrary to early expectations, the apparently gender-free evaluation of women in the workplace is used to reinforce gender biases. Because the value system by which men and women are judged is still deeply rooted in the traditional patriarchy, women are still perceived as inferior to men. In traditional China, they were inferior, because women were not permitted to participate in any profession as independent individuals and financially they had to rely on men as their providers. In contemporary China, their participation in all kinds of professions continues to prove their inferiority. Since women *are not* men, they cannot be measured as equals in these professions whose male-centered standards remain unchanged.[13]

Their position as official signifiers of Communist ideology has in a sense deprived women of any subject voice, since their voices have been objectified and appropriated by the party. Therefore, only after the collapse of this ideology have women started gaining subject voices. In the post-Mao era, articles and books on women's oppression in both the old Confucian as well as in the modern socialist society have emerged.[14] Because of the demystification of the emancipated socialist woman, gender oppression in contemporary China has ceased to be a taboo.

The collapse of communism has not, however, necessarily dissociated women from their representational roles in Communist discourse. Because of women's function in minority discourse, certain attacks, supposedly directed against communism, are actually directed against women, as if they were indeed identified with communism. As we have seen, the almost nonexistent foreign population of East Germany and the Jewish population, which is on the verge of disappearing in the former Soviet Union, still serve as the target of xenophobia or of anti-Semitism in these regions. Similarly, the party's power to represent women, which has prevented women from speaking as subjects in Communist discourse, has been used to justify a prevailing misogynistic discourse in post-Mao China. Moreover, as is the case with nationalism in Eastern Europe, misogyny in China can be said to be largely motivated by fear. In the past, masculine superiority was secured by the thousands of years of Chinese civilization that excluded women from any respectable social profession except for that of reproduction. Women's massive participation in various professions as financially independent individuals has thus threatened the sense of masculine superiority. Because this discourse is often associated with subversion of communism, we must avoid condemning it simplistically, following a black-and-white logic.[15] In order to examine the formulation and function of this discourse in contemporary China, the present study focuses on its manifestations in literature, particularly Chinese experimental fiction of the late 1980's, in which misogyny serves as both a basis for and a limit on its subversive function vis-à-vis communism.

Fiction and Women in China

Unlike poetry, which has a long critical tradition dating from the first Chinese work of a single author devoted to literary criticism, Liu Xie's *Literary Mind and Carving of Dragons* (*Wenxin diaolong*) of the fifth century, fiction (*xiaoshuo*) has always been treated as secondary, so insignificant that it was deprived of a clear-cut definition or any kind of rigorous categorization. It was defined either against a higher literary genre, poetry, or against an epistemologically lofty form of writing, history. Moreover, in traditional China fiction was defined not only negatively (as in opposition to) but also casually (mentioned in passing). Not until the fifteenth century did radical scholars begin promoting vernacular fiction as an alternative to classical Chinese. At this historical moment, the decline of the imperial examination system, which served as the political basis of Confucian ideology, weakened the status of classical Chinese as the only official written language. The examination system, which had initially had a positive effect on social mobility, became more and more inadequate as the population increased rapidly and the economic structure changed radically. At the beginning of the twentieth century, the

May Fourth movement promoted "fiction written in the spoken language" (*baihua xiaoshuo*), since its language was presumably more accessible to the masses. Moreover, fiction in this context connoted the progressive West in its bourgeois ideology of liberalism and individualism. Unfortunately, the only promoters of fiction in Chinese history, either Ming and Qing revisionist Confucian scholars or May Fourth Westernized intellectuals, seemed unconcerned with the Confucian concept of "rectification of names" (*zhengming*) for *xiaoshuo*. Consequently, even today, fiction has been relatively loosely defined in China in comparison with its Western counterpart. As a habit, we translate *xiaoshuo* as "novel," although *xiaoshuo* in Chinese includes short stories and novellas, as well as novels. Sometimes, even reportage is described as one kind of *xiaoshuo*, "truthful fiction" (*jishi xiaoshuo*). For want of a better term, I have chosen *fiction* as a compromised translation for *xiaoshuo*. At the same time, I hope that its looseness may help illustrate the traditionally lower status of fiction in China, which has deprived it of any elaborate definition.

Like the nationalism dominating most Eastern European countries, the misogyny prevailing in contemporary China can be explained by the need to search for a different and oppositional Other onto which the source of all social problems can be projected. At the same time, misogyny can be traced back to the most significant traditional Chinese ideology, Confucianism.

In China, fiction and women have shared a common attribute, *xiao*. *Xiao*, as a diminutive in Chinese, can be translated as "little," "mean," or "inferior." In the *Analects*, Confucius stated: "Only inferior men [*xiaoren*] and women are difficult to deal with."[16] In other words, women are equal to diminutive versions of men, inferior in terms of both social status and morality. Interestingly, this diminutive term *xiao* is also used to qualify fiction.[17] In Chinese, "fiction" (*xiaoshuo*) literally means "little talk" or "little narrative" in contrast with the great narrative.[18] As a means of consolidating the social hierarchy, "rectification of names (words or titles)"[19] is a major component in Confucian thinking.[20] According to the theory of the rectification of names, the behavior of each individual in a Confucian society should be determined by the morality implied in names (titles), such as father, son, ruler, or subject.[21] As a result, "writing must carry the great principle" (*wen yi zaidao*)[22] in order to preserve the purity of names crucial to Confucian morality. In traditional China, the great narrative was supposedly expressed in its objective form, history, or in its subjective form, poetry. Given such a hierarchical concept of society and culture, it should not surprise us that in traditional Chinese society the subordination of fiction as a decentralizing little narrative in relation to the great narrative parallels the subordination of women as equivalents of little men in relation to "great men" (*daren*).[23] Furthermore, the analogy between fiction and women extends much further than semantics. In many respects, fiction and women in China have shared the same fate. Both have not only been the objects of contempt in official history and orthodox society but have also served as weapons used by different generations of Chinese intellectuals in rebellion against the existing patriarchal order, be it Confucian or Communist.

In traditional China, from different perspectives, fiction writing was dismissed as a lower type of writing vis-à-vis poetry and history. In the "Catalogue of Artistic Writings" in the *Book of Han* (*Hanshu* "Yiwen zhi"), by the Latter Han historian Ban Gu, which is considered the first catalogue of written works, fiction writers were labeled the "lowest-ranking officials" (*baiguan*). Yan Shigu, a Tang commentator, glossed this term as "being in charge of taking notes on insignificant gossip on the street."[24] By contrast, poetry was perceived as a means by which the poet expressed his ideals.[25] Naturally, fiction as gossip was not comparable with this prestigious high genre. Furthermore, until the Tang dynasty, *xiaoshuo* was not considered part of literature. One of the Chinese words used to designate fictional writings is "wild history" (*yeshi*).[26] "Wild" (*ye*) in Chinese suggests barbaric, unreliable, in bad taste, anonymous, obscene, and irresponsible. Therefore, the expression "wild history" situates fiction in opposition to an official history supposedly written by an important official, the "official historian" (*shiguan*).[27] This official historian, as spokesman for Heaven, was supposed to defend the truthfulness of his account of current events for the sake of future generations even against his current ruler and at the price of his own life. By contrast, "wild history" as sourceless gossip was indefensible and unreliable.

Thanks to the low status of both women and fiction in Chinese culture and society, from the Ming dynasty to the present, they have constantly been used by Chinese intellectuals to mark subversiveness and progressiveness. In modern Chinese history, fiction and women have shared a common fate in various political and intellectual movements. The common attribute and common fate of fiction as a genre and women as a gender are interrelated. Largely because of their inferior status in orthodox ideology and official culture, they can easily be used as spokesmen of marginalized and subversive positions. At the same time, their insignificant roles in official history have, to a large extent, facilitated the roles of fiction and women as flexible ideological signifiers. Lacking a proper meaning and place in history, they can more easily be shaped and manipulated to their users' content.

In the fifteenth century, radical intellectuals in a branch of Wang Yangming's School of the Mind (*xinxue*) (a Ming neo-Confucian school that tended to center the universe on the human mind)[28] moved away from the Confucian ideological monopoly by promoting the idea of the synthesis of Confucianism, Daoism, and Buddhism.[29] This move was partly achieved by some of Wang Yangming's disciples in the late Ming, who enthusiastically endorsed and promoted vernacular fiction as a more direct voice of self-expression than the Confucian classics, which were written in classical Chinese.[30] Because of vernacular fiction's emphasis on sensual experience, women occupied an important place in it. Moreover, certain promoters of fiction, such as the sixteenth-century iconoclast Li Zhi, claimed that men and women should be regarded as equals in their ability to judge.[31]

In the early twentieth century, May Fourth intellectuals sub-
stituted the vernacular language—especially in writing fiction—
for classical Chinese, which at that time remained the standard
written language. This reform has been interpreted as an important ideological statement of the iconoclastic position of the May
Fourth intellectuals vis-à-vis Chinese tradition.[32] However, unlike the late Ming and early Qing promoters of vernacular fiction,
the May Fourth intellectuals were strongly influenced by Western
culture. These intellectuals, a large number of whom had studied
in the West or Japan, believed that writing fiction in the vernacular language marked a radical departure from traditional Chinese
culture. They felt that this departure was urgently needed because
the majority of May Fourth intellectuals, despite their iconoclasm, were still implicitly determined by traditional Chinese culture due to their early intensive training in Confucianism.[33] Moreover, thanks to its connections with ideologies considered Western, such as realism and humanism, May Fourth writers
perceived modern fiction as an imported weapon in the fight
against the rigid hierarchical Chinese society dominated by the
old-fashioned Confucian ideology.[34] At the same time, women's
oppression, also associated with the hierarchical Chinese society,
served as a perfect emblem of this evil tradition. Consequently,
the inequality between men and women occupied a predominant
space in these intellectuals' writings. Like modern fiction, gender
issues became a mark of their Westernized modernity.

During the 1920's and 1930's, the character of Nora in Ibsen's
Doll's House became an important archetype for the Chinese
woman in search of independence.[35] In 1918, on the eve of the
events that sparked the May Fourth movement, Hu Shi published
an influential essay entitled "Ibsenism" ("Yipusheng zhuyi") in
the leading literary journal of this movement, *New Youth* (*Xin
qingnian*).[36] In this essay, Hu Shi, one of the three leaders of the
movement, treated Nora as a symbol of individualism, since the
housewife was bold enough to seek her independence by leaving
her family. By means of an interesting process of identification,
the individual self sought by the Norwegian housewife became

an indirect expression of the Chinese male scholar's subjectivity. This subjectivity was largely based on a value system that Hu Shi had acquired during his graduate studies in America, namely, independence and responsibility.[37] Lu Xun, the leftist satirical writer, also praised Ibsen.[38] Nevertheless, the well-known radical writer was much more socially oriented than the famous scholar and pointed out the flaw in Nora's leaving her husband as a solution by asking: How could a Nora survive in Chinese society without financial independence?[39] Nora, as an expression of Hu Shi's individualism, was turned into an expression of Lu Xun's concern for social justice. Mao Zedong, an avid reader in his youth of both *New Youth* and of Lu Xun's works, found an answer to Lu Xun's question: commit suicide.[40] In Mao's logic, the death of a young woman rebelling against an undesirable marriage was convincing proof of the evil nature of traditional Chinese society. Thus, the act of a woman's suicide contributed to legitimizing Mao's revolutionary power.

Since 1985, experimental fiction (*shiyan xiaoshuo*) has emerged as a significant genre in mainland China. In the late 1980's, the term *xiaoshuo* again came to be used to designate this newly emerging literary form, which includes short stories, novellas, and a few novels, written by a select group of mostly young novelists. Their works are characterized by a common desire to subvert the conventions of socialist realism, which has dominated mainland Chinese literature for about half a century. Half a century ago, inspired by the Russian Revolution, a large number of radical May Fourth writers sought a complete Westernization as a mark of their collectivism; their underlying concern was to save China as a nation by modernizing it in accordance with Western standards. In contemporary China, however, collectivism has been demystified and discredited along with communism. Contrary to the notion of their May Fourth forebears, for contemporary experimental writers the West has become the emblem of individualism. In their works, the extreme form of Western individualism, highlighted by violence, perversion, and death, exemplifies the ideological vacuum in post-Mao

China. This vacuum has been created by the agony of the Communist father following the patricide of the Confucian grandfather several decades ago.

As the title of their leading literary journal, *New Youth*, indicates, the May Fourth generation intended to reverse the father-son hierarchy, which had been secured by a central notion of Confucianism, filial piety, for thousands of years. For these young rebellious intellectuals, youth represented the future. By the 1980's, the previously hopeful youth had become aged fathers. This change makes their sons' position even more difficult to define; although their rebellion may resemble that of their Communist fathers, opposition to the father may by contrast lead them back to the Confucian grandfather. How can the sons, caught between their fathers and grandfathers, find a space of their own between the silenced but no less deep-rooted Confucian tradition and communism, which was originally iconoclastic? They can choose to change their fathers' logic—namely, adopt a more radically democratic attitude and renounce the desire to establish their own objective order, a new hierarchy. Or they may choose an oppositional politics following the logic of their fathers—namely, trying to justify the objectivity of a potentially new social order in which sons take the place of their fathers. Most experimental fiction writers seem to have chosen the second option as an easy solution by uncritically endorsing misogynistic tendencies in contemporary China.

Partly due to this choice, the majority of experimental fiction writers have articulated their disillusionment with communism as an implicit revival of the Confucian patriarchy by means of misogynistic discourse. In this discourse, women symbolically return to their status as inferior men as defined by the Confucian tradition. Interestingly, women, in their long representational journey associated with the fate of fiction, have come full course. The revived Confucian (grand)father, however, is disguised as a Westerner—as Adam, for example, the pen name used in 1986 by a Chinese male essayist in an article entitled "Adam's Bewilderment" ("Yadang de kunhuo") that asserted masculine superiority. A number of Chinese male readers welcomed this article as the best ever published by the journal *Chinese Women* (*Zhongguo funü*), because, according to them, it served as an outlet for men's anger.[41]

Each of the three intellectual rebellions in recent Chinese history was followed by political changes—which were very often brought about by violent revolution. During the seventeenth century, the libertinism of Wang Yangming's disciples was cited as the cause of the fall of the Ming dynasty—the last empire dominated by Han Chinese.[42] The May Fourth movement at the beginning of the twentieth century can be perceived as a prelude to the Communist revolution. One of the three leaders of the movement in 1919, Chen Duxiu, participated in the founding of the Chinese Communist party two years later.[43] Chen was also the editor of *New Youth*, to which Li Dazhao, another founding father of the Communist party and Mao Zedong's teacher, was an active contributor during the late 1910's and early 1920's.[44] Furthermore, a large number of May Fourth leftist intellectuals joined the Communist party, which, at that particular historical moment, they considered the only possible catalyst for radical change in China and in its relationship with Western imperialism.[45] In contemporary China, discontent similar to that expressed in experimental fiction during the 1980's largely motivated the student demonstrations in Tian'anmen Square, which led to the crackdown on June 4, 1989, by the Communist regime. It is not an exaggeration to take Chinese experimental fiction as a literary expression of this movement, despite its writers' declared contempt for politics in favor of a pure literature.[46] Their contempt for politics is itself highly political, since it aims to subvert the slavery of literature to communism imposed by the Communist party.[47]

In these three historical moments, radical intellectuals in China have, to different degrees, used women to represent their ideological closure. A case in point is the transformation of Ibsen's Nora into different images of the Chinese woman in search of independence during the early twentieth century. A sinified Nora signified individualism for the humanist Hu Shi, the demand for social justice for the leftist Lu Xun, and the justification for a violent revolution for the Communist Mao Zedong. As a mostly silent sex, the women portrayed in their writings iconize and stabilize certain meanings that serve as a problematized and fictionalized ground for the male writer's ideological stance or subjective identity. Women's inferiority vis-à-vis their saviors or their rapists is crucial in each of these forms of fiction in order to make the world of fiction "meaningful." Some radical scholars of the late Ming were accused of raping other people's wives.[48] The May Fourth radical intellectuals, and later the Communist party, represent a version of women's salvation.[49] Furthermore, for three of the contemporary experimental male writers studied in this book, Mo Yan, Su Tong, and Yu Hua, rape is a both favorite and favorable theme in their portrayals of sexual relations. In the writings of Zhaxi Dawa, the fourth contemporary writer studied here, women's bodies are transformed into pure signifiers either of the ultimate truth in a mysterious sense or of an impossible harmony between ancient Tibet and the modern West. As a result, their transformation into bearers of meanings for a sacred cause often makes women's bodies untouchable. In the final analysis, their saviors and rapists are not so different in regard to women. In both cases, women's silent sufferings are instrumental to the male writers' representations of their projected self-images. The female body is a locus on which male subjects attest their power—either benevolently or malevolently. To a large extent, despite their benevolence, the saviors are not necessarily less indifferent toward women as their saved objects than are the rapists toward them as objects of sexual violence; both are satisfied as long as they can prove their points. In both cases, after the instrumental uses of their bodies, women—who have never truly formulated subject voices—are bound to be forgotten.

An Unstable Balance Between Freedom and Equality

Ironically, the great revolutionary praised by Mao Zedong and his party, Lu Xun, adopted a rather skeptical attitude toward revolution. His deeply rooted skepticism, expressed more than seven decades ago, is today proving highly insightful. Lu Xun's skepticism resulted from a rather pessimistic view of human nature at a moment when humanism prevailed among Chinese radical intellectuals. For Lu Xun, revolution represented hope because it could destroy traditional Chinese society. At the same time, an underlying question remained: Since the revolutionaries will replace the old rulers in a revolution, why should the people trust their new rulers more than the old if human beings in power cannot surrender their possessive nature?[50] Several decades after Lu Xun's death, his hope for revolution has been fulfilled to the extent that the old evil society has been destroyed by the Communist party. At the same time, his fears have also been realized—the socialist revolution, which to a large extent amounts to a transition of power from one emperor to another has not altered the fundamental power structure.[51]

To a certain extent, *Hegemony and Socialist Strategy* by Ernesto Laclau and Chantal Mouffe can be seen as a tentative response to the question that underlies the works of the Chinese radical writer of more than half a century ago.[52] According to Laclau and Mouffe, one needs to have recourse to hegemonic practice to avoid violent and useless transitions of power. For them, hegemonic practice is a basic function in a democratic society, since it constantly enables dispersed subjects to articulate and rearticulate themselves as equal participants in the process. Instead of searching for an objective order that dominates society, hegemonic practice constitutes and limits a social order as "an absent totality."[53] As a result, no social order, forced to reveal itself in its historicity and contingency, can claim an objectivity that allows it to silence voices different from its own. For Laclau and Mouffe, relativization of the social order makes a radical democratization possible. In other words, democracy must function in accordance with a logic of equivalence instead of a logic of dominance. The logic of equivalence implies "a radical pluralism," in which "each term of this plurality of identities finds within itself the principle of its own validity, without this having to be sought in a transcendent or underlying positive ground for the hierarchy of meaning of them all and the source and guarantee of their legitimacy."[54]

Since all transcendent signifiers—God, the Mandate of Heaven, the Communist paradise—have lost their magic ability to preserve a stable image of social order, post-socialist society reveals its inherent impossibility.[55] This impossibility can also be interpreted as an open-endedness or as an absence of totality, which constitutes and limits what we call society. Due to an increasing demystification of the idea of objectivity in the social order, a society based on a spurious transparency between the spokesman of its people and the "objective interests of different groups" can no longer survive in our increasingly decentralized world, which is at the same time less and less bound by geopolitical divisions. Meanwhile, the trend toward pluralism encourages more and more diversified subject positions to articulate and to rearticulate themselves. Therefore, an extreme model of liberalism based on "possessive individualism" is also bound to be destroyed by the increasing number of different, potentially conflicting, subject positions.[56]

Laclau and Mouffe's theory may help us better understand the cause of the ideological vacuum in post-socialist countries. This situation can be considered highly promising, since it has created an "organic crisis"[57] that makes hegemonic articulation unavoidable. Although hegemony does not amount to democracy, hegemonic articulation, by its open-endedness, makes democracy possible provided the articulation is based on a dynamic balance between individual freedom and the equalitarian imaginary.[58]

Without this balance, however, the "organic crisis" may lead to the formation of a new discourse that again privileges one dominant voice either in the name of egalitarian ethics or individual freedom. In this case, hegemonic practice risks becoming a *mauvais infini*, in which successive hegemonic articulations alternately emphasize collectivism or individualism without changing the fundamental structure of society. Whether collectivist or individualistic, the newly established order is still based on the suppression of difference. To a large extent, the history of modern China provides a good example of the *mauvais infini*. Without too much success, numerous revolutions in one way or another have attempted to democratize China over the course of the twentieth century.

These failed revolutions may partly be explained by their failure to acknowledge the precarious nature of any social order, especially the one the revolutionaries were in the process of establishing. In other words, subversive subjects believed in and tried to assert their new order, not by means of a legal system to which, along with other people, the subjects themselves must submit, but by means of the "objective" superiority of their new order. The new order thereby often became as inflexible as the old hierarchy, if not more inflexible. As a result, numerous revolutions amounted to nothing more than a power transition in which new emperors with different names replaced the old without changing the fundamental structure of the empire. Viewed in this light, Lu Xun's skepticism about revolution is particularly perceptive.

Nowadays, the vacuum left by the collapse of communism has generated an organic crisis. Will the different antagonistic forces be able to move in the direction of democratization? At a similar historical moment of generalized crisis, Lu Xun and his generation of radical intellectuals failed in their attempt at democratization by finally letting the party speak for the people. They did so partly because they tried to play the roles of saviors by speaking for the silent and oppressed Other, such as women, instead of engaging in dialogues with the victims they intended to save.[59] Will the new generation of advocates for democracy repeat the same mistake from a different perspective by letting their possessive individualism speak in the name of individual freedom? This mistake includes, as in the case of experimental fiction, their search for male subjectivity in the degraded image of woman as the objectified Other.

Despite their desire to subvert Communist discourse, most works of experimental fiction are characterized by pronounced misogynistic traits. Mo Yan's utopia of a masculine kingdom is based on a reconstruction of a past that depends largely on a clear-cut gender hierarchy. Zhaxi Dawa often uses the female body as the only possible signifier in his attempt to regain a mystical totality, which has been lost at either the cultural or the religious level. Su Tong blames women's animality for men's sexual failures, although the same animality serves as the most significant mark of the inferior sex in his system of sexual differentiation. In Yu Hua's world of violence, women are often reduced to abstract numbers or pieces of meat that to various degrees satisfy men's sadistic sexual appetites. From different perspectives these writers are participating in the formation of a misogynistic discourse, which prevails among a large number of Chinese (male) intellectuals. This formation follows an implicit logic: since women's emancipation is part of the Communist legacy, the subversion of communism to a large extent justifies the effort to force women to return to their traditional position as the inferior sex. These intellectuals can thereby create a convenient Other onto which they project their social problems, as if the largely imaginary empowerment of women were the genuine source of the disempowerment of men. The uncritical endorsement of misogynistic discourse necessarily limits the subversive potential of these writers. Since this endorsement implies an unconditional acceptance of at least one hierarchy, that of gender, their subversion of the party's hierarchy becomes more limited and less effective. The legitimation of the sisters' oppression by their brothers inadvertently justifies the sons' oppression by their aged fathers.

Naturally, experimental fiction does not necessarily amount to the democratic movement in China. But as arguably the foremost avant-garde literary form during the late 1980's, this movement can at least be said to be an indirect expression of the subversive trend in contemporary China. Moreover, a number of advocates of experimental fiction were actively involved in the student demonstrations in 1989.[60] On the one hand, the endorsement of prevailing misogynistic discourse by experimental fiction writers largely limits their subversive potential, since "the cultural construction of sex into gender and the asymmetry that characterizes all gender systems cross-culturally (though each in its particular ways) are understood as systematically linked to the organization of social inequality."[61] Sexism in China cannot be isolated from the racism and social prejudice against the working class manifested in the student movement during the late 1980's.[62] On the other hand, despite their shocking degradation of women, there is still a certain hope (paradoxically because of their hopelessness and negativity) in these experimental writings, which can be perceived as a sample of contemporary intellectual trends in China.

The May Fourth radical intellectuals in general, except for Lu Xun and a few others, were much more faithful to their belief in social justice as an objective and objectifiable order by which every action could be rationally measured. Moreover, this rationality, which became a kind of natural law for most May Fourth radicals, was based largely on a somewhat superficial importation of Western values. In general, the May Fourth writers were much less willing to question the objectivity of their own implied order than were their descendants of the 1980's. The disillusionment with communism as a means of collective salvation has generated a much deeper skepticism among contemporary experimental writers vis-à-vis any objective order. Because of their deeply rooted skepticism, they cannot in good conscience ignore the relativity of any discourse, including their own. Supported by certain ideas of Western individualism, their effort to search for a firm ground in the traditional gender hierarchy results more from nostalgia than from any faith. Even their misogynistic portrayal of women has, to a certain extent, pointed out the hopelessness of such an attempt. Mo Yan's kingdom of masculinity based on sex and violence can be located only in a utopian past. Zhaxi Dawa's use of the female body as the ultimate signifier of religion and culture reveals a radical relativization of all ideological and cultural values. In the final analysis, the presumably sacred signified that sustains the identity of the male subject is no less empty than its signifier, the female body. Su Tong's attempt to reinforce sexual hierarchy by means of a debasement of femininity is symptomatic of a fundamental crisis in the very notion of masculinity, since the sexual dead-end cannot avoid affecting male subjectivity at least as much as it does its female objects. Yu Hua's order of violence can only be established on the condition of a conspicuous exclusion or abstraction of women, whose absence silently questions this order. In a sense, their misogynistic gesture is all the more aggressive largely because these authors are, at a deeper level, aware of the fictionality of the traditional gender hierarchy that is used as a firm ground for their search for male subjectivity. In the final analysis, their search becomes a nostalgic expression of an "objective" order that can never be restored.

At the beginning of the century, Lu Xun talked about the hope for destruction, exemplified by revolution. At the end of the century, Chinese experimental fiction writers speak of the destruction of hope by means of revolution. The absence of any hope for the foreseeable future forces the new generation of writers to practice a kind of involuntary pluralism, which is in its turn constantly subverting, and subverted by, the prevailing misogynistic discourse. To this extent, the discourse itself becomes potentially open-ended, because it cannot avoid undermining its own basis. As a result, the inability of these works to effect any closure inadvertently leaves room for the expression of other voices, among which we may count Can Xue's.

As a woman writer, Can Xue's daring experiment with language questions both communism and the assumption of a masculine monopoly of language that prevails among contemporary Chinese experimental writers. This double subversion, in its own perverse way, has attracted and angered a number of Chinese critics, essentially male, who have for the most part attributed Can Xue's originality to her imagined madness. In China the controversial status of Can Xue's works makes them all the more interesting since they open a new alternative to the majority of male writers' painstaking and somehow useless effort to search for solid ground.

Furthermore, the dead-end of gender hierarchy portrayed by these writers unwittingly demonstrates the impossibility of promoting pluralism by reinforcing the gender hierarchy. The more pluralized a general trend becomes, the more people will be able to realize that the slavery of the Other can, neither in theory nor in practice, be constructed as a solid basis for their own individual freedom, because in the end they themselves cannot escape the same logic. Chinese reformers are attempting to reinvent and exploit a convenient Other to justify and establish the objectivity or superiority of their own potential order. Sooner or later, I hope, direct or indirect advocates of democratization in China will learn to accept and to respect the differences among people. Naturally, this change cannot occur without fundamental changes in economic, political, legal, and social structures. However, unless would-be reformers realize the need to respect the largest minority group in terms of power distribution in China—women—in their specificity and difference, no change they make will be truly fundamental or radically democratic.

As the nineteenth-century French historian Alexis de Tocqueville pointed out, "It is impossible to believe that equality will not finally penetrate as much into the political world as into other domains. It is not possible to conceive of men as eternally unequal among themselves on one point, and equal on others; at a certain moment, they will come to be equal on all points."[63]

CHAPTER I

Revolution:
Hope Without Future or
Future Without Hope?

An iconoclast par excellence, Lu Xun spent his entire life fighting against the idols of Chinese tradition, which he considered the source of China's numerous problems. Ironically, he was my childhood idol, and his way of thinking still has a strong impact on me and on Chinese intellectuals of my generation. A number of contemporary Chinese experimental writers, including those studied in this book, have acknowledged Lu Xun as their only Chinese master, despite their pronounced contempt for their countrymen in literature. To a certain extent, the present essay may be perceived as an attempt to imitate Lu Xun's iconoclastic gesture of more than six decades ago—namely, to hold an idol, in this case Lu Xun himself, responsible for China's current problems.

However respected he is by his young and disillusioned disciples, Lu Xun differs from writers of the 1980's in one respect: despite his deep skepticism, he still remained an idealist and humanist, because of his belief in social justice and human value. We may call him a skeptical humanist or idealistic nihilist. However, at the end of the twentieth century, humanism and idealism have faded away and left behind skepticism and nihilism. Too many critics of Lu Xun, partly for ideological reasons, have emphasized his idealism and humanism and perceived him as a radical critic of traditional society. By contrast, the present chapter intends to explore the darker side of Lu Xun's works, a side that connects him to the contemporary generation of Chinese experimental fiction writers. Unlike the later disbelievers, however, Lu Xun was desperately and honestly severe on himself. He seldom excluded himself from the target of his skeptical scrutiny: traditional Chinese society. In most cases, he included himself as part of the traditional society he wanted to destroy.

Distinguished from the works of his contemporaries by his perspicacity, uncompromising stance, and cultivation, Lu Xun's works are among the best illustrations of the New Culture movement (*Xinwenhua yundong*). This movement, from which the Chinese Communist party originated, largely determined the direction of China during the twentieth century. Lu Xun's spirit (Lu Xun *jingshen*)—as Mao Zedong admiringly called it—still haunts contemporary China in its negativity, destructiveness, self-contradiction, and pessimism. The May Fourth movement has taken an unexpected turn. Although the iconoclastic spirit still prevails among the present generation of intellectuals, the old Confucian idols have been replaced as objects of attack by the new Communist ones. In this sense, one of the utopian dreams of Lu Xun and his contemporaries has been realized. As a generation versed in classical Chinese culture, Lu Xun and his radical friends attacked Confucianism as experts, albeit rebellious experts, on this culture. By contrast, as the generation who lived through the Proletarian Cultural Revolution, or the Destruction of the Four Olds (*po sijiu*),[1] contemporary Chinese intellectuals have often attacked the same cultural tradition without having a clear picture of it. Chinese tradition has thus become a fantasy or a phantom onto which these intellectuals project their psychological, political, and ideological frustration, especially when the political situation makes it more dangerous to attack current idols or communism.[2]

Since the May Fourth movement at the beginning of the century, cultural nihilism—the negation of China's entire cultural heritage—has been a dominant mode of thinking among radical Chinese intellectuals. A number of May Fourth intellectuals proposed "complete Westernization" (*quanmian xihua*) as a means of transforming China into a powerful nation. This implied that China had to abandon its traditional culture in order to replace it in every aspect by Western culture. In this regard the Communist party seemed to follow the May Fourth radicals, not to mention the Western origins of Marxism itself. As Mao Zedong succinctly stated: "There is no construction without destruction" (*bupo buli*). "Destruction" (*po*) of traditional society and culture has always been perceived as the precondition for the success of the revolution and one of the main functions of the Chinese Communist party. A large number of contemporary Chinese intellectuals, as demonstrated by the works of the experimental writers studied in this book, still remain in the same mode of cultural nihilism. Very often these writers compete with each other in portraying perversion, violence, and destruction, as if the one who can prove most effectively the nullity of any value system is the captain of his or her team.

Although traditional Chinese culture has repeatedly undergone destruction, the ghost of China's past has never ceased to haunt the modern nation. In the meantime, destruction motivated by different forms of cultural nihilism has turned into an empty ritual in which a great number of people are sacrificed in vain. This ritual, contrary to the predictions of different generations of radical Chinese intellectuals, does not lead anywhere, except to a hopeless return of what has been destroyed. The socialist revolution in China offers an excellent example of this return. Mao Zedong, as a champion of cultural nihilism,[3] exercised his power as leader of the Communist party and the Chinese nation in the manner of a totalitarian emperor. Indeed, Mao compared himself to all the famous emperors in Chinese history.[4] Ironically, cultural nihilism in this case has literally led to a repetition of history in its most conservative and regressive aspect, the imperial system.

Curiously, despite all the failures caused by the practice of cultural nihilism, the belief in destruction as the path to salvation is still strong among contemporary Chinese intellectuals. The difference between them and their May Fourth forerunners is that the past serving as the target of their supposedly revolutionary act of destruction is more complicated—because it includes communism—and more indefinable—because traditional culture has become formless. On the one hand, their cultural nihilism is inherited from one of the targets of their criticism—communism. On the other hand, the other target of their criticism, traditional culture, has already repeatedly been nullified in modern history. In other words, these intellectuals are imitating their ideological enemy, the party, in their attempt to destroy a cultural phantom, an already destroyed past.

In a certain sense, however, cultural nihilism originates from a predicament of traditional Chinese culture in its search for moral purity. In Confucian China, a loyal minister was supposed to die in order to force a confused emperor to return to his senses or simply to protest his wrong decisions. According to a definition generally accepted in traditional China, a great hero was not necessarily a brilliant strategist who successfully helped the emperor defend the empire but was more likely a general who died on the battlefield[5] or was mistakenly killed by the confused emperor he so loyally served.[6] Therefore, moral integrity has historically been associated with a certain destructive drive. The most well thought of heroes in Chinese history, such as the civil minister of the Chu kingdom, Qu Yuan,[7] or the military general of the Song dynasty, Yue Fei, owe their high stature mainly to their tragic ends. Moreover, both official and popular histories have portrayed them as stubborn searchers for death, as if (self-)destruction were all that counted in their lives. Their stubborn search for death had little to do with the construction of a better future; it is as if death were the ultimate proof of their heroic righteousness and moral integrity. There are certain similarities between these traditional Confucian heroes and modern radical intellectuals. Both esteem sacrifice for a lofty cause, and both moralize destruction as an ultimate goal in itself.

In his stories and essays Lu Xun expressed skepticism about this destructive heroism. Thanks to their author's pessimistic view of Chinese culture and his lucid reflections on the dead-end to which destruction motivated by cultural nihilism leads, Lu Xun's works are a mirror of Chinese intellectual radicalism in the twentieth century. On the one hand, as a Chinese intellectual deeply rooted in his culture, Lu Xun could not help searching for a higher value, an ideological Big Other. This search motivated him to participate in a political movement that aimed to destroy the past in the hope that this destruction would open a space for the realization of a much better social system. On the other hand, he saw the fallacy of such a higher value, whatever form it might take.

In his writings Lu Xun often complained of his inability to communicate with the oppressed, who belonged either to the laboring class or to the opposite sex. Despite this lack of communication, he sincerely but unsuccessfully tried to avoid the trap of using the other as a proof of his higher value system and as a way out of his cultural and ideological dilemma.[8] Obsessed by the idea of destruction, oscillating between hope and desperation, Lu Xun exemplifies the contradictory, hopeless, and painful path taken not only by the May Fourth intellectuals but also to a large extent by their followers at the end of the twentieth century. Furthermore, his lucidity—or abilities at "self-dissection" (*jiepo ziji*), as he put it—allows us to understand the insoluble dilemma faced by a modern Chinese intellectual. Lu Xun did not attempt to criticize Chinese culture as an outsider. Even in his most vehement attacks on this culture, he always included himself as a product of it, and not simply a distant observer. Because of this unique combination of various contradictory qualities, Lu Xun's works powerfully and tragically attest to the failure of the practice of destruction supported by cultural nihilism.

Cultural nihilism in modern China has been expressed in one of two forms of cultural absolutism. In one form, represented by modern radical intellectuals, including Lu Xun, China must transform its old cultural identity into a new one in order to survive in the modern world. In the other, Chinese culture is seen as so superior that it does not need to engage in a dialogue with other cultures. The first form still prevails among a number of contemporary Chinese intellectuals in search of a Westernized identity. The second can count among its supporters certain sinologists in China as well as in the West.[9] These two forms, despite appearances, are not contradictory but overlapping and complementary. As two versions of the same inferiority complex, cultural absolutism has hindered modern China from engaging in genuine and equal dialogues either internally among different groups or internationally with other cultures.

Dead Fire as an Image of Revolution

For the majority of leftist intellectuals of Lu Xun's generation, revolution or radical change was a vague hope for ending the agony and humiliation of China, which they blamed on the evil Confucian tradition. This may explain the intimate and intricate connections between the New Culture movement, in which most progressive intellectuals of the 1920's and 1930's participated, and the socialist revolution led by the Communist party. In fact, the May Fourth movement is considered one of the main impetuses for the formation of the Chinese Communist party.[10] Chen Duxiu, one of the three leaders of the May Fourth movement and the founder in 1915 of what was to become the leading literary journal of the movement, *New Youth*, also participated in the founding of the Communist party in 1921. In his youth, Mao Zedong not only read *New Youth* avidly but also published an article in it.[11] As Maurice Meisner states, "A young Mao Zedong was the intellectual product of the first cultural revolution, and an aging Mao was the political promoter of the second."[12] During the 1930's, a large proportion of prominent left-wing writers who had participated in the New Culture movement, such as Mao Dun, Rou Shi, Ding Ling, and Xiao Jun, joined the Communist party.[13]

Although Lu Xun never joined the party, his name has been

used on both sides of the Taiwan Strait as the symbol of "literary revolution" (*wenxue geming*). On many occasions Mao Zedong praised Lu Xun as a model for Chinese revolutionaries. In his "Talk at the Yan'an Forum on Literature and the Arts" ("Zai Yan'an wenyi zuotanhui shang de jianghua"), the article that has determined the literary conventions of socialist realism in China for more than four decades, Mao Zedong again enthusiastically endorsed the May Fourth radical writer.[14] Thanks to Mao's promotion, the author of *Call to Arms* (*Nahan*), whose mind was supposedly "in communion" (*xiangtong*) with Mao's own, has been sanctified and worshipped as a national hero in socialist China since 1949. On the other side of the Taiwan Strait, Lu Xun, for the same reason, was regarded as a dangerous enemy and his works were proscribed for decades.

Indeed, Lu Xun's uncompromising critique of traditional society made him a perfect fellow traveler of the Communist party, which represented a destructive force par excellence as a dissident party. However, the fellow traveler could not follow the party to the end, because Lu Xun's hopes, which were often equated with revolution in his writings, were by nature negative or destructive, whereas the Communist party believed that destruction of the past has a teleological function—to lead to the construction of a better future under the direction of a new center, the party itself.

This difference is exemplified by Lu Xun's metaphor "dead fire" (*sihuo*) for hope or for revolution in contrast to the metaphor "raging fire" (*liehuo*), which is used in socialist realism to indicate the same idea.

> This was dead fire. Despite its blazing appearance, it remained perfectly immobile. It was completely frozen—in the form of branches of coral. There was coagulated dark smoke at the end of each branch; the dead fire was shriveled as if it had just come out from a burning hell. The fire was mirrored on all sides of the icy wall, which in its turn reflected back and forth; its image was transformed into numberless shadows, coloring the icy valley with a coral red.
>
> During my childhood, I loved to watch the foam and waves

left by swift ships and raging flames darting out from a blazing furnace. Not only did I love to watch them, but also I wanted to retain clear pictures of them. Unfortunately, they changed every second, never stable in shape. Although I gazed and gazed, they never left any distinct trace.

Dead fire, I have finally seized you![15]

Dead fire embodies the childhood longings of the narrator and the dreams of the adult poet. Dead fire is characterized by two contradictory qualities: a stable or even static form combined with an extremely dynamic force, or the image of death saturated with life. In other words, life, no longer measured by temporality, is spatialized and frozen in the form of an aesthetic object through death. One may say that Lu Xun also hoped for this impossible combination, a finalized change or a change so constant that it finally becomes unchangeable. Lu Xun's relationship to revolution can be illustrated by the poetic image of dead fire as a finalized image of change. Dead fire can only preserve its dynamic form in congelation; in the process it loses its dynamic force. The eternal congelation will soon make the dead fire "perish."[16] The aestheticization of dynamic, changing, and destructive force implies an etherialized choice—confining Lu Xun's subversive drive within the realm of a harmless aesthetic game. Nevertheless, like the dead fire in the narrator's dream, Lu Xun preferred immediate destruction to the slow death by coagulation. The image of immediate destruction invokes the action of revolution in its radical negativity, as the conversation between the narrator and the dead fire demonstrates:

"I would like to bring you out of the icy valley so that you will never be frozen again but will remain burning forever."
"Alas, I will burn out!"
"I would feel sorry for you if this happened. Well then, let me leave you here."
"Alas, I will be frozen to death!"
"So, what can we do?"
"How about yourself, what would you do?" the fire asked me.
"I have told you, I would get out of this icy valley ..."
"So let me burn out."

The dead fire suddenly jumped up like a red comet, taking me along out of the icy valley. A big stony car unexpectedly ran toward me; I was crushed under its wheels. Before I had time to see that car, I fell into the icy valley.

"Ha ha, you will never meet dead fire again!" I laughed triumphantly, as if this were what I had wished.[17]

The dead fire's choice is also the narrator's choice in his dream—namely, to destroy the self along with the surrounding world regardless of the consequences. Like the dead fire, Lu Xun faced a dilemma. He would have liked to destroy traditional society, which he perceived as the source of China's problems, but this destruction could not avoid a certain amount of self-destruction, since Lu Xun belonged to the world that he intended to destroy just as the dead fire belonged to the icy valley. Lu Xun's concept of revolution was as elusive as his childhood image of burning fire; it consists of a destructive force that ceaselessly renews itself in death. Nevertheless, the image of dead fire that originated in Lu Xun's childhood memory also implies a return to a forsaken past. This return endows the image with an undertone of nostalgia. Like a child's game, this image is aimless. It may be projected into a past but not into the future. Revolution in Lu Xun's terms is thus a futureless destructive game. Choosing revolution is tantamount to choosing destruction and self-destruction with a devilish laughter—like the narrator dying along with the dead fire. The past is finished, and so is the destructor as part of this past that he must destroy.

If the narrator equates dead fire with hope, the icy world represents society. The fire in the icy world can only play a decorative role by coloring the otherwise colorless world. The fire cannot have any impact on the world unless it is destroyed along with part of the frozen world. The narrator's happy laughter in his dream is a laughter of death that represents the last step in a desperate rebellion. Death can be perceived as the failure of the rebel, since it marks the end of his rebellion. However, it can also be considered the mark of victory, since the world against which he rebels can no longer exercise any power over him. This mark of victory illustrates the pessimism in Lu Xun's writings: rebellion is presented more as a hopeless gesture of destruction than as a teleologically constructive act.

The Madman as Revolutionary

Not surprisingly a large number of May Fourth intellectuals ended their ideological wandering by anchoring themselves in communism. Despite their radically iconoclastic attitude toward Confucianism, the ideological world of most intellectuals of this period was still implicitly influenced by the Confucian training of their formative years. Their nihilistic attitude toward their cultural heritage did not necessarily allow them to overcome the determination of their cultural heritage. On the contrary, in repressing their connection to the past, they were even more haunted by the ghost of this heritage, since they had not settled accounts with their personal share in the Chinese cultural tradition. Lu Xun, for example, suggested to the younger generation that they completely ignore classical Chinese literature.[18] At the same time, he could write his diary only in classical Chinese, the medium in which he expressed some of the most intimate details of his personal life. His choice of classical Chinese indicates that Lu Xun remained a "native" of this culture. The connection between the May Fourth iconoclasts and the Confucian tradition can be found in their commonly shared belief in collectivism. Confucianism, as a collective ideology, emphasizes the social responsibility and moral mission of each individual. For Confucius and his disciples, an individual exists mainly as an embodiment of the social relations and functions implied by his titles: father, son, minister, etc.[19] As a Western collective ideology, communism was particularly attractive to May Fourth intellectuals, who urgently wanted radical change for their nation but were nevertheless unable to eradicate the ideological influences of their formative years.

Despite his apparent similarity to his generation of radical intellectuals, Lu Xun still represents an exception among them. Most May Fourth intellectuals who joined the Communist party believed in the function of collective salvation. Lu Xun, however, associated the Communist party, the most powerful dissident organization, with negation. He identified revolution with hope, not because he believed that revolution was hopeful but because he considered hope as illusory as revolution. Since he hoped mainly to destroy, this hope would very likely be destroyed by its realization.

Lu Xun was not the only pessimist among the May Fourth radicals. The works of a large number of May Fourth writers, such as Ba Jin's *Family* (*Jia*), Yu Dafu's *Sinking* (*Chenlun*), and Rou Shi's *February* (*Zaochun eryue*), evince a similar pessimism concerning the constructive function of any individual action. In the eyes of these writers, because the individual is reduced to a powerless victim by society, society must take the blame for events and the environment. The image of a powerless individual facing a powerful society implies that the individual subject need not be truly responsible for what happens to the objective and the subjective world. Despite their avowed individualism, Lu Xun's contemporaries tended to let the nation or some other collectivity shoulder responsibility for their personal problems. Lu Xun's attitude, however, differed. For him, destruction was not only a passive outcome of the subject's victimization but also an active choice in which the rebel's subjectivity was formulated. Lu Xun's rebellion might well be aimless and fruitless, but it was not irresponsible. Despite his sense of disorientation, the rebel must assume responsibility for his choice as well as for the outcome of his unavoidable failure. In this sense, Lu Xun's pessimism gains a tragic dimension.[20]

Most of Lu Xun's contemporary radical writers attributed their personal desperation to the political and economic situation of their nation. For them, the destruction of the evil tradition would solve both personal and national problems.[21] This may partly explain the appeal of communism for many Chinese radical intellectuals of the May Fourth movement, who considered the Russian Revolution an example of collective salvation. By contrast, collective salvation was never truly part of Lu Xun's agenda. In his opinion, traditional Chinese society was hopeless not only because it oppressed individuals, but also because corrupted or corruptible individuals were the products and carriers of this tradition. Lu Xun's protagonist in "The Madman's Diary" ("Kuangren riji") is a good example of the individual rebel limited by his own connections with his intended object of subversion—in this case, traditional society. In this story, the hero protests against the practice of symbolic cannibalism; the other, submissive members of society, including his family, regard him as mad. In the end, however, his protests do not prevent the madman from joining the "eaters of human beings" (*chiren de jiahuo*) in traditional society, and he regains his sanity by becoming a potential member of officialdom (*houbu daotai*).[22] The madman's rebellion does not substantially shake the foundations of traditional society. On the contrary, it turns into a journey toward his own integration with, and submission to, the evil society.

If the madman, initially a determined rebel, cannot avoid participating in the cannibalism practiced by traditional society, how can we expect such rebels to save us from the same tradition? The madman's transformation from determined revolutionary to official reveals Lu Xun's skepticism of collective salvation. A savior beyond traditional society and free from the present power structure does not exist in reality. At the same time, no one, including the author himself, escapes contamination by the evil tradition.

Lu Xun was revolutionary to the extent that he transformed revolution into a synonym for negation—ceaseless negation of both the objective and the subjective world. The double negation distinguishes Lu Xun's view of revolution from the teleological notion of a constructive revolution promoted by the Communist party. Ironically, the myth of Lu Xun as a great revolutionary created by Mao Zedong and his party serves to cancel out his subversive or revolutionary potential, which depends largely on the double negation of the world and the self.

The Uncertainty of Negation

In 1925, Lu Xun wrote to his student and wife-to-be, Xu Guangping:

> This fantasy cannot for certain be proved to be a fantasy. Consequently, it may be taken as a consolation, as God in the eyes of his believers. You seem to read my works very often, but they are too dark. Although I constantly sense that only "darkness and emptiness" do "truly exist," I still cannot help resisting them desperately. As a result, my voice sounds rather radical. Very likely, this belief may have something to do with age and experience and may not be true, since in the end I am unable to prove that only darkness and emptiness truly exist.[23]

Lu Xun still had hope because he was unable to disprove the existence of hope with certainty; in contrast the existence of the polar opposites of hope, darkness and nullity, cannot be proved. Just as Pascal based his faith in God on an intellectual bet on God's providential existence in order to preserve the possibility of his own salvation, Lu Xun took refuge in a fantasy of hope. Although he understood his own desperate situation and that of his nation, Lu Xun did not want to sink into darkness and emptiness prematurely, in case the future were not as dark and as empty as he imagined. Like Pascal, Lu Xun hedged his bet by pointing to his failure to find substantial justification for his desperation.

At the end of "My Old Home" ("Guxiang"), Lu Xun presented hope as a beautiful dream, beautiful precisely because it was unreal.

> While lying down, I listened to the water rippling beneath the boat and realized that I was following my own path. I thought: although Runtu and myself had become so distant, the next generation could still communicate with each other. Right now, was Hong'er not thinking of Shuisheng? I hoped that they would not like us become distant in the future. . . . At the same time, I also hoped that in order to maintain their closeness, they would not have to toil restlessly like me; nor toil to the point of stupefaction like Runtu; nor, like others, have to toil for the sake of dissipation. They should be able to enjoy a new life, a life we never experienced. . . .

I thought about hope and suddenly felt frightened. When Runtu wanted to keep the incense burner and candlestick, I secretly laughed at him. He always worshipped idols and could not forget them for a single moment. Now, what I called hope—was it not also an idol that I myself created? The only difference was that his wish was close and tangible, whereas mine was distant and elusive.

With my dreamy eyes, I saw a stretch of emerald green sand bordering the ocean and extending under the golden full moon in the dark blue sky. One cannot be certain whether hope exists or not. This is just like the case of roads in this world. Originally, there were no roads on earth. Only because a great number of people have passed by have roads taken form.[24]

After twenty years of wandering, the narrator returns to his hometown in order to help his family move. Despite the gloomy atmosphere in his childhood home, which has already been sold to a new owner, the narrator arrives with the hope of seeing a childhood friend, Runtu, a peasant of his own age. The narrator values this friendship because it crosses class boundaries and represents for him the hope of overcoming the lack of humaneness engendered by the traditional social hierarchy. The encounter with the adult Runtu, however, brings disillusionment. As a prematurely aged peasant and the father of five children, Runtu, burdened by poverty, natural disasters, and taxation, has become an *ordinary* peasant, and respectfully calls his childhood playmate, the narrator, "master" (*laoye*). When the narrator's mother asks Runtu why, he replies that as a child he did not understand the "rules" (*guiju*). The conventionalization of the relationship between the two childhood friends from different social backgrounds shatters the narrator's hope, which is based on a romanticized version of the past. After witnessing his nephew and Runtu's son befriending each other in a re-enactment of his and Runtu's equalitarian relationship, however, the narrator ends his short story with an image of new hope. But it is no longer possible to substantialize this hope, either in his memory or in an idealized future. It becomes "dreamy" (*menglong*), "distant and elusive" (*mangyuan*).

Before the narrator meets the adult Runtu, his hope is epitomized by the image of a twelve-year-old boy in the middle of "a stretch of emerald green sand bordering the ocean and extending under the golden full moon in the dark blue sky." Following the narrator's encounter with the true peasant, this portrait of the "little hero" (*xiao yingxiong*) becomes "blurred" (*mohu*).[25] The old image of Runtu in the middle of a limitless natural world is replaced at the end by another image of hope, a similar image of the natural world, but one from which human beings are excluded. The image of empty nature exemplifies the narrator's hope in its total negation. Hope will emerge only after the destruction of the current world, as the point of departure, or the degree zero.

The narrator's idealized memory of Runtu as a child in a sense deprives Runtu of a subject voice, since that image is primarily the narrator's subjective projection. Like the beloved lady in the romance of courtly love, the peasant Runtu, as the representative of the laboring class, becomes an empty sign onto which the narrator may project his subjectivity.[26] In the final scene, which summarizes the narrator's hope for a classless society, even this empty sign is excluded. Runtu, the representative of the Other, is not the only one to be excluded, however; the narrator himself, as the author's spokesman in the story, also does not have access to the world of hope. Beautiful nature, as a reconfiguration of hope at the end of the narrator's journey, refuses entrance to any inhabitant of the old world.

What would this new life look like? The narrator's description of the new life, "a life we have never experienced" (*wei women suo weijing shenghuo guo de*), consists of three neologisms that negate the existing modes of life. It should not be like the narrator's own life of "restless toil" (*xingku zhanzhuan*), nor like Runtu's of "toiling to the point of stupefaction" (*xingku mamu*), nor like others' of "toiling for the sake of dissipation" (*xingku ziwei*).

The three neologisms offer a fresh perspective on the society. This perspective, independent of the conventional symbolic system, makes the narrator's value system relatively autonomous. Life is reclassified and reevaluated by the invention of three expressions that grant the narrator a critical distance from conventional language as the basis for social discourse. Because of their idiosyncratic nature, the three expressions are self-referential within the context of the story and will become meaningless once displaced into a context of common language. As the life-style of an idealistic reformer determined to fight against the existing social hierarchy yet unable to escape from the same social structure, the narrator's mode of life described in the story endows the first expression with a vivid image. With his wooden face and emotionless language, Runtu, a worn-out middle-aged peasant, brings the second expression to life. By means of her vulgar but colorful language and greedy but amusing manner, Beancurd Xishi illustrates the third expression. At the same time, one cannot accurately describe these images invoked by the three phrases verbally. "Toiling" (*xingku*), the first two Chinese characters of each expression, serves as a critique of society in general. By repeatedly using this term, the narrator seems to imply that every member of society toils uselessly, regardless of his or her social origins and ideological beliefs. His refusal to use a conventional expression may be interpreted as a mark of protest against the hierarchical society inherent in this language. In other words, *toiling* puts people of different social classes on an equal footing, sharing the same negative position as a somewhat aimless slave in relation to society. Although the equalization of people of different origins expresses hope for a utopian equality, this gesture also expresses desperation, since the rebellion is realized only in language—the negative language of fiction.

Lu Xun's ability to invent these three neologisms was, however, largely due to mastery of classical Chinese. As in classical Chinese poetry, the concision of these expressions and the lack of conjunctions create a highly suggestive effect and invoke a dreamy image of what the narrator calls hope. Like the three neologisms, hope in Lu Xun's writings can hardly be translated or explained by any intelligible terms of conventional language. At the same time, the similarities to word formation in classical Chinese tinges the image of hope created by the three neologisms with a nostalgia for a golden past.

A Spiritual High Wall

In his "Preface to the Russian Translation of 'The Official Story of A Q'" ("A Q zhengzhuan ewenban qianyan"), Lu Xun wrote:

> Although I have tried, I am still not certain about my ability to draw a truly accurate spiritual portrait of our fellow citizens. As for others, I am unable to learn with certainty. But as for myself, I seem always to sense the existence of a high wall that separates each of us from others. The wall isolates us and makes communication impossible. This is because our intelligent ancestors, called sages, divided people into ten different categories, each of which was classified in a hierarchical structure presumably in accordance with its degree of superiority. Nowadays, although we no longer use the same titles, the ghost of this hierarchy is still alive. Moreover, the isolation has developed further, and it has even extended to the different parts of the human body, so that the hands even become contemptuous of the feet. The creator of human beings was already ingenious enough to make us insensitive to others' physical pain. Our sages and their disciples even further perfected this creation by making us insensitive to others' emotional pain.[27]

Although Lu Xun considered the spiritual high wall the source of many social problems in modern China, he also realized that he himself, as the product of traditional culture, was imprisoned within this wall. Like most of his contemporaries, Lu Xun was haunted by the ghost of the traditional hierarchy. But unlike most of them, Lu Xun suggested that it was not enough to destroy the social hierarchy in order to establish a new society, since the social hierarchy was inherent in everyone's subjective world, including his own. How could one destroy the past without destroying the rebel's subjective world, if the rebel was part of this past? At the same time, if the destruction must affect not only society but also the rebellious individual, who will be left to construct a less hierarchical society in the future? Will those who are left after the total destruction be able to escape the traditional hierarchy? In other words, Lu Xun was suspicious of destruction,

since it was initiated by individuals who belonged to a world subject to destruction. Lu Xun differed from his contemporary iconoclasts, because he did not believe that one could purify his subjective world by drawing a line between the self and society. At
the same time, he was no less obsessed by the urge to free the
world completely from its evil past. He was lucid enough to understand that totality and purity did not exist, since any clear-cut
category, including the one dividing old and new, was artificial
and conventional. But he was unable to give up his dream of a
new society that would emerge only after the total destruction of
the old. The keen awareness of the impossibility of his dream and
the persistent unwillingness to give up this impossible dream
made Lu Xun the most original and at the same time most tragic
writer of modern China.

Lu Xun's short stories are often told from the perspective of
a first-person narrator. The narrator always presents certain strikingly autobiographical elements. Furthermore, despite his position as observer, the narrator usually feels a deep compassion for
the victims of society, be they members of the opposite sex or the
laboring class. At the same time, the narrator's compassion never
succeeds in overcoming the gap between observer and observed.
Lu Xun's narrator is so emotionally and physically distant from
the lower-class victims that any genuine communication between
the two parties is impossible.

Marston Anderson points out that the narrator's attitude toward Sister Xianglin in "The New Year Sacrifice" ("Zhufu") is
similar to Lu Xun's attitude toward Qian Xuantong in Lu's preface to *Call to Arms*.[28] Sister Xianglin, the protagonist of Lu Xun's
story, is a laboring-class woman. As a commodity, she is sold as
a child bride to a family. After the death of her first husband, she
is sold by her mother-in-law to her second husband, with whom
she conceives and gives birth to a baby. After the death of both
her second husband and their son, she returns to the household of
the narrator's uncle in order to resume her past job as maid. Perceived as unchaste since she was married twice and as a bearer of
misfortune since both of her husbands died, Sister Xianglin is un-

welcome in the narrator's hometown. By the time the narrator meets her on the street, she has become a beggar. On the verge of death, Sister Xianglin asks the narrator if there is an under-world where the souls of dead people meet. The narrator, taken by surprise and frightened by the prospect of becoming respon-sible for what happens to her in the future, offers an ambivalent answer: "I can't say for sure" (*wo shuo bu qing*).[29] Despite his belief in social equality and his compassionate description of her life, the narrator cannot communicate with her, since the only words he can articulate are a mark of failure of communication. This mark further suggests a condescending attitude—the educated male narrator should not tell the truth to the uneducated female protagonist in order to protect her from deep disillusionment. To this extent, the high wall separating them is also of the benevolent narrator's own making. Despite his position as reformer, deep in himself the narrator still does not believe that a laboring-class woman can communicate with him as an equal partner. As a re-sult, any genuine communication between them becomes im-possible. Sister Xianglin is never granted a subject voice, and like her body, her language is commodified in the story.

Fiction of Gender Equality

Most progressive May Fourth intellectuals criticized wom-en's oppression in traditional China, and Lu Xun was no excep-tion. Nevertheless, as usual, Lu Xun is distinguished from most of his contemporaries by a strong sense of irony, which some-times even led him to question the political belief in which his own works originated. In his "How Would Nora Manage After Leaving Her Family?" ("Nala zouhou zenyang"), Lu Xun rightly pointed out that women could not be independent if they re-mained financially dependent on men.[30] To this extent, for Lu Xun women's emancipation can be achieved only with a fundamental change in economic structure that gave women access to financial independence. Coincidentally, the same path was taken by the Communist party several decades later in its women's emancipation movement. For both ideological and economic reasons, women, with only a few exceptions, must work in socialist China. However, this change, contrary to Lu Xun's prediction, has not truly liberated Chinese women.[31] Still, we can detect in Lu Xun's works some traces that may help us explain the failure of the women's emancipation movement in China.

Even though Lu Xun's narrators cannot communicate with a laboring-class woman, as in "New Year Sacrifice," are they able at least to deal on an equal footing with a woman whose origin is similar to their own? In Lu Xun's work on romantic love, "Regret for the Past" ("Shangshi"), communication between the two sexes also appears impossible.

In this story, Lu Xun describes a failed romance between a young writer, Juansheng, and his girlfriend, Zijun. The story is supposedly written in a confessional mode from Juansheng's perspective to commemorate his former lover. The plot is rather simple. Several months after they decide to live together despite family opposition, the narrator tells his lover, who depends on him for a living, that he no longer loves her. His statement leaves her no other choice but to return to her father's house, since their relationship is based on free choice and unbound by any social contract. Because of her "independent" decision to cohabit with Juansheng, however, Zijun has become an outcast in the family. Apparently, the unbearable situation of living with her father's daily reproaches and her lover's abandonment leads to her death a few months later.

At the beginning of their romance, Juansheng is deeply moved by Zijun's expression of independence: "I belong to myself; none of them has any right to interfere in my life." As he comments, "Her sentences shook my soul. Several days later, they still rang in my ears. I felt exuberant, since I understood that Chinese women were not as hopeless as predicted by those misanthropes. In a near future, we would see brilliant daybreak."[32]

"Brilliant daybreak" (*huihuang de shuse*) is a metaphor for bright future. Since the subject is ambiguous, this expression can be understood as referring to women or to the nation, which belongs to its male citizens. Since this statement is made by the narrator from a subjective point of view, we may assume that the future in question will include himself as a viewer of the daybreak. As in the case of the socialist revolution, woman's independence becomes a representation of a "larger" political agenda to the extent that this independence at most has only a symbolic function.

Nevertheless, after Zijun shares Juansheng's apartment, the symbol becomes "real." The symbolic or verbal independence with which Zijun echoes Juansheng's speech on Western literature must be tested against the reality of Chinese society. In the end, it turns into a desperate dependency on her lover. Instead of the brilliant daybreak of an idealistic world, Zijun is finally perceived by her lover as a burden. Her cooking skills and housewifely competence cannot solve his problems, especially because he no longer has a job. Zijun remains a traditional housewife, and Juansheng does not truly differ from a traditional scholar in providing for his family by means of his literary skills. Zijun's independence, which does not change traditional gender roles, is a fiction written by the narrator himself in imitation of Western writers such as Shelley and Ibsen. The fiction is written on Zijun's memory. Later on, Juansheng does not want to admit the fictionality of his own writing, but Zijun's memory faithfully reminds him of his own story:

> However, she remembered everything: as if she had revised my words so many times, she could recite them endlessly. As if my actions were projected on an invisible movie screen, she described them in a lively fashion and in detail—naturally including the superficial shots that I would like to forget. At night, it was time to rehearse. Very often, I was interrogated and examined. I was ordered to repeat the words of the past, which more often than not need be completed and corrected by her—as if I were a mediocre student.[33]

From the very beginning, the "truth" (*zhenshi*) of their love is a fiction, or to be more precise, it is a copy of fiction that imitates certain ideas from Western literature. Zijun recites words that Juansheng has borrowed from Western authors. Zijun does not seem to understand the words she herself pronounces, and the Western works her romantic teacher tries to explain to her remain no less foreign to him. The fictionality of their love can be perceived as the only truth in their relationship. Consequently, their love must be expressed by some means related to fiction—either in a symbolic world as a narrative constantly recited by the two lovers or in a visual world as a feature film projected onto an invisible screen in front of them. Any attempt to make this romance part of their life experience is doomed to fail because of the inherent contradiction between the fiction of gender equality and the reality of an unchanged traditional gender hierarchy.

Juansheng understands the fictionality of his romance only in terms of its duplication, namely, in Zijun's words and actions. He does not realize that his own work from the very beginning has been a fiction. Therefore, he blames his lover/student for lacking independence and authenticity, and she has to carry the burden of emptiness. He does not realize that her dependency is implicitly written in his work from the outset; it is as if by pretending to be a mediocre student of his past speech, he could blame his own lack of independence and authenticity on Zijun, his faithful student. If he still believes in his ideal, which is expressed in the form of free love in this context, the silent admiration of his female student will confirm the truth-value of his ideal. If he starts to doubt his belief, the student carries the blame for not embodying his ideal. In both cases, the ideal is preserved and protected to the detriment of the woman. The man remains the superior knowledge-holder and the teacher; the woman, the inferior knowledge-receiver and the student. Nevertheless, the teacher must also depend on the student; only through the student's unconditional reception can the teacher's truth be proved. This would in the future become a model for the relationship between a male party member and his less consciously revolutionary female worshipper in a large number of works of socialist realism.

After Zijun's death, Juansheng deeply regrets having told his lover the "truth": "I should not have told Zijun the truth. We had loved each other; I should always have offered my lie to her. If truth were worthwhile, it should not have burdened Zijun as emptiness. Naturally, lie is also empty. Nevertheless, in the end it would at the most have been as heavy as this truth."[34]

At the end of the story Juansheng expresses a longing for his dead lover. Although this longing is no less intense than his love at the height of their romance, the narrator seems to believe that the truth is he no longer loves her, even if his feelings contradict his belief. Love itself becomes an ontological truth bestowed only on the narrator. Zijun, despite her role as Juansheng's lover, does not have access to this truth. Inherently, the romance lacks a minimum equality between the two lovers, and free love can only be an empty phrase. If Zijun is incapable of learning the truth of her own feelings, how can she make any choice by her free will? Freedom belongs only to the truth-holder, the male subject, whereas Zijun's freedom lies only in her ability to copy her lover's words and actions.

Although he claims to have made a mistake in not withholding the truth, Juansheng is a rather confused truth-holder. To a large extent, Juansheng can make such a claim precisely because Zijun believes in the authenticity of his speech. Zijun is his only listener whose complete approval makes the "truth" possible. The narrator succinctly explains: "I loved Zijun, on whom I relied to escape from loneliness and emptiness."[35] Silently and admiringly, Zijun listens to his speech on Western writers, such as Shelley and Ibsen, as well as to his statements on gender equality. Like an echo, she transforms his speech into her "own" expressions: "I belong to myself; none of them has any right to interfere in my life." In the end, Zijun as a loyal believer can no longer be appreciated by her truth-holder, since what she believes only reminds him of his past statements which he now sees as false.

In this relationship, Zijun is caught in a dilemma. She has to be independent in order to have the right to attest to the narrator's role of truth-holder. Despite the emphasis on her independence, any sign of lack of compliance on her part may be interpreted by the narrator as lack of understanding. She can "understand" truth only through the truth-holder, whereas she herself should not expect understanding in return, because she cannot offer anything worthy of being understood. She needs to be completely independent from her family members, such as her father and her uncle, in order to depend unconditionally on her lover. This lover, however, is not dependable. From the beginning to the end of their romance, it never occurs to Juansheng that Zijun, "independent" as she is, may have a voice or needs different from his own. At the end of their romance, Juansheng reproaches Zijun for losing her independence. Consequently, she no longer deserves his love. But from the outset, Zijun's independence exists in Juansheng's dictionary only as a ritualistic term. Independence does not change Zijun's traditional role as commodity. As a woman, she is transferred from her father to her male lover. This transaction differs from the traditional one only in not being authorized by the father. Juansheng is a rebellious son who refuses to sign the marital contract with the family and society. The bill for his rebellion, however, is paid mainly by the woman, who loses her family's support without obtaining the guarantee of a financially dependable husband. Furthermore, the lack of parental consent is, in the man's point of view, compensated by the expressions of Western authors, who replace the Chinese father as supporting authorities. Since Zijun's independence is based on a myth, which originates from a broken contract between the two generations of men, the eventual demystification should come as no surprise. When both her father and lover are no longer dependable, Zijun has no choice but to leave this world.

In one respect, Lu Xun's love story resembles a traditional romance between the talented young man and beautiful young lady, such as "The Biography of Yingying" ("Yingying zhuan") written by the Tang poet Yuan Zhen. In this story, Yuan described the illicit romance between him and his cousin. Despite his initial infatuation, he abandons her after having physical relations for a short period, since he claims that such a beauty is harmful to any man. "The Biography" served as basis for the famous play *Romance of the Western Pavilion* (*Xixiang ji*).[36] The play is one of the best-known pieces of traditional Chinese "romantic drama" (*chuanqi*). In Yuan's story, some people reproach him for "initial seduction and final abandonment" (*shiluan zhongqi*), a phrase that can be used to describe Juansheng's conduct in Lu Xun's story. In this sense, their relationship is nothing more than a conventional story of seduction in a patriarchal society where the burden of responsibility for an illicit romance falls mainly on the woman. The main difference is that the relationship in Lu Xun's story has been romanticized by a fictional vocabulary borrowed from Western literature.

Nevertheless, from a subjective point of view, Lu Xun as a May Fourth writer differs from Yuan Zhen as a Tang poet. Yuan's romance is narrated in a self-congratulatory tone; Lu Xun's narrator expresses poignant regret. Juansheng's regret at telling Zijun the truth is further portrayed with skepticism by the author, who points out all the confusion, contradiction, and superficiality in the narrator's "truth" statement. Moreover, the content of this statement is never revealed to the reader, except as the names of certain Western writers. This emptiness shakes further the truth status of Juansheng's statements. Despite a certain sense of identification between the narrator and the author—as suggested by the subtitle of the story, "Juansheng's Personal Writing" ("Juansheng shouji")—the author keeps a safe ironical distance from his narrator.

The narrator's truth, which is subjected to Lu Xun's skepticism, represents one of the most fashionable life-styles of May Fourth progressive intellectuals, namely, free love. In traditional Chinese society, where a legitimate marriage had to be arranged by the parents through a matchmaker, a male intellectual's decision to live with a woman indicated his individualism, independence, and liberalism. Free love represented the idealized value system of the West in the eyes of a majority of May Fourth radical intellectuals and seemed to offer a means to escape the restrictions of their Confucian upbringing. Lu Xun was aware of the illusory nature of this doorway to freedom, yet at the same time he was unaware of the reasons for this state of affairs. By attributing a purely instrumental function to the woman, the male intellectual, like Juansheng, basically remains a prisoner of the Confucian patriarchy from which he would like to break away. In reducing the woman to her traditional role under new circumstances—a voiceless object—the male intellectual merely recreates the past.

The romance between the male intellectual and his "independent" lover is to some extent analogous to the relationship between the Communist party and its "emancipated" women. In both cases, women must submit to a new ideology that rebels against the traditional patriarchy. The act of rebellion, however, does not necessarily make the new ideology less patriarchal. In the battle of succession between the aged father and the rebellious son, women mainly play instrumental roles by offering their bodies as voiceless objects by means of which the new ideology can be represented and defined. When the new ideology can no longer fulfill its promise, women are held responsible for its failure, either by the disillusioned believers such as Juansheng or by the disillusioned sons rebelling against their already rebellious fathers, as in the case of contemporary experimental fiction writers.

Lu Xun's generation tried to save women from their oppression, either by means of free love or communism. Both can be taken as somewhat equalitarian ideologies imported from the "progressive" West. If both attempts at women's salvation have failed, it is largely because gender equality has served as a signifier of a much more "significant" political agenda, either individualism or communism. At the same time, despite the emphasis on gender equality, women have never been granted the opportunity to raise their own voices. They have to "be spoken" by male subjects either as objects of oppression or as objects of salvation. A new gender hierarchy between the male speaking subject and female spoken object has implicitly been reestablished in the very name of women's emancipation.

Several decades after Lu Xun, communism has lost its subversive function. The rebellious youth of the May Fourth movement have become authoritarian fathers. Gender equality is no longer a password for radical intellectuals; instead, it connotes the agonies of communism. Gender equality, which at best existed at a symbolic level, serves to identify women's rights with the party line for some contemporary Chinese intellectuals. By means of this identification, they return to the traditional misogyny that Lu Xun's generation tried to subvert. In most contemporary experimental works, for example, women are no longer objects of salvation but representations of a threat to male subjectivity that must be dissipated, or elements of disorder that must be returned to their original inferior positions. The current disorder in society is blamed on women, who have caused political confusion by destroying the boundaries of the traditional gender hierarchy.[37] In other words, the radical discourse that failed to liberate women more than a half century ago ironically provided a new generation of radical intellectuals with an excuse to use women as scapegoats for cultural failure.

CHAPTER 2

'Red Sorghum':
Limits of Transgression

Among Chinese experimental writers of the late 1980's, Mo Yan stands out as a transitional figure. His 1986 novella *Red Sorghum* (*Hong gaoliang*)[1] was an immediate sensation among Chinese readers and literary critics.[2] A year later, Zhang Yimou, a Chinese director of the "Fifth Generation" (*di wu dai*),[3] adapted Mo Yan's story for the screen. The film, also entitled *Red Sorghum*, won a Golden Bear Award at the Berlin International Film Festival.[4] Mo Yan was the first experimental writer to become famous. Moreover, his popularity among Chinese readers is still much greater than that of his younger colleagues.[5] Because *Red Sorghum* contributed greatly to his popularity, I have chosen it for study in this chapter in order to situate Mo Yan's success in its particular historical context.

The story concerns the romance between the narrator's grandfather, a bandit, and grandmother, a rich landlady, as well as their participation in the anti-Japanese war in the northeastern country of Gaomi. As a teenager, Grandma is married to a rich leper by her parents. Three days after rescuing her from a kidnapper and potential rapist, Yu Zhan'ao, the chief sedan carrier for her wedding and the future Grandpa, imitates the murdered kidnapper's action and rapes her in the sorghum field. At this point, the line of demarcation between lovemaking and rape becomes blurred. Seemingly, Grandma submits to Yu after discovering his identity. Interestingly, even romantic passion must initially take the form of rape. Yu later murders her father-in-law and her legal husband. As a result, Grandma becomes the owner of her dead husband's winery, and Yu becomes a bandit and the owner of the woman. When their son, the product of their romance in the sorghum field, reaches the age of fourteen, the Japanese invade their country. Liu Luohan, Grandma's manager and possibly her lover, is skinned in public by Japanese soldiers. Incited by Grandma's eagerness for revenge, Grandpa decides to attack Japanese trucks using rather unconventional methods. At the beginning of the battle, Grandma is killed by Japanese bullets while carrying food to Grandpa and his team in the sorghum field. Her son and her lover, hidden among the sorghum plants, end the battle by killing a famous Japanese general.

Mo Yan's novella differs greatly from socialist-realist works in its ideological, discursive, and narrative structures. The choice of outlaws and adulterers as anti-Japanese heroes mocks the Communist party's self-portrait of the national hero in the anti-Japanese war. Supernaturalism, which occupies a large space in the story, goes against the basic assumption of socialist realism, namely, faithfulness to reality. The story is narrated by an "I" who presumably never participated in the events of the story. The narration is further complicated by the perspectives of the narrator's father and grandmother, whose reminiscences are intertwined with the events situated in an already remote past. This manipulation of complicated narrative perspectives transgresses the convention of a seemingly objective and objectifying narrative framework in socialist realism. Nevertheless, *Red Sorghum* remains traditional in comparison with the works of Mo Yan's followers, not only because it is more "realistic"[6] but also because the author's effort to subvert socialist realism is so transparent that it constantly calls attention to itself.

However, the transitional stage in literary history in which the novella is situated contributed greatly to its popularity.

Emerging at a historical moment when a radical change in Chinese fiction was badly needed, Red Sorghum offered an image of change that was not too unfamiliar and too shocking for a readership who, despite its resentment, was accustomed to socialist realism. Furthermore, the implicit familiarity was disguised by an effort to defamiliarize the socialist realism expected by the reader and to shock by sheer difference. What can be more seductive than a difference that does not require a fundamental change in reading habits? It may fulfill the longing for novelty without intolerably provoking the natural resistance to change.

The transparent linkage to its object of subversion, socialist realism, and its transitional function in Chinese experimental fiction make Red Sorghum all the more interesting. Understanding certain devices at work in Red Sorghum may help us grasp how much Mo Yan and his generation of Chinese experimental writers, despite the apparent influences of Western avant-garde literature, are largely (counter)products of the Communist domination in China.

Nostalgia for a remote past—exemplified by the narrator's exclusive interest in his grandparents' life in Red Sorghum—often leads contemporary Chinese experimental writers to explore an origin apparently free of any Communist influences. Since this origin cannot truly be traced to any remote past but is rather in the mind of its author,[7] it may be perceived as a fantasized origin serving as a counterimage or a reversed mirror image of the Communist culture.

Ambivalent and undefinable, this fantasized origin has from the outset been lost. The irrevocable loss of the origin, however, does not prevent Mo Yan's work from being haunted by a more historically situated past, the orthodox Chinese tradition. The ideological and cultural past, which is more truthfully connected to a historical origin, differs totally from the past that serves as a fantasized origin in Mo Yan's work. The author prefers to reject, or at least to hide, the historical past—which for the sake of convenience I will call the "first past." The first past contradicts the author's belief in the value of an individual self, whereas the second past, the imaginary origin recreated by him, glorifies his belief in individualism.

The implicit image of the first, unwanted past exists in *Red Sorghum* by means of a refraction of the Communist rejection of China's old traditions. This implicit image exists either as a counterpart to, or as an accomplice in, communism. Mo Yan's romanticization of the traditional sexual hierarchy through the relationship of the narrator's grandparents provides an example that functions as a counterpart to the women's rights movement sponsored by the Communist party. At the same time, his contempt for traditional ethics and social institutions manifested in the glorification of rebellious forces more subtly acknowledges the legacy of the Communist ideology of class struggle.

In the narrator's praise of his grandmother as a "pioneer of individual liberation" (*gexing jiefang de xianfeng*; HGL, p. 112), it is precisely the first past—the orthodox Chinese tradition—that Mo Yan tends to reject as restrictive of individual freedom. After all, the story is about outlaws and adulterers who daringly challenge social structures and marital institutions. In the light of Western individualism and, less conspicuously, of Communist ideology, the author considers certain conventions of the Chinese culture backward. However, as we shall see, this intentional rejection does not necessarily detach Mo Yan's world of fiction from the historical past, which still indirectly controls its two rebellious descendants, Communists in their political and social hierarchy, and most contemporary experimental writers in their sexism.

The Socialist-Realist Legacy

On the surface, the contradictory male desire projected onto Grandma is as ancient as any civilization, namely, the desire for a woman who functions as both mother and prostitute.[8] In fact, this traditional paradox is further complicated by the desire for woman's subtly limited independence, which may be traced to the socialist-realist legacy.

The movement to emancipate women initiated by the Communist party has encouraged Chinese writers to portray women as rebellious, independent, and daring. Be they female students like Lin Daojing in *Song of Youth* (*Qingchun zhige*),[9] country girls like Chunlan in *Genealogy of the Red Flag* (*Hongqi pu*),[10] professional revolutionaries like Jiangjie in *Red Rocks* (*Hongyan*),[11] or housewives like Xiaomei in *New Heroic Biographies of Sons and Daughters* (*Xin'ernü yingxiong zhuan*),[12] women in socialist-realist literature are generally characterized by their outspoken, unconventional, and strong personalities. This kind of strong personality can also be traced to Lu Xun's Zijun in "Regret for the Past," who, at the beginning of her romance with Juansheng, firmly believes in her independence.

The socialist-realist novel *Bitter Flowers* (*Kucai hua*), for example, written in 1958 by Feng Deying, is about an oppressed peasant woman, named Mother, who supports her daughters and sons in their decision to join the socialist revolution and treats everyone in the revolutionary army as her own child.[13] At the beginning of the novel, the chief of her clan reproaches Mother for letting her eldest daughter, Juanzi, participate in social activities.[14] In the old man's eyes, Juanzi's behavior is against Confucian ethics, which forbids women to play a role outside their households, in the name of "three submissions and four virtues" (*sancong side*).[15] In this sense, a woman's participation in the revolution implies independence vis-à-vis traditional ethics, especially Confucianism.

In Mo Yan's *Red Sorghum*, Grandma's independence also subverts Confucian ethics. As a daughter, she disregards her father's plans for an arranged marriage. As a wife, she uses a pair of scissors to defend herself from her husband. Moreover, she commits adultery with the murderer of her legal husband. In other words, Grandma literally transgresses the rules of the "three submissions" imposed on Chinese women by Confucian ethics, which require a woman to obey her father before marriage, her husband after marriage, and her son after her husband's death. In this respect, Grandma resembles her revolutionary sisters in socialist-

realist literature. If the chief of the clan in *Bitter Flowers* had lived
in the world of *Red Sorghum*, he would have used exactly the same
terms to reproach Grandma, Mo Yan's "pioneer of individual liberation," as he did Juanzi, Feng Deying's woman revolutionary.

But whereas revolutionary women become independent
from traditional social norms in order to serve the Communist
cause, Grandma gains her independence apparently in order to
enjoy sexual freedom. Like the contradictory male desire for a
woman who can play the roles of both mother and prostitute, the
notion of women's independence in socialist-realist literature is
inherently contradictory. A woman needs to be independent so
as to serve as an oppressed voice against the old society, but this
voice enjoys freedom only to the extent that it depends on the
leadership of the Communist party in order to be heard. In this
case, women's independent attitudes toward the old society must
be strictly disciplined by the party. Mo Yan's portrayal of the sexually "free" woman inherits the contradictory notions of the independent woman in May Fourth literature as well as in socialist-
realist literature: Grandma's apparent freedom in *Red Sorghum*
must be subjected to severe restrictions by masculine power.

Although every socialist-realist heroine chooses her lover or
husband according to her personal feelings, her love is always justified by the lover's revolutionary qualities and the collective approval of these qualities. In *Bitter Flowers*, Jiang Yongquan, who
initiated Juanzi into the revolution and is also her leader, talks
about revolution enthusiastically. His speech makes Juanzi realize
that she is indeed in love with her teacher: "Every word rapped
at Juanzi's kind and tender heart. She became excited, saturated
with hatred and love, as well as with strength resulting from her
passion. She hated—she hated the enemies to death. She loved—
she loved the unknown revolutionary companions, the martyrs
who had sacrificed their last drop of blood."[16]

Afterward, Juanzi continues to meditate on her feelings for
Jiang Yongquan. She loves him because every revolutionary loves
such a good person. She loves him all the more because he is her
"leader, comrade, companion" (*lingdao tongzhi zhanyu*). Her love

for his body is instrumental in her love for the revolutionary cause, since her love is not personal but collective, shared by anyone who belongs to the larger revolutionary community. Moreover, the object of her love is not just her lover but every unknown revolutionary who has his same qualities. Paradoxically, however, even though every male revolutionary may have virtually the same qualities, Juanzi must remain loyal to her chosen lover.

Mo Yan's portrayal of Grandma in *Red Sorghum* deliberately transgresses this stereotype of the revolutionary woman in socialist realism. Apparently, Grandma is not concerned with any moral values when she chooses Grandpa as her lover. Nevertheless, the evocations of individualism before Grandma's death are strangely reminiscent of Juanzi's revolutionary slogans.

Grandma says: "Heavens! What is chastity? What is justice? What is good? What is evil? You have never told me. I have behaved in accordance with my own will. I love happiness. I love strength. I love beauty. My body belongs to me. I am my own master. I am afraid neither of crime, of punishment, nor of your deepest hell" (*HGL*, p. 167).

Grandma's self-justificatory refutation of social conventions on the verge of death are matched in artificiality and hyperbole by the revolutionary slogans in Juanzi's description of her love. The overflowing passion and overdramatic language mask a sense of emptiness or of indifference, because the speakers in both cases, instead of being the subjects of their own statements, serve mainly as spokeswomen of lofty causes. In *Bitter Flowers*, as a teenager from the countryside falling in love for the first time, Juanzi thinks mainly about her passion for all her lover's unknown companions. In *Red Sorghum*, as a countrywoman who has never seriously been concerned with ethical values, Grandma spends her last precious moments intellectualizing about the meaning of her transgressive sexual behavior. Just as Juanzi's expressions of love for her lover illustrate the author's political stance in *Bitter Flowers*, Grandma's confessional voice, which makes a great effort to justify her romance, displays Mo Yan's belief in individualism.

Juanzi in *Bitter Flowers* loves Jiang Yongquan because he represents the revolutionary cause. Grandma in *Red Sorghum* loves Yu Zhan'ao because he personifies masculinity by his strength and power. "[Her] own will" (*ziji de xiangfa*) is nothing more than the masculinist ethos to which Grandma must submit. Grandma becomes his lover only after Yu Zhan'ao abducts her and forces her to make love to him in the sorghum field. Since the individualism of *Red Sorghum* is based on physical strength, Grandma is condemned as a passive victim or as a location on which brutal masculine power displays its force. In both cases, sexual desire, especially when expressed by a woman, must be justified by a lofty or a more serious cause, which is the manifestation of the author's ideological stance. To this extent, individualism in Mo Yan's fiction can be considered a subversive descendant of Communist ideology, thanks to shared forms of moralizing slogans and clichés.

This sentimental hyperbole was called "revolutionary romanticism" (*geming langman zhuyi*) by Mao Zedong, who stated that "revolutionary realism must be combined with revolutionary romanticism." As illustrated by the quotation from *Bitter Flowers*, revolutionary romanticism is characterized by extreme lyricism and passion while remaining impersonal. The lyricism and passion expressed in literary works must be directed toward a collective cause: revolution. Although in *Red Sorghum* Mo Yan often maintains the same mood of revolutionary romanticism, his passion and lyricism are individualistic. Naturally, the subject of his individualism must be gendered as masculine.

However, the same kind of exaltation of the self in the mode of revolutionary romanticism is not completely absent in the previous works of socialist realism. Mao Zedong's poems can be taken as good examples. In his poem "Snow" ("Xue"), Mao wrote:

> Mountains and rivers are so magnificent,
> That they attract numberless heroes
> To compete for them at the price of their lives.
> In the past, the Emperors Qinshi and Han Wu

Slightly lacked sophistication.
The First Emperors of Tang and Song
Somehow needed cultivation.
Counting every genius
The best of all still live in modern times.[17]

As is common in romanticism, nature in Mao's poem becomes part of the poet's subjective world. At the same time, nature, represented by mountains and rivers, is also politicized by means of their Chinese connotation of territory. As the modern "emperor," the former Communist leader considered himself unique in comparison with his most famous predecessors in Chinese history. In the final analysis, revolutionary romanticism in China is not so different from the exaltation of the self in Western romanticism. However, the only legitimate subject who could *openly* express passion for his individual self in revolutionary romanticism without risking his political life in Mao's China was the leader of the party or the Communist emperor. Mo Yan's *Red Sorghum* democratizes the subject of self-exaltation by extending it to other men, but the legitimate subject of individualism in *Red Sorghum* is not simply any man. Like the emperors who compete for political control of China's magnificent mountains and rivers in Mao's poem, Grandpa Yu Zhan'ao must also prove his superior masculine power through violent conquest of the female body. Mao Zedong reserved subjecthood for the man who controls the empire, whereas subjecthood for Mo Yan belongs to the man who conquers the most desirable woman. Mao expresses his individual passion by means of mountains and rivers, and Mo Yan, by means of the female body.

The hero of socialist-realist literature does not need to conquer his sexual partner through violence, because the heroine must remain loyal to the lover of her choice. *Song of Youth*, written by Yang Mo in 1959, describes the student movements of the 1930's. This novel is considered one of the most influential works of socialist realism written during the late 1950's and early 1960's. After several years of separation from her first Platonic lover, Lu Jiachuan, a Communist leader of the student movement at Bei-

jing University, Lin Daojing, the heroine, learns from a female
friend that he has died in prison. In preparation for their future
relationship, her potential second lover, Jiang Hua, is carefully described by the narrator as Lu Jiachuan's close friend and comrade,
who has the same revolutionary qualities as his predecessor. Because of his unlimited respect for Lin Daojing's feelings for his
predecessor, Jiang Hua postpones expressing his love for years.
When the two lovers finally decide to make love, the memory of
her first lover still creates strong feelings of guilt in the heroine.[18]

   Genealogy of the Red Flag is another important socialist-realist
work of the late 1950's and early 1960's. The novel describes peasants' lives in the pre-Communist countryside. Like the revolutionary student Lin Daojing, Chunlan, a country girl, has the
same kind of everlasting passion for her lover, Yuntao, who is
condemned to life imprisonment for his revolutionary activities.[19]

   On the surface, Mo Yan's heroine differs from these revolutionary women in that she does not *intend* to remain loyal to anyone. On various occasions, the narrator refers to Grandma as a
sexually liberated woman (*HGL*, pp. 106, 112). This sexual liberation is, however, limited to a verbal and intentional freedom.
From the beginning to the end, Grandma remains physically loyal
to her lover, Yu Zhan'ao, despite the narrator's allusions to the
contrary. Female sexuality both in socialist realism and in Mo
Yan's *Red Sorghum* serves as an interesting test case of the limits
of women's independence.

   In socialist-realist fiction, women must channel their sexual
desire to the revolutionary cause. Like nuns, they are married to
their god, revolution. The ideological marriage desexualizes
women's desire. Even the objects of their love, revolutionary
men, function primarily as their teachers of Communist theory.
Lin Daojing in *Song of Youth*, Juanzi in *Bitter Flowers*, and Chunlan
in *Genealogy of the Red Flag* become revolutionaries thanks to the
teachings of their lovers, to whom they remain eternally loyal.
Their love is a religious devotion to the preachers of communism.
Often the preachers are inseparable from the cause they preach.

Interestingly, despite the pronounced ideology of equal rights between the two sexes in Communist China, teacher-student relationships in most socialist-realist works are still based on a strict sexual hierarchy. In this hierarchy, only a politically and ideologically decadent woman like Bai Liping in *Song of Youth* can enjoy sexual freedom. Her betrayal of Luo Dafang, her revolutionary-teacher-lover, amounts to betraying the revolutionary cause.[20] Like their sexuality, women's independence is strictly controlled by the party line. Female characters in socialist-realist literature are independent mainly in regard to the traditional norms that differ from Communist ideology. Their alleged independence serves as a weapon to be used by the Communist party against the traditional society. Naturally, a weapon has to be carefully guarded in order to avoid hurting its owner.

Since Grandma in *Red Sorghum* is praised as a "pioneer of individual liberation" (*HGL*, p. 112), it is difficult to expect from her the same kind of self-censorship in her sexual behavior that is expected from her revolutionary sisters in socialist-realist works. Nevertheless, her sexuality is no less strictly guarded—not by the party line but by masculine power and violence. In exchange for a mule, her father marries her to a leprous husband (*HGL*, p. 164). On her wedding night, her husband attempts to sleep with her against her will (*HGL*, p. 163). Yu Zhan'ao, Grandpa, kills her potential rapist, a bandit in the sorghum field (*HGL*, p. 143). Later on, he himself imitates the potential rapist by kidnapping and raping her in the sorghum field (*HGL*, pp. 165–66). The rape turns into lovemaking, since apparently Grandma submits after recognizing Yu's face. Then, Yu kills her husband and father-in-law. In imitation of his father, her son at the age of fifteen tries to shoot the person who expresses sexual desire for his mother (*HGL*, p. 128). As the successive and carefully guarded property of her father, her husband, her lover, and her son, Grandma's loyalty is miraculously preserved for the physically most powerful man, Yu Zhan'ao, by means of his violent struggles. Her "own will" is meaningful only as long as it corresponds to Yu's will—

to consider himself the only man who can monopolize Grandma's sexual desire.

As mentioned above, in socialist-realist works such as *Song of Youth, Bitter Flowers,* and *Genealogy of the Red Flag,* sexual relations often parallel teacher-student relations. As we saw in the preceding chapter, this teacher-student relationship existed in May Fourth literature between the somewhat Westernized male intellectual and his "independent" girl friend. The knowledge of Communist theory is in this context transformed into masculine power that demands women's total submission to a different patriarchal order, the Communist party. In *Red Sorghum,* however, masculine power appears in the much more naked form of violence. In both cases, women must obey their masters, who are portrayed as their saviors and protectors, regardless of what kind of power they wield.

Despite the Communist ideology of women's emancipation and Mo Yan's representation of Grandma as a "pioneer of individual liberation," sexual hierarchy remains deeply rooted in Communist culture and in Mo Yan's world of primitive origin. In socialist realism, women's independence is a well-controlled weapon used against the Communist enemy, traditional Chinese society. In the world of *Red Sorghum,* dominated by masculine power and violence, Grandma's alleged sexual freedom can serve either as a harmless decoration for her feminine attraction or as a weapon against Communist puritanism—provided that this weapon is not turned against its owner, the male subject. By treating women as mainly instrumental, both the revolutionary cause in socialist-realist literature and Mo Yan's reconstruction of the liberating second past—an idealized and fantasized past—as a counterpart to the communist culture, lead to an implicit submission to the first past, which both parties apparently intend to reject—namely, the traditional Chinese patriarchy.

Red Sorghum is especially interesting in its contrast between a negatively hidden origin and a positively reconstructed origin, since this stance is common among Chinese contemporary experimental writers. The contrast between the first and second pasts highlights the novella's complicated, often self-contradictory, relationship with different axiological systems: Chinese tradition, Western liberalism, and communism.

Linguistic Subversion of Communist Discourse

In *Red Sorghum*, Mo Yan attempts to reconstruct the second past in the image of the narrator's home county, Gaomi. The narrator's description of Gaomi at the beginning of the story reveals the contradictory nature of this reconstruction:

> In the past, I passionately loved my northeastern county Gaomi, and I also passionately hated it. Once I grew up, I diligently studied Marxism. I was finally enlightened: undoubtedly, my northeastern country Gaomi is the most beautiful and the most ugly, the most noble and the most earthy, the most sacred and the most dirty, the most heroic and the most vile place on earth, where one can drink and love to one's heart's content. My countrymen love sorghum, and every year they plant a great amount of it. In the eighth month in the middle of autumn, the limitless sorghum field reddens, transformed into an immense ocean of blood. The sorghum is tall, dense, and splendid; sorghum is melancholic and lovely; sorghum is passionate and loving. (*HGL*, pp. 103–4)

What does the narrator's perception of his home county as a paradoxical entity have to do with his "diligent study of Marxism" (*nuli xuexi makesi zhuyi*)? At a superficial and literary level, it seems to refer to Marxist dialectical materialism, an important component of Chinese Marxist-Maoist discourse. One of Mao Zedong's three major philosophical works is entitled "On Contradictions" ("Maodun lun"), and for the narrator to invest the image of his home county with all kinds of contradictory values apparently acknowledges his respect for this Marxist-Maoist principle.

However, the "diligent study of Marxism" can be understood as ironic at a different level. Since "Marxism" has become a political metaphor for the party line in China, to study Marxism can be interpreted as a political expression of a person's loyalty to the dominant ideology. Born in a family of "upper-middle peasants" (*shangzhong nong*), Mo Yan seems obsessed by his politically disadvantageous background in his writings.[21] In *Red Sorghum*, the narrator's parents can only be second-class citizens in contemporary China, because of their financial situation as well-to-do peasants in "old society."[22] In this context, "to study Marxism" implies that at least for a short period in his life, the narrator tried to reject his milieu—the countryside, which represents the marginalized "natural world"—by adopting the opposite value system, that of the city, which is also the political and ideological center of the Communist party.

The narrator's "passionate love and hatred" (*jiduan chouhen jiduan re'ai*) for his county metaphorically describes his oscillation between the values of the countryside, or "natural earth," and the values of the city, or "cultural center." His choice of the earth in the end expresses a return to his original milieu and a deep disillusionment with his experience of "studying Marxism." However, his disillusionment does not prevent him from remaining deeply enmeshed in Marxist-Maoist discourse, in spite of, or because of, his conscious subversion of it. At a deeper level, his literary and ironic identification with the Marxist-Maoist discourse comes back to haunt the author of *Red Sorghum*. His emotional attachment to his home county as a paradoxical emblem certainly has its roots in Marxism. Because Mo Yan carefully distances himself from realism or materialism by taking refuge in supernaturalism, these roots, however, are not necessarily found in Marxist dialectical materialism but in the author's use of language.

Mo Yan's use of language often reveals his contradictory relationship with the dominant discourse. "The most" (*zui*), for example, is an expression frequently used by Mao Zedong and his followers. Fifty years ago, in order to establish the norms of socialist realism in China, Mao Zedong wrote: "The source of literature and the arts resides in people's lives. Despite their primitiveness and coarseness, these materials are the liveliest, the richest, and the most essential. In this sense, they outshine any literature and the arts. People's lives are the unique source of literature and arts, a source that is inexhaustible. They are the sole source, outside of which no any other source may survive."[23]

In this passage, Mao used "the most" (*zui*) three times to describe "real life" as the source of literature and arts, "the liveliest" (*zui shengdong*), "the richest" (*zui fengfu*), and "the most essential" (*zui jiben*). In addition, "unique" (*duyi wu'er*), "sole" (*weiyi*), and "that is inexhaustible" (*quzhi bujin yongzhi bujie*) are also superlatives.

The abundance of superlatives exemplifies the logic of the Communist party, which takes upon itself the role of owner and guardian of the absolute truth. The logic of "the most" is also the logic of the totalitarian state and of its indisputable authority. Despite his inclination to dialectical materialism, Mao Zedong rarely allowed anyone to apply dialectical principles to the authority of the "correct" party line, of which he was the permanent personification.

Interestingly, Mo Yan's description of Gaomi conforms to Mao's canon of literary creation in this particular linguistic aspect. For instance, the narrator uses "the most" ten times to describe the open country. Nevertheless, the same word creates a different image, due to the juxtaposition of the "most" opposite qualities. Mao uses *zui* in a single direction, a monological world of the Great Leader of the party that is further limited by its adoption as dogma by his faithful followers. Mo Yan's *zui* presents a world of insoluble contradictions, disorientation, and fragmentation. The logic that combines "the most beautiful" (*zui meili*) and "the most ugly" (*zui choulou*) is a logic of paradox and absurdity. The world in which Mo Yan and his contemporaries live is indeed an absurd world. Ironically, the absurdity has largely been created by the party's logic of *zui*, which tried to repress differences and oppositions. Under a homogeneous surface, divergences existed more persistently than ever during the three decades of Communist domination. During the Cultural Revolution, the Chinese people became deeply disillusioned with the reigning order, because the events of that period amounted not only to a further destruction of traditional culture but also to a self-destruction of Communist ideology through endless struggles between various political clans.

After the Cultural Revolution, the Communist party tried to reestablish its credentials by utilizing Western technology in its campaign for modernization. But contrary to the expectations of most Communist leaders, the new program provided a counter-reference to communism: Western bourgeois liberalism. This development shook the ideological foundations of Communist China even further. Since the appearance of unity can no longer be maintained, Communist China has become ideologically fragmented. As a result, Mo Yan's subversion of monological discourse is caught up in its linguistic pattern, which reflects the current fragmentation. By attributing "the most" contradictory qualities to his home county, Mo Yan makes this linguistic figure polemical and disrupts a seemingly closed system of discourse. There is no longer a single highest order. On the contrary, different, or more precisely, conflicting orders exist in this fragmented world to the point that the world itself is disoriented. The coexistence of contrasting values in Mo Yan's description of his home county can be taken as a metaphor for the China of the 1980's, in its dispersal of, and disillusionment with, the power that dominated China for more than thirty years. The linguistic disruption of the party's monological "highest order" can thus be seen as an accurate presentation of the collapse of Communist ideology, which is paralyzed by its exposed contradictions and oppositions. In this respect, Mo Yan's use of the superlative *zui* as a polemical feature is far more realistic than the conventional language of socialist realism.

However, Mo Yan's description of his home county is not specifically aimed at the duplication of the agony of communism in China; rather, it is intended to create an image of life full of primitive energy and strength. Mo Yan's generation of writers, born after the establishment of the Communist power, witnessed the dissolution of communism. For them, this image of abundant life can more easily be found in a past apparently free of Communist influence.[24] But questions remain. How could Mo Yan and his generation of writers, experimental or not, recreate this past, which is necessarily remote from their own life experiences? More specifically in the context of this chapter, how could Mo Yan reconstruct the past by using a language heavily saturated with Communist discourse? "Natural life" in Mo Yan's fiction, defined by its object of subversion, originates largely from the fragmentation of the same object, Communist ideology. In other words, the "original" world exists in opposition to the dominant discourse and is determined by its oppositional nature. One thing is certain in this world of confusion: from a subjective point of view, Mo Yan's notion of original life has little to do with the historical past, or as I have called it, the first past. In this case, what is the second past, this fantasized origin created by the author of *Red Sorghum*?

The disintegration of communism after years of domination will not bring about a return to the original world. On the contrary, its fragmentation is accompanied by a fragmentation of Chinese culture, be it popular or elite, because its domination was established on the violent destruction of the old world. The death of a murderer cannot bring his or her victim back to life; it is only a "settling of accounts," or the symbolic death of the victim, a "radical annihilation of the symbolic texture through which the so-called reality is constituted."[25] In other words, instead of restoring the beauty of the "original life" in China, the settling of accounts means a second death for the old tradition—death in memory. Under the Communist regime, the educational system did not make the younger generations familiar with traditional culture, the "symbolic texture" through which a nation's past "is constituted." On the other hand, the collapse of communism made memory lose its *raison d'être*, namely, as a form of resistance among certain Chinese intellectuals to the dominant ideology.

In this sense, Mo Yan's reconstitution of the beauty of original life in the image of the immense sorghum field is necessarily utopian, because this is by no means a return to the past. It is, rather, a negation of modern life. For this reason, Grandma, who embodies the beauty of this life, has to die in her prime to show that a return to the past is forever impossible.

The Sorghum Field and the Female Body

To a large extent, Grandma exemplifies the author's impossible desire for a return to an imaginary past. Her name is rarely mentioned. "Grandma" remains her only name, except for one time when she is named by an old countrywoman reciting a folk rhyme to her grandson about Grandma's contribution to the battle against the Japanese invaders (*HGL*, p. 112). Moreover, this folk rhyme is extradiegetic. The absence of her name reveals the paradoxical nature of the author's desire for an eternally desirable female body that is simultaneously an efficient tool for the reproduction of male descendants. Because she is less a person of flesh and blood than a conceptualized object of male desire, the heroine must remain nameless. By situating her in a past to which her grandson, the narrator, has no access, she is securely free from the contamination of communism. By attributing his father's birth to his grandmother's unlawful romance in the sorghum field, the narrator rejects the family ethics of Confucian China. By depriving her of life at the age of thirty, her grandson can desire her well-preserved image of youth and beauty, untouched by the erosion of time.

Like the landscape of the narrator's home county, Grandma's body becomes a location on which his most contradictory values converge. These values deny and reject other value systems, such as communism and traditional Chinese ethics. However, the contradictions, negations, and rejections miraculously emerge as a positive image of life through the premature death of Grandma. Since her death reconciles past generations with youth, seduction with reproduction, prolonged sensual desire with its sublimation, Grandma is transformed into an image that functions as a utopian solution for the author's desire to reconstruct a new world based on the fragments of the old. Furthermore, because Grandma's body is identified with Gaomi, a symbol of natural force and primitive energy, the new world represented by the female body is perceived as an idealized origin supposedly free of Communist influence, "the second past," in contrast to the first past, a historical past explicitly rejected by the author.

On the verge of death, Grandma remembers the consummation of her passion with Grandpa. Both the act itself and the act of remembering occur in the sorghum field. Through her dim eyes, the sorghum field is viewed as a supernatural stage for her dying consciousness. To a large extent, this stage is identified with her body, or more precisely it becomes her body's extension:

> Father left, running. His footsteps were turned into soft and tender whispers, and then were transformed into the music from paradise that she had just heard. Grandma heard the voice of the universe, coming from the red sorghum plants. She gazed at them. Through her dim eyes, the sorghum plants were marvelously beautiful and had fantastic shapes. They moaned, twisted, shouted, and intertwined. Sometimes they resembled demons, and sometimes they resembled members of her family. In Grandma's eyes, they intertwined like knots of snakes, and then brusquely expanded. Grandma was unable to describe their splendor. They were red and green, white and black, blue and green. They laughed loudly, they cried loudly. The tears they shed, like raindrops, rapped at the desolate desert of Grandma's heart. Between the sorghum plants, fragments of the blue sky were inlaid; the sky appeared at the same time so elevated and so close. Grandma felt that heaven, earth, human beings, the sorghum plants, everything was woven together, covered by a gigantic shade. (*HGL*, p. 168)

At different levels, this passage reminds us of the narrator's perception of Gaomi. Grandma's vision of the sorghum field is similarly characterized by paradoxes. The difference is that the geographical location, Gaomi, is described by the narrator as an object. Its contradictory nature is revealed by adjectives—as static qualities. In contrast, in Grandma's perception the sorghum field manifests its paradoxical nature through verbs—as actions.

In both cases, Gaomi and the sorghum field remain identical

not only at the literary level but also in their symbolic function as the representation of an original world characterized by unsolved contradictions. The change occurs not at the level of the geographical location but rather at the level of its relation to the two different subjects. For the male narrator, the location is still mainly a stage for his actions, such as "drinking" (*hejiu*) and "loving" (*ai*), shared by his "countrymen" (*fulao xiongdi*). Since the sorghum plants in the narrator's description are humanized by the use of static verbs such as "melancholic" (*qiwan*) and "passionate" (*aiqing jidang*) (*HGL*, p. 104), the humanized natural world remains passive. Therefore, there is still a clear-cut line of demarcation between the male subject and the landscape. For his female ancestor, however, the sorghum field, humanized by action verbs, becomes a stage for her consciousness, where the sorghum plants, like herself, perform their contradictory actions. In this case, the line of demarcation between the female subject and the objective world is blurred and on the verge of disappearing. In a process of identification, the subjectification of the sorghum plants objectifies Grandma's body by transforming it into a stage for action. Like Gaomi, the county of the red sorghum, Grandma is the object of the "countrymen's" love (*HGL*, p. 104) shared by the narrator.

Grandma views the sorghum plants as part of the objective world. The objective world, however, is not completely separated from the viewer's subjectivity. On the contrary, the subject and object of viewing become largely identical in a metaphorical world of mutual reflections. The actions of moaning and twisting attributed to the plants are actually carried out by the wounded Grandma on the verge of death. This kind of shift—combining an inanimate subject with an animate verb, or combining an animate subject with an inanimate predicate or verb—is one of Mo Yan's intentional manipulations of conventional language and a transgression of socialist realism. In this passage, the positions of things and human beings are reversed. Grandma is reified as a static eye or as a theatrical stage, whereas the sorghum plants, humanized, display their activities on the stage. They are capable both of dynamic actions—"They intertwined like knots of snakes in Grandma's eyes, then brusquely expanded" (*tamen zai nainai de yanli panjie cheng she yiyang de yituan, you hulala de shenzhan kailai*)—and of complex emotions—"They laughed loudly, they cried loudly" (*tamen haha daxiao tamen haotao daku*). The humanization of sorghum creates a double layer of surrealism by its fantasy and also through contrast. In other words, the sorghum plants are presented not only as human beings but as more powerful than people, since they can at the same moment perform the most contradictory actions—expanding and restraining themselves—and experience the most conflicting emotions—laughing and crying. The ability to experience the most paradoxical actions and feelings deifies the sorghum plants as the quintessence of the original world.

Deification of the sorghum plants enables Mo Yan to romanticize Grandma, as plants and her consciousness merge in this world of primitive energy. Both the sorghum field and the female body represent the world of paradox. To a large extent, paradox in Mo Yan's fiction is turned into a symbol of strength, energy, and freedom, since it leads to dynamism, tension, and movement. In this world of paradox, constant motion destabilizes any possible authority. This may explain Grandma's nonconformity and the sorghum field's limitless possibility of action, since the world of paradox breaks rules and restrictions. Nevertheless, the female body, like the landscape with which it identifies, is largely excluded from the world of dynamic movement. The representation of paradox by her body makes a woman's participation in the paradox highly improbable, if not impossible, since the female body serves mainly as a stage for paradoxical actions, not as their agent. As a result, Grandma's first sexual act, even with her lover-to-be, must be disguised as an act of rape. Furthermore, she must die at the very beginning of the battle against the Japanese—mortally wounded by the first Japanese bullet. In the story, this battle is the most important action highlighting the paradoxical nature of the world of the red sorghum—the world of extreme hedonism and heroism in their most basic forms. In both love and war, her body is used as a sacrificial victim—which passively represents the action but does not actively participate in it.

The deification of the heroine parallels her objectification. There is a chiasmatic relationship between Grandma and the sorghum plants in this passage. Explicitly, by viewing the sorghum field from a woman's perspective, the reader seemingly is invited to enter Grandma's subjective world. Implicitly, this subjective world is already pre-empted by nature, represented by the sorghum field. Grandma's consciousness, deified by its reflection of the sorghum plants, is objectified by the same act of reflection. Like the sorghum plants, her actions are devoid of any subjective agency, since they are mainly manifestations of nature.

Grandpa's initial act of lovemaking with Grandma starts as an act of rape. Disguised as a bandit abducting her to the sorghum field, Grandpa begins the sexual sacrifice of the woman by treading violently on a number of sorghum plants (*HGL*, p. 165). This action symbolically unifies the object of sexual violence, the female body, with its sacrificial altar, the sorghum field. The rape of the woman is equal to the violence done to the sorghum plants.

Like Grandma, the sorghum field is portrayed as "marvelously beautiful" (*qijue guili*) in its "splendor" (*huihuang*). Like Grandma, it is the object of people's desire, or of her countrymen's love (*HGL*, p. 104). The agitations of the sorghum plants metonymically remind us of Grandma's suffering at the last moment of her life. At the same time, they can also be interpreted as her orgasm, echoing her sensuality in their frantic movements of moaning, twisting, shouting, and intertwining. In this sense, not only are the images of the sorghum plants and of the woman identical, the images of life and death are also indistinguishable. In a sense, the desire for the woman's body is also the desire for her absence or her death, because the glorification of the male subject's actions can be sanctified only by the sacrifice of the female body as the object of desire. Grandma's premature death makes her representational value as paradox everlasting. The sacrifice of her youthful body, which has already accomplished its reproductive task by giving birth to a son, eternalizes her function as the icon of male desire. Because of her premature death, her image is glorified in two paradoxical ways. On the one hand, the narrator, her grandson, is a living image of her past, through his biological tie and also by his act of storytelling. On the other hand, she remains the object of intense male desire. Even her grandson can worship her as a sexual object—safely and glamorously. Nevertheless, even in a remote past, the femininity Grandma embodies is highly contradictory and can be preserved only through the premature death of the heroine, in order to reconcile her social function—son-bearer—and her imaginary function—eternal object of male desire.

This reconciliation is reinforced by a symbolic gesture, fetishization of Grandma's bound feet. Lovingly described by the narrator at considerable length, her feet are supposedly the major source of her sensual and feminine qualities. She is selected by her future father-in-law for marriage because of her impeccably bound feet, and Yu Zhan'ao, the future Grandpa, is also attracted to her by the sight of her bound feet. In traditional China, bound feet literally made women less than men by imprisoning them within a restricted world. Traditional Chinese masculinists used to argue for the irresistible beauty of deformed feet by bestowing on them the rather erotic name of "three-inch golden lotus" (*sancun jinlian*). The contradictory desire for an erotic object that is not sexually threatening is realized in this ultimate mark of beauty, Grandma's mutilated feet. This mark constrains its bearer within a small world, namely, the household. The confinement of the beauty contributes to her domestication for her sexual counterpart. By means of this tour de force, her attractiveness is not contradictory but complementary to her motherly function.

Can Xue, a woman experimental writer of the same generation as Mo Yan, provides a hilarious burlesque of his predilection for bound feet. She claims that 800 heroic bandits with the same kind of masculinist aesthetics live in a "primitive" village atop a mountain. They are so energetically masculine that they attract some blond Western girls disappointed by the lack of masculinity among men in their own culture. These Western girls have decided to search for the village of perfect masculinity while carrying their own food. Can Xue makes the following "compassionate" comments:

> They [the Western blondes] have an insurmountable obstacle: their feet. They should know that the 800 heroic bandits love only women with bound feet. This is the quintessence of traditional Chinese aesthetics and cultivated taste, which will never change. The size of their feet affects their way of walking and consequently the way of their potential lovers' "leisure cultural life" [*yeyu wenhua shenghuo*, which means sexual intercourse in Can Xue's vocabulary]. Unsuitably sized feet may very well turn these men off. Then they will become unaffectionate and cruel. The naive girls who are so passionate have never thought about the problem of their feet. I do rather hope they will never be able to find the mountain village, or eat all their food long before they reach their destination. If not, they will have journeyed in vain.[26]

This passage can serve as a prelude to the next chapter on Can Xue. It may help us understand why this woman writer is not well loved by her male colleagues in China. Can Xue is keenly aware of the contradiction inherent in the works of Mo Yan and other contemporary male writers in search of masculinity. Mo attempts to recreate an idealized origin based on what he perceives as the value system of the individualist West, while rejecting what he considers China's historical past. In the end Mo's reconstructed past is not so different from the historical past, since his attitude toward women as sexual objects inadvertently coincides with that of his most conservative and masculinist ancestors.

CHAPTER 3

Can Xue:
What Is So Paranoid
in Her Writings?

Equality between men and women cannot be realized without *considering gender as sexual* and without rewriting the
rights and duties of each sex in terms of *the differences* in their
social rights and duties.

—Luce Irigaray, *Je, tu, nous*

In the Confucian concept of the "rectification of names"
(*zhengming*), the act of correct naming or purity in language is
perceived as capable of maintaining the social structure. According to the *Great Learning* (*Daxue*), one of the Confucian Four
Books: "If names be not correct, language is not in accordance
with the truth of things. If language be not in accordance with
the truth of things, affairs cannot be carried on to success. If affairs be not carried on to success, proprieties and music cannot
flourish. When proprieties and music do not flourish, punishments will not be properly awarded. When punishments are not
properly awarded, the people do not know how to move hand or
foot."[1]

In classical Chinese, "name" (*ming*) also designates words.
The "rectification of names" means to readjust a linguistic sign
to fit its original reference. As Xunzi, a Confucian scholar of the
third century B.C., explained in his essay "On the Rectification of
Names" ("Zhengming pian"): "Kings are the ones who define

names. The names of criminal law were created in the Shang dynasty. The names of official titles have been formed since the Zhou dynasty. The names of ritual ceremonies originated from Zhou's *Book of Ritual*."[2] The reference need be objective, as long as the subject, such as a prince, a king, or a sage, who decided the original meaning of a word was endowed with enough social authority.

Moreover, in the Confucian tradition, writing or literature (*wen*) must be a vehicle for principle (*Dao*).[3] Despite their claims to modernity, a large number of Chinese avant-garde critics of the 1980's and 1990's still believe in this Confucian didactic view of language and literature. This belief, however, is more often than not disguised by a modernized and Westernized theoretical vocabulary. For example, Li Tuo, an avant-garde critic, writes: "A Q [the protagonist of Lu Xun's 'The Official Story of A Q'] and the discourse formulated on the basis of A Q's personality are now reshaping many Chinese people's mentalities. Because of this discourse, they feel embarrassed by their Chineseness. Moreover, I believe that this ideological 'avalanche' has just begun. In the near future, A Q's discourse will more deeply influence the Chinese and thus encourage radical changes in their concepts."[4]

In Li's logic, writers are supposed to rectify "names" (*ming*) in order to invent a discourse that corresponds to the "correct" way of thinking. Like kings and princes in ancient China, good writers are able to create "names" in order to dictate how the Chinese people should perceive and understand current reality. Li Tuo and some other Chinese critics have promoted experimental fiction as an open-ended and modern form. Nevertheless, they have also attempted to establish a new order, which in many ways resembles the old patriarchal order it is intended to replace.[5] However modernized and Westernized they may be, for these critics, experimenting with language necessarily implies a mastery of the object of subversion—language—on the part of the subversive subject. And from a masculinist point of view, women are supposed to be mastered by language, but not to master it.

In this context, Can Xue's writings inadvertently challenge

and subvert preconceptions about language imposed by a newly established patriarchal order. By 1985, at the age of 33, Can Xue was a relatively well recognized experimental writer in China, although she had started publishing her fiction in Chinese literary journals only shortly before. Can Xue is among the few Chinese women who enjoyed such a reputation.[6] Because of her works' shocking and puzzling effects on readers, a large number of avant-garde critics have paid tribute to this woman writer. As a subversive voice within the supposedly subversive order, Can Xue's position is doubly subversive—vis-à-vis the dominant official ideology *and* the institutionalized male-centered subversive position among Chinese intellectuals. This particular position may help explain why her works both fascinate and disturb her mainland Chinese critics. In this chapter I attempt to pinpoint the ambiguity inherent in their comments on a woman's successful experiments with language, even when measured by a heavily masculinist standard, and at the same time to approach Can Xue's works from a different perspective.

In order to overcome their uneasiness toward Can Xue's double subversion, a number of Chinese male critics have adopted a common strategy: they attribute the originality of Can Xue's texts to madness. Interestingly, these critics can detect symptoms of her hysteria only in her works but not in her life. Tautologically, her fiction serves as both the proof and the result of her alleged insanity. This logic is not, however, as puzzling as it may appear. A woman's experimenting with language amounts to an attempt to master a masculine property—language. From a masculinist point of view, any attempt to disrupt the masculinist rationale is in itself maddening, not necessarily for the female intruder but for the newly established male order. Consequently, Can Xue's success cannot be explained in terms other than inherent madness.

Cheng Yongxin, editor of *Selections of New-Wave Fiction in China* (*Zhongguo xinchao xiaoshuo xuan*), has commented: "None of Can Xue's works can avoid a fundamental undertone: the delirium of a paranoid woman, afraid of being hurt by other people.'"[7] Cheng Depei, a well-known critic of the literary journal *Shanghai Literature* (*Shanghai wenxue*), expresses the same opinion in a more sophisticated vocabulary. In his article "The Dream That Tortures Can Xue" ("Zhemo Can Xue de meng"), he describes her characters as "scopophiliac" (*kuishikuang*):

> The skepticism and crisis of a scopophiliac character only prove that his/her target is very likely illusory. The dispersal of illusion will eventually reveal that his/her target is no one else but him/herself. As a result, hidden behind this scopophilia is an exhibitionist with a narcissistic tendency. The madness expressed in this form of scopophilia proves that his/her exhibitionism has reached an uncontrollable degree. For us, the truth-value of images of a mother, of a husband, or of a father in this dream is insignificant, because dreams can never truly reflect the reality of our daily life; at the most they can vaguely verify the reality and history of a psyche.[8]

Of these two critics, Cheng Yongxin at least has the frankness to term Can Xue a "paranoid woman" (*huanyou kuangxiangzheng de nüren*). Interestingly, according to the same critic, the fear that in Can Xue's works earns her the name of "paranoid woman" is transcended by Yu Hua's masculine imagination. The "transcended" fear in Yu Hua's fiction "reminds" Cheng Yongxin of Robbe-Grillet's novels and Antonioni's films.[9] Given the fetishization of the West among contemporary Chinese intellectuals, the names of a French novelist and of an Italian filmmaker indicate less a tangible quality of Yu Hua's works and more an unreserved endorsement of them. Ironically, Cheng Yongxin's endorsement of a male writer is based on the very element that allows him to condemn a woman writer as insane, namely, the portrayal of an omnipresent fear in their works.

With all his fancy psychoanalytic terms, Cheng Depei basically tries to make a similar statement. Cheng Depei's floating signifiers do not, however, necessarily endow his statement with more scientific accuracy than Cheng Yongxin's straightforward curse. At the most, this effort only reveals his fetishization of the West; it is as if a Westernized vocabulary were all it took to prove the truth-value of his diagnosis of a Chinese woman writer's mental illness. Like the Chinese "Adam" who published "Adam's Bewilderment,"[10] a general identification with the West helps the male critic regain his masculinity, thus allowing him to treat women as Confucian inferior men. Ironically, by privileging the truth-value of a meaningful world over a woman writer's experimental quality, these avant-garde critics, despite their claimed modernist stance, cannot avoid falling into the old trap of socialist realism.

In fact, Cheng Depei's diagnosis that Can Xue's scopophilia hides exhibitionism and narcissism may be used as a weapon against himself. The fancy vocabulary may endow his passage with a simulacrum of dignity, since no one in China or in the West (probably including himself) can fully understand what he means. But this simulacrum of dignity is the extent of his statement's truth-value. His painstaking effort to play the role of an observing doctor reveals his own fear of the unknown world created by Can Xue's special sensitivity to the nightmarish reality of daily life in contemporary China. Her sensitivity results not only from an intent to subvert the party line, but also from her double marginality as a woman writer in both Communist ideology and its subversive partner, Chinese experimental fiction. Thanks to her first marginality, her writings recreate a world that crystallizes the absurd logic of Communist discourse. Thanks to her second marginality, she need not acknowledge or follow any particular master, Western or Chinese, as is normally the case with male experimental writers.[11] In this case, her femininity among a group of male writers and critics with an implicit or explicit masculinist ideology becomes a mark of marginality that is related to, but not limited by, gender identity.[12]

I would argue, against the grain of this trend of literary criticism, that Can Xue's works are interesting not because of her (or her works') madness, but because of her (or her work's) lucidity. Her writings capture the reality of contemporary China through her "feminized" language's marginality or "fluidity"—to borrow Luce Irigaray's expression.[13] This reality is paranoid since the ideological vacuum in post-Mao China has deeply shaken the basis for even daily communication by depriving language of any commonly acknowledged referentiality. The disappearance of any master signifier makes Can Xue's fluid language an excellent tool for exploring the nightmarish situation in contemporary Chinese society. I base my argument on a textual analysis of three short stories by Can Xue: "A Mei's Melancholy Thoughts on a Sunny Day" ("A Mei zai yige taiyang tian li de chousi"), "In the Wilderness" ("Kuangye li"), and "What Happened to Me in That World—To a Friend" ("Wo zai nage shijie li de shiqing—gei youren").[14] Each of the three stories was first published in a literary journal in 1986.[15] Each story deals with sexual relations in a different form: marriage as a process in "A Mei's Melancholy Thoughts," the routine life of a married couple in "In the Wilderness," and a strangely idealized love in "What Happened to Me in That World."

Insanity and Reality

In "A Mei's Melancholy Thoughts on a Sunny Day," the narrator, A Mei, matter-of-factly reports on her marriage. As with most families in mainland China, after eight years of marriage, A Mei lives with her son and her mother. The only strange circumstance is that following the birth of the son, Big Dog (Dagou), her husband disappeared.

The two main expressions in the title of the story sound somewhat contradictory. In classical Chinese, "melancholy thoughts" (or "longing") (*chousi*) may evoke a poetic and romantic image of a beautiful woman who, from a distance, longs for her lover or husband.[16] However, A Mei's melancholy thoughts about her absent husband could not be more prosaic and dispassionate. Moreover, in the Communist vocabulary "a sunny day" (*taiyang tian*) connotes hope and happiness in life.[17] But the story describes a life completely devoid of any happiness. By not fulfilling the readers' expectations formed either by classical Chinese literature or by socialist realism, the title sets a transgressive tone for the story at various levels: language, culture, ideology, and politics. Furthermore, given that one of the flattering names for Mao Zedong during the Cultural Revolution was the "red sun" (*hong taiyang*)[18] or even the "reddest, reddest sun in our hearts" (*women xinzhong zuihong zuihong de hong taiyang*),[19] the subversive implications of Can Xue's short story become apparent. Like the unfortunate sunshine, marriage, instead of evoking happiness as in a supposedly normal situation, becomes nonsensical.

Before the marriage, Old Li, the narrator's absent husband-to-be, has a close relationship with his future mother-in-law. After a period of intimacy between the two, Old Li offers to marry A Mei, with whom he has barely had any previous contact. A Mei describes this scene:

> It was very hot in July. Everywhere in the house there were little insects. One day, he decided to propose to me. That day, I went to the kitchen to fetch water. He came in by surprise. As I was getting ready to escape, he unexpectedly opened his mouth:
>
> "Hey, you, do you have any objection to me?" ...
>
> Then, he asked me whether I was willing to marry him immediately. While talking, his entire body was twitching uncomfortably. Later on, he found a stool. The stool was dark and oily, and one of its legs was already loose. He sat there shakily. Again and again, he repeated the same arguments; the most important one being that my mother owned a house. If he married me, he could live in this house and no longer needed to look for an apartment. At that moment, I tittered. He blushed immediately. With a stern look he angrily asked me: "Why did you laugh?"
>
> "At first, I had intended to leave and to write a letter. But I have stayed here for such a long time listening to you."
>
> With a sense of relief, he said, "Oh! I see." (*HDPXS*, pp. 302–3)

In fact, this apparently absurd scene is a concise and realistic picture of marriage in contemporary China. Most marriages are no longer arranged, but many of them are still suggested by the parents. In China parental intervention is often crucial in a child's marriage. As a result, the acceptance of a marriage proposal may

depend more on the satisfaction of the prospective parents-in-law
than that of the potential spouse. Naturally, the way to please a
potential spouse's parents varies. Can Xue's portrayal of the implied sexual relationship between A Mei's mother and her future
husband seems, on the one hand, to push this logic to its extreme
and, on the other, to emphasize the absurdity inherent in this
form of marriage. The increasing materialism of Chinese society
is also expressed in marital relations. Possession of certain objects
has become one of the commonly accepted preconditions for
marriage. Because of the scarcity of available housing in China,
a large percentage of married couples still live separately. Under
these circumstances, Old Li's choice of housing as the most important motivation for marriage can easily be justified.

The expression used by Old Li to begin the conversation—
"Do you have any objection to me?" (*ni duiwo you shenmo yijian*)—
is certainly not unfamiliar to a reader from mainland China. Before the 1980's, this expression was widely used in personal conversation. The word "objection" (*yijian*) originally indicated
ideological criticism. The sentence supposedly expresses the
speaker's desire to receive ideological criticism from one's inter-
locutor in order to improve one's political behavior in accordance
with the party line.

Since personal interests in Mao's China of the 1960's and
1970's had a suspicious undertone, any personal ties constantly
needed to be justified by revolutionary interests. The process of
constant camouflage greatly altered the nature of communication
in both private and public life in China. Personal relationships
were politicized (a woman, for example, must marry a man because of his loyalty to the revolution; see Chapter 2), and a large
number of revolutionary slogans were also transformed into substitutes for personal expressions. The constant confusion between
public politics and the personal world led to a trivialization of the
former and an impersonalization of the latter. As a result, both
political and personal language resemble meaningless noise,
which conveys nothing but a simulacrum of communication.

Because of the motivation (sexual relations between the future mother-in-law and son-in-law), the justification (housing), and the use of language (the personal use of politicized language), Old Li's marriage proposal appears highly absurd, especially to a reader accustomed to a much more romanticized or rationalized image of marriage. However, the absurdity in sexual relations, which differs from Mo Yan's romanticized version of masculinism (see Chapter 2), Su Tong's exploration of the dead-end in sexual relations (see Chapter 5), and Yu Hua's sadism (see Chapter 6), marks Can Xue's sensitivity to the nightmarish reality of contemporary China. Instead of looking for transgressive models mainly in predominantly Western literary works, Can Xue more consciously and lucidly manipulates materials found in contemporary Chinese society in order to subvert the existing conventions of socialist realism.

By crystallizing the logic of communism in its daily manifestations, Can Xue succeeds in capturing the absurdity inherent in this logic. In Old Li's relationship with his future mother-in-law, a defective process of naming (to become the daughter's husband) is a cover for an unnamable reality. In his desire to obtain a room by means of marriage, Old Li reverses the relationship between a goal and its means. In his use of impersonal language, the tie between signified and signifier has been broken. Can Xue's apparently surrealist world epitomizes the logic of Communist ideology in its camouflage, reversal, and fragmentation.

The Disappearance of Boundaries

Can Xue's short story "In the Wilderness" describes the married life of an anonymous "her" and her equally nameless husband, "him." Both of them suffer from somnambulism. The story is apparently told from her perspective and consists of an endless and aimless game of hide-and-seek between her and him from the house to the wilderness. The final contact between the couple entails a fatal destruction. Although the destruction occurs

mainly in the imagination, its effect is no less substantial. In Can
Xue's world, there is no demarcation between dream and reality,
and an imaginary death is equal to death *tout court*.

From the beginning, the relationship is presented in an interesting light:

> In the evening, she went to bed. Suddenly she realized that she was
> not sleeping. Therefore, she got up. Without light she wandered
> around the room. As she walked, an ominous noise arose from the
> rotten floor. In the dark, a black lump, similar to a bear, knelt in the
> corner. The lump was moving and noisily tramped on the floor.
>   "Who is that?" Her voice was frozen in her throat.
>   "It's me," her husband answered in a frightened voice. They
> were afraid of each other.
>   Ever since then, like two ghosts, every night they wandered in
> darkness through the many rooms of the big house. During the
> day, she lowered her head, as if she could not remember what had
> happened during these nights.   (*HDPXS*, p. 319)

On the one hand, the house offers no protection to its inhabitants. Neither husband nor wife seems to have the slightest sense
of security that the shelter of their own house should provide. As
indicated by the title, the home is an extension of the wilderness.
To this extent, the line of demarcation between nature and culture
has disappeared. On the other hand, the lack of protection does
not prevent their house from functioning as a prison. Moreover,
the wilderness is also an extension of the prisonlike house. The
wilderness, in this respect, resembles civilized society in that it
forces individuals to face each other in a kind of unfriendly, even
hostile, atmosphere. As a result, the identification of nature and
culture is tantamount to a synthesis of the worst qualities of both
entities. Neither culture nor nature can provide shelter for human
beings who live in a threatening world. Neither nature nor culture can offer an open space where one individual may escape
from the threatening presence of the Other. An individual living
in such a house cannot avoid both the horrifying sense of an invincible loneliness and the threatening presence of the Other. The
individual feels lonely as if she or he were lost in a wild world of

nature. At the same time, the individual feels threatened by his or her numerous neighbors, who, hostile or not, are interested in everyone's private life, as is common in a highly populated society such as China's.

The synthesis of the most negative features of nature and culture in Can Xue's story is epitomized by the apparently routine life of the couple. It is difficult to imagine a more negative relationship between human beings than their nightmarish situation. They are both absent and present to each other; absent because any actual contact is impossible, and present because each remains an ominous force in the other's imagination. The psychological impact of this environment is so powerful that it affects human beings not only mentally—by provoking an invincible fear—but also physically—by materializing the threat through a fearful imagination. At the end of the story, in the husband's imagination, a formless hand (very likely his wife's) touches the husband's painful toe. This imaginary hand, however, finally destroys the clock, the flywheel of which symbolizes the phallus, or the husband's masculinity. In this context, the line of demarcation between imagination and reality has disappeared, since the psychological effect of fear is so intense that it becomes "real."

Since the line of demarcation is blurred in every aspect of Can Xue's writings, a reader could legitimately ask: Is the story about a reality or a dream? In Can Xue's story, everything, including reality, is a dream. The heroine of "In the Wilderness" says:

> "A dream, which came through that little window, follows me. It swam into the room like a shark and blew cold air behind my neck. I couldn't sleep these days. You see, my skin became wrinkled. Taken by surprise last night while trying to escape from the carnivorous fish, I broke the paperweight. How long will this game of hunting and chasing last?" she complains inadvertently. "I can no longer distinguish dream from awakening. I raved in the office, scaring all my colleagues to death."
>
> "Who can understand this kind of thing? Some people perpetually live in similar situations all their lives. They have no choice but to sleep while walking and talking. Perhaps we will finally become like them." (*HDPXS*, p. 321)

Again, like the narrator of "A Mei's Melancholy Thoughts," the female protagonist of "In the Wilderness" deliberately uses solipsistic language to refuse to play a role in communication in post–Cultural Revolution China. In fact, both she and her husband recognize the impossible nature of such communication. Her husband, however, participates in the simulacrum of communication more willingly. He feels that since many people are asleep while talking, their own situation can be considered perfectly normal. The nightmarish situation created by defective communication is normalized through repetition in the eyes of the male protagonist, whereas the normalized situation is again problematized and unmasked as nightmarish by the female protagonist's idiosyncratic language or refusal to take part in communicative discourse. In the final analysis, a kind of madness lies in the impossibility of social communication, but each participant pretends to ignore this in order to continue the game. In this context, the female protagonist's idiosyncratic language is not necessarily a mark of her madness—as Cheng Yongxin and other critics have claimed—but a mark of lucidity that allows her to uncover the insane logic of social communication. The difference between her language and the object of its imitation, communicative discourse, is that her language acknowledges its solipsistic nature, whereas communication's normal function depends on the participants' ignorance of its true nature. Logically, her language, which duplicates social communication in post-Mao China by making its impossible nature explicit, is necessarily delirious—or at least idiosyncratic. Consequently, it does not surprise us that the female narrator shocks her colleagues by her ranting, because her language does not address anyone but herself. Her monologue is an acting-out of communicative discourse, whose true nature people must ignore in order to keep functioning in such a system.

Given their intention to unmask the impossible nature of social communication in Chinese society, Can Xue's writings tend to deconstruct most boundaries that are normally taken for granted, such as those between signified and signifier, dream and reality, life and death. As a result, in her fiction Can Xue captures the absurd essence of the world of post-Mao China, where any well-defined value system has been dismantled, discredited, and dissimulated.

In this world, even dream itself is no longer spontaneous and becomes the fruit of an imaginary will. As the husband protested loudly:

> "This is merely a dream, a dream I myself wanted," he was frightened by her approaching footsteps.
>
> The footsteps stopped near him, but no one was there. In the wilderness there was no one. The footsteps were only the product of his imagination. The imaginary footsteps stopped near him.
>
> An invisible hand deliberately touched his painful toe. Despite himself he could not avoid it. His frozen body hair stood up—like numerous pins.
>
> After the last ring, the wall clock broke. The gear wheel, like a little bird, flew to the sky. The distorted rubber tube stuck tightly to the dirty wall. A pool of dark blood oozed onto the floor. (*HDPXS*, p. 323)

By claiming that the dream originates from his will—"a dream I myself wanted" (*wo ziji yuanyi de meng*)—the husband perceives dreams as products of rationalization and will. Interestingly, this is the only point where the male protagonist invokes the notion of will. In the story, the will of the male protagonist may be considered the only mark of masculinity; without will a man cannot exercise his power. Ironically, the will is not only equal to the dream, but it is also powerless within the dream. Finally, this dream as a product of the masculine will ends in the destruction of the clock, whose gear wheel flies away like a little bird. The Chinese character for bird (*niao*) can also be read (*diao*), meaning the male sex organ. In other words, the final picture of this product of masculine will symbolizes the destruction of the phallus. In addition, both the fish, as a metaphor for her haunting dream, and the bird, as a metaphor for his clock, remind us of the image of the phallus, from the female and the male perspectives, respectively. The fish, which comes through a small window and follows the woman, suggests rape. By contrast, the destruction of the bird as a substitute for the phallus can be interpreted as an image of castration.

By transforming marriage into a daily practice of rape and castration, the story presents the most legitimate form of sexual relationship, marriage, in a most destructive light. Since referent and referee can no longer be distinguished from each other, language has lost its function of differentiation. As a result, the distinction between legal and criminal sexuality has also disappeared. Furthermore, because the house is an extension of the wilderness, culture becomes nature. At the same time, nature resembles culture by restricting the freedom of human beings. Even the wilderness can offer only limited space, where the runaway husband must encounter his castrating wife.

Fluid, Ice, and Solid Ground

Usually, Can Xue's world is submerged in a darkness generated by fear, hatred, and death. The darkness, however, is not absolute. In her short story "What Happened to Me in That World—To a Friend," a strange light breaks into the usual darkness. Unlike the repulsive sunshine in "A Mei's Melancholy Thoughts on a Sunny Day," the pure and immaculate light originates from icebergs and icicles floating on the sea. The world of ice may be considered a limitless mirror that not only reflects the narrator's image but also extends her subjective world to infinity. Both the mirror and the narrator's body are equally fluid and shapeless.

However, even in this particular story, love and light exist only in "that world"—the imaginary world—where the memory of a remote past is reflected by an icy surface. In contrast to that world, this world—the "real" world—is submerged in darkness. In "What Happened to Me in That World," the overwhelming presence of darkness in this world subtends the transparent and icy light of that world. As in Can Xue's other stories, in this "real" world, strange and revolting individuals constantly wage wars in order either to destroy each other or to conspire against the narrator. In opposition to this world crowded with mysterious individuals, that pure and transparent world of ice includes only two human beings, you and me, or more precisely only myself, waiting for your arrival. As Can Xue describes the situation:

> I close my eyes, and withdraw into a corner. Friend, I am thinking about that iceberg. I believe that, as soon as the ocean unfreezes, the iceberg will start moving. I lift my head from the water, watching the iceberg move like a solemn meditating white whale. Icicles under the sky drip down, "pitter-patter, pitter-patter." "Crack," a sky-high icicle breaks. Pieces of broken ice glitter with a blue luster and swiftly draw arcs, which disappear at a glance. The brilliance of icicles is eternal and dazzling. Friend, have you ever had a similar experience? When your chest is open and your head becomes a reflector, thousands and thousands of stars suddenly darken. Even the sun becomes puzzled, alternately brightening and darkening. I lift my head from the water, shake little pieces of broken ice from my hair, and narrow my eyes. Frost drips from the sky. Softly I say to myself: "One morning, I will say 'This is how it is.'" Then, everything will start again. The earth again becomes a unified entity. Under the immense and hairy carpet, vague desires and strange emotions grow. Plants gradually are drenched in lascivious green. But I cannot start again; I have already entered this world. The brilliance of icicles is eternal and dazzling. Frightened comets fall on the ground, turning into ugly stones. The silent iceberg is luminous. I stubbornly stay in this world. Friend, I am growing in order to become one of these numerous sky-high icicles. While the glimmering reflection shines, my body is itching all over, just as if numerous sprouting leaves were on the verge of exploding from the inside. I shake my head and hear the cool breeze whistle in between the leaves. Abundant fluid floats out my armpits. ("WZNS," pp. 367–68)

In this passage, there is a recurrent pattern: actions that require more mental than physical effort, such as thinking and speaking, are presented as a *mise en abyme*. That world appears only after the narrator directs her sight inward to an imaginary image, the icy ocean and the meditating white whale as a metaphor for the iceberg. In this context, that world may be perceived mainly as the product of her thinking. At the beginning, she is "thinking [*xiang*] about the iceberg," which "moves forward, like a solemn meditating [*chensi*] white whale." In the middle of the passage, the narrator "says to herself softly: 'I say: this is how it is' " (*wo qingqing de dui ziji shuo wo shuo jiu zheyang*). The *mise en abymes* of the actions of thinking and speaking emphasize the subjective aspect of the imaginary world, since both actions are doubly self-reflexive. In the first instance, the white whale as a metaphor for the iceberg also represents the narrator's body. Both, equally submerged in the icy ocean, move slowly while thinking. At the same time, the iceberg as well as the icy world originates from the narrator's act of thinking. Thinking engenders itself in this boundless ocean. The second instance is even more striking. The narrator tells herself that she is pronouncing a sentence.

Whiteness, transparency, silence, cold, and loneliness suggest a world of negation and of nothingness. To a large extent, that world, purified by unusually colorless images, serves as a negation of reality. In Can Xue's story reality is represented by this world. Negation is also a process of poetization by means of which images and words are purified. In the process of poetization, since imagination, sensation, emotion, and vision are no longer separated, the subject and the object of observation often merge into a single unit. Due to their interchangeability and constant merging, that world is tantamount to her subjective world: the act of observation itself becomes narcissistic. While closing her eyes, the narrator imagines herself watching the mirror image of her body move in the icy ocean. Like the young Parque in Valéry's poem,[20] she accomplishes an endless cycle of seeing herself seeing.

In the icy and taciturn subjective world, one can hear only the lifeless sound of dripping water and breaking ice. For the narrator, this peace indicates merely a state of waiting—waiting for a man, who will share her experience. In other words, the narrator would like to merge not only with the imaginary iceberg, a symbol of an objective world, but also with an equally imaginary male friend—a specifically gendered other. In the latter case, the act of merging bears a strongly sexual undertone. Even though she appears to be the only living being in that icy world, when she speaks, the narrator constantly addresses her friend rather than herself. Moreover, the story's subtitle "To a Friend" (*gei youren*) suggests that it is written in a vaguely epistolary form. The masochistic image of opening the chest has both sentimental and erotic implications, since the chest is metaphysically the source of passion and physically a female erogenous zone.[21] The head, usually containing the faculty of reason, turns into a reflector. As a result, the source of rationality becomes simply a mirror of nature in its coldness, colorlessness, randomness, and transparency. The imaginary merging with her male friend is so unusually luminous that in contrast to their (erotic) union both stars and the sun lose their luminance. At the same time, since the "you" in this dialogue remains silent and unresponsive, the luminous merging is only a mirage and does not affect the narcissistic nature of that world. In the end turning into an echo of her own voice by absolute solitude, the narrator has no choice other than to talk to herself. Even the masochistic gestures, which are potentially liberating, such as opening the chest and turning the head into a reflector, cannot help her substantiate the intensely desired imaginary merging. As a result, the failure of communication in that world makes sexual union impossible.

Nevertheless, the sensual language used in the narrator's monologue expresses a boundless desire for union and for love. This desire, according to the narrator, can be realized only through the birth of a new world. At the same time, the idea of that birth is already conditioned by the imaginary existence of that world as the point of departure from which the narrator can imagine the birth. The multilayered imagination in Can Xue's story accentuates the fictionality of that world. The story, despite its apparently epistolary form, is only a monologue, succinctly illustrated by the sentence "I say to myself: 'I say.' "

The friend exists in the story mainly as a symbol of masculinity—with his "body reeking of cigarettes" (*hunshen doushi nazhong yanweier*)—and of otherness—as a silent listener. Functioning as a mirror and as the focus of her intense desire, the friend is

shapeless and without any fixed identity. In this love story, un-
common in Can Xue's fictional works, the abstract nature of the
friend epitomizes the impossibility of love between man and
woman. Love is expressed not in the form of dialogue but in the
form of monologue, since the only possible lover is a silent mirror
of the narrator's subjective world. Since the narcissistic love lacks
any warm feeling that could potentially bind two individuals together, passion can exist only in the lifeless world of ice.

The narrator makes an appeal: "Friend, now is the time. Listen! Burning hailstones [*ranshao de bingbao*] fall like a torrential
rain. Large transparent trees wave their spotlessly white canopies.
The water of the ocean ripples sensually. You and I, hand in hand,
emerge from the sea. Bathed in the light and flames of ice [*bing de
guangyan*], we narrow our eyes. We sing 'Mother's Shoes' with
voices deep inside our chests." ("WZNS," p. 370)

Both "burning hailstones" and the "light and flames of ice"
are oxymorons. The combination of ice and fire suggests the in-
compatibility of love and reality. The language Can Xue uses to
describe this romance is characterized by a large number of oxymorons. Apparently disconnected or contradictory images are
combined in order to convey an uneasy sense of discontinuity,
fragmentation, and nonsense. Throughout the story, this sense is
so persistent that it finally establishes its own continuity and co-
herence. Like the water of the ocean, the language that "ripples"
is highly sensual. Rationality, metonymically indicated by the
head transformed into a reflector, ceases to function and cedes its
voice to the body. In "What Happened to Me in That World," the
language of the body is expressed by the images of the white
whale, the open chest, and finally, the two lovers, hand in hand,
emerging from the ocean. The essentially imaginary and figura-
tive language poetizes the body as both the subject and the object
of love:

> When the ocean wriggles slightly, my back emerges from the sur-
> face of the water. A burning intense light expands my heart. Turn-
> ing back, I look for the mirror and, with a quick glance, discover
> that my eyes have been transformed into two violets. The white

whale's meditation will never be interrupted. At a distance, pieces of broken ice run into one another. The icy world does not distinguish day and night. I raise my head from the water and try very hard to open my chest. Sparks as white as snow dart toward the heavens. The iceberg also emits purple smoke, with a deep rumble. ("WZNS," p. 369)

In this story, that world is composed of certain recurrent images: the ocean, ice, the woman's body and chest. As we saw in the other passage, the narrator is finally united with the friend in her imagination by sharing the imaginary experience of opening the chest. Here, again, sparks as white as snow dart from her open chest. "Mother's Shoe" ("Mama de xiezi"), which is repeatedly sung by the lovers, may be considered a strange theme song of their love. The story ends with the same song being sung by the lovers in voices deep inside their chests. Emotion, represented by sparks and song, can be expressed only through a fragmentation of the body, which symbolizes sterility and death.

In that cold and sterile world, ice is shapeless, broken, and moving. In this sense, ice is similar not only to fire in its burning heat but also to liquid in its fluidity. Can Xue's image of ice is itself a perfect oxymoron in its combination of heat and cold, and of solidity and fluidity. The water and ice of the ocean have become one single unity. In this boundless world even a faint line of demarcation tends to disappear. Liquid, fire, and solid bodies are transmutable into one another. Even the narrator's eyes are transformed into violets. To a large extent, the world of transformation is also a world of liquefaction in which everything turns into drops of water in the limitless and shapeless ocean. Female subjectivity, flexible and indeterminate, emerges from the ocean.

A Chinese Woman Writer and a French Feminist

In traditional China, since the time of the *Book of Changes* (*Yijing*), one of the most ancient Chinese books, water has been considered a *yin* element, and thus associated with femininity.[22] In addition, the colloquial expression "fluid nature" (*shuixing*) has been used for centuries to describe the changing nature of women. Interestingly, a modern French feminist, Luce Irigaray, also uses the expression "fluidity" to define femininity as a subversive element in opposition to the Western male-centered metaphysical tradition, which can be traced back to Greek mythology and philosophy.[23]

Irigaray has taken the association of women with water from the Western metaphysical tradition where fluidity, representing shapeless and useless femininity, has been devalued in comparison with solidity, representing constant, rationalized, and valuable masculinity.[24] Over the course of Western civilization, judged by a phallocentric standard, the female sex has not existed, even in such supposedly subversive discourses as Freudian and Lacanian psychoanalysis or Marxist political socioeconomic theory.[25] Since the phallus serves as the ultimate signifier and the basis for the construction of language, woman, the nonexistent sex in a patriarchal society, cannot truly have access to language unless she accommodates herself to the role of serving as an echo or mirror of the world of male subjectivity.[26] Thus, fluidity by its connection with femininity must be subservient to solidity, which exemplifies masculine rationality. In the same vein, the tangible, related to the mother-material in the Platonic metaphysical tradition, must be subservient to the intelligible as related to the father-ideal.[27]

For Irigaray, because language in a patriarchal society is structured on the prerogatives of the phallus, demanding equality is not sufficient for women. An equality that ignores sexual differences still implicitly or explicitly privileges masculine standards, which are inherent in linguistic, cultural, ideological, social, and economic structures. Such an equality still requires women to renounce any hope of asserting their subjectivity, since the ignorance of sexual differences in a patriarchal context implies women's acceptance of being judged as men and by masculine standards.[28]

A possible way out for women, in Irigaray's opinion, is to begin by changing the basic patriarchal assumptions of language.

Since, according to her, the female sex is not one, but plural,[29] women should create a language that, free from hierarchical implications, does not privilege any ultimate signifier. The language should be fluid, avoiding the rigid dichotomies and hierarchies on which patriarchal language is usually predicated. This language will eventually enrich modern culture, which in most cases is still based on "the sole pole of sexual identity."[30]

Although Can Xue's works stem from a different language and cultural tradition, they and their fate in a highly patriarchal society can test the functionality and limitations of Irigaray's theory. In fact, the reception of Can Xue's works in China shows that an equality between the two sexes that ignores gender differences remains to a large extent fictional. The judging of women by masculine standards during the thirty or forty years of the women's emancipation movement in Communist China has provided the current misogynistic discourse with the excuse of feminine inferiority. A woman's difference is tantamount to her inferiority—as demonstrated by the comments of a large number of Chinese male critics on Can Xue's works.

However, if the ability to earn an income is not enough to win women's equal rights, can a utopian language recreated on the basis of so-called femininity solve the rest of women's problems? To what extent can a writer claim to write or to speak as a woman? Are there any characteristics that may define a woman's writing without reversing, thus duplicating, the structure of the patriarchal gender hierarchy? These are some of the questions explicitly addressed by Irigaray in her theoretical writings and implicitly but no less provocatively raised by Can Xue in her experimental fiction.

In "What Happened to Me in That World," female subjectivity, expressed in the form of love, is associated with the fluid world of the ocean. Conventionally, woman's love is used in literature to provide the male subject with firm ground for its solidification, since supposedly her love must originate from her lover's higher degree of masculinity, whatever that may mean. As in Mo Yan's *Red Sorghum Family* (*Hong gaoliang jiazu*), women's attachment to a man, Yu Zhan'ao or grandfather, proves the existence of his highly valued masculinity as the source and justification of their love. Ironically, his masculinity in this context is expressed by his ability to kill.[31] Under these circumstances, by situating her narrator's love in an exclusively fluid world of female subjectivity, Can Xue deliberately marks a refusal to provide the male subject with firm ground for its solidification by means of a sexual relationship. Furthermore, since there are no fixed or fixable rules in her world of transformation, the father's logic is absent.[32]

However, this absence of the name of the father[33] in Can Xue's fiction largely duplicates the situation in contemporary China. Since the patricide of the Confucian father by the socialist revolution in 1949, the Communist father has also gradually become an agonized figure, wounded by the political struggles within the party, by the economic problems in the country, and by a resulting disillusionment with the current regime. Similar to other experimental works of the late 1980's, Can Xue's writings belong to post-Mao China where the name of the father as cultural authority has become increasingly absent.

Nevertheless, in the perverse, destructive, and subversive world of fiction created by most male experimental writers, one can always detect a vague sense of nostalgia for an origin. Generally speaking, most male writers, however timidly, still attempt to seek solid ground and a firm foundation, which is implicitly or explicitly based on a father's logic. Mo Yan's narrator, for example, attempts to reconstruct a pre-Communist past in which his grandfather's masculinity is kept intact in an idealized world (see Chapter 2). Zhaxi Dawa's characters embark on numerous quests for something that may eventually combine an ancient Tibet and a modern West. Nevertheless, this combination has never truly been found (see Chapter 4). Some of Su Tong's heroes desperately try to break away from the dead-end of sexual relations between men and women by having recourse to male bonding. Unfortunately, male bonding has in the end proved to be another dead-end (see Chapter 5). Yu Hua, however, tends to establish a rigorous new order of violence, uncannily reminiscent of the old order of Communist domination (see Chapter 6).

Contrary to all these male writers' search for solid ground, the liquefaction of all solid materials in the fatherless world of Can Xue's story is daringly celebrated as an exuberant renewal or even a rebirth. Can Xue's world offers no firm ground on which the subject, male or female, may search for an origin. The narrator's recognition of her fluid nature in a boundless world of ocean is the point of departure for a possible birth of her subjective world. The possible birth is based on a refusal to serve as a solid mirror for the male subject—a "pure and simple image fashioned by the father's spirit."[34] By means of its constant refusal and denial, the world of female subjectivity is identified with the boundless and shapeless ocean. Like the ocean, it can no longer be contained within the boundaries of any specific discourse.

At the same time, the world that denies the paternal authority also cuts itself off from any maternal ties, since the female narrator's refusal to solidify her body is expressed by a rejection of motherhood. In Can Xue's fatherless and motherless universe, the lonely voice of the female subject, deprived of any social, family, or personal ties, cannot provoke any response other than its own echo. In this sterile world of imagination, motherhood is strictly associated with phallic power, defined by Irigaray as "a phallic maternal."[35] In Can Xue's stories, the mother is often described as an authoritarian, hostile, and repulsive figure. To mother a child—especially a male child—is often part of a conspiracy to start a shameful and incurably doomed sexual liaison. Apparently, physical pleasure and motherhood in Can Xue's writings are mutually exclusive.

Can Xue's special resentment against motherhood may be perceived as a rebellion against the significant role of mother assigned to Chinese women by the traditional culture. In traditional China, the only legitimate social function for a Chinese woman was to give birth to male descendants, and motherhood was the only respectable identity for women. This identity, to a certain extent, could be considered a firm ground for a traditional

Chinese woman in her otherwise in(de)finite world of liquid.[36] Furthermore, as carrier of the husband's son, she also performed the role of a mirror for the male ego.

In "A Mei's Melancholy Thoughts on a Sunny Day," the narrator gives birth to a son, but does not feel at all motherly. The role of mother is assumed by the narrator's own mother, who is particularly hostile to her. Moreover, the grandmother uses her grandson to maintain a suspicious and hopeless liaison with her son-in-law. Similarly, in "What Happened to Me in That World—To a Friend," motherhood is as usual personified by an old woman. Identified with a tung oil tree, the old woman usurps the place of the narrator, who from time to time takes the form of a camphor tree. As soon as she takes the place of the camphor tree, the old woman is turned into cement. Thus, in Can Xue's story, the female body is solidified by two different processes: transformation into cement in this world, and into ice in that world. The former is irrevocable; the latter is always subject to fluidification.

Transformation into cement can be perceived as an equivalent to motherhood. Woman, identified by her reproductive function, loses her fluidity—feminine identity—which is regarded as changeable, indefinable, and unreliable in a patriarchal society. Moreover, as the bearer of the male sign (the son), the mother's "cemented" body has also been transformed into the father's mirror. In contrast, the sterile process of glaciation in the narrator's imaginary world can be taken as an attempt to formulate a new kind of female subjectivity. Constantly changing, the narrator's imaginary world deconstructs the boundaries and definitions assigned to women by a patriarchal culture. The rejection of motherhood symbolizes a radical denial of woman's instrumental position in a patriarchal discourse. By means of this denial, female subjectivity emerges in its shapelessness and indeterminacy. The denial of motherhood largely cuts the traditional tie that binds a woman to a man as a sexual partner or, even more strikingly, the tie between women exemplified by the mother-daughter relationship. At the same time, a new tie either between the two sexes or between women has not yet been formed. As a result, Can Xue's world of female subjectivity can be said to exclude any man or woman, unless it is at a completely abstract level as in the case of the nameless and faceless friend. In other words, the male friend is transformed by female subjectivity into a formless liquid—a drop of water in the immense ocean.

In her "Power of Discourse," Luce Irigaray writes:

> This "style," or "writing," of women tends to put the torch to fetish words, proper terms, well-constructed forms. This "style" does not privilege sight; instead, it takes each figure back to its source, which is among other things *tactile*. It comes back in touch with itself in that origin without ever constituting in it, constituting itself in it, as some sort of unity. *Simultaneity* is its "proper" aspect—a proper(ty) that is never fixed in the possible identity-to-self of some form or other. It is always *fluid*, without neglecting the characteristics of fluids that are difficult to idealize: those rubbings between two infinitely near neighbors that create a dynamics. Its "style" resists and explodes every firmly established form, figure, idea or concept.[37]

Like the ultimate signifier, the phallus in a Lacanian sense, which breaks into pieces at the end of Can Xue's "In the Wilderness," every firmly established form, figure, idea, or concept explodes in her writings. In accordance with a changing idiosyncratic map of identities, words are repeatedly broken and reconstituted so that every form—be it linguistic, stylistic, narrative, or metaphysical—is constantly subject to fragmentation. To use Irigaray's words, Can Xue's language "is never fixed in the possible identity-to-self of some form or other." The linguistic lack of identity-to-self is due to Can Xue's keen awareness of her identity as a woman or, more precisely, to her awareness of her lack of identity as a woman writer.

The lack of identity in a phallocentric discourse is precisely the "proper(ty)" of Can Xue's fiction. Can Xue's language of the body acknowledges no authority or order predicated on the ultimate signifier, the phallus. By privileging sensation and touching over rationality and vision, her language questions the traditional fetishist concept of women. In Chinese patriarchal society, women are frequently used either as visual and representational images or as reproductive instruments. In the first instance, women serve as images in which the male subject invests his erotic desires or ideological beliefs. In the second instance, the female body is treated as a reproductive instrument by means of which the father's image can be multiplied in time and space. Thanks to the radical deconstruction of women's traditional position in patriarchal cultural and social discourse, Can Xue's language goes beyond any existing discursive boundaries.

It should thus not surprise us that her works are perceived as paranoid by a great number of Chinese avant-garde critics. To a large extent, the word *paranoid* may more properly be applied to those critics themselves, since their inappropriate use of this word reveals their own intense fear of a world created by a woman writer that exceeds their expected discursive boundaries. Most of these critics still believe that men actively shape language, whereas women are passively shaped by language. The experimental writings of a man reflect his consciousness or subjectivity, whereas those of a woman are the products of her unconscious and the symptoms of her mental illness. As a result, most male experimental writers, such as Yu Hua and Ge Fei, have received enthusiastic praise from leading Chinese critics for their lucidity, discursive disruption, and courage to challenge readers' expectations.[38] In contrast, Can Xue's daring experiments are interesting to the same critics mainly as symptoms of her paranoia.

As Frederick Engels points out: "The first class opposition that appears in history coincides with the development of the antagonism between man and woman in monogamous marriage and the first class oppression coincides with that of the female sex by the male."[39] Class oppression, however, does not simply coincide with gender hierarchy. To a large extent, gender hierarchy, perceived as biological and natural, can be used to justify any discrimination by one group against another in the name of differences in race, social position, or sexual orientation.[40] Those who want to be masters of slaves cannot avoid being subject to the same logic, a logic that eventually leads to their own slavery. The use of women as subhumans in a large number of experimental fiction works leads to a certain worship of the "master" by these writers. Therefore, the male writers' misogynistic discourse largely limits the subversive potential of their works by reducing them to products of a newly established patriarchal clan. The clan can still present itself as dynamic and subversive mainly because it has not yet truly acquired political power.

In this context, Can Xue's marginalized position as a woman writer within the male order provides her with an edge to overcome the limits imposed on most of her male colleagues by a clan-oriented mentality. Her carefree attitude helped Can Xue break through the barriers that tended to exclude women from the world of experimental fiction. Since then, the lack of support from important literary critics has liberated Can Xue from the obligation to pay tribute to any master. Her success in experimental fiction mocks at the masters' efforts to monopolize this genre under the guardianship of certain new patriarchal figures. Moreover, her success also shows that the masculine monopolization of language is only another fiction by means of which the masters tend to justify their misogynistic discourse.

However, Can Xue's solitary voice, which demystifies the newly established phallological discursive order, does not consciously acquire any positive feminine identity. By choosing absolute solitude, her voice refuses to reverse the patriarchal order or to replace male bonding by female bonding as an easy and simple solution. This choice may be perceived as a gesture of radical disbelief. As Irigaray says: "No one should believe,"[41] although her statement itself suggests a belief in the pluralism of woman's (re)writing. One question remains: Can women formulate a language without truly taking any position? Irigaray's expression "attention and faithfulness to experience"[42] already implies a responsibility based on a belief (*croyance*). A certain amount of belief, as long as it is not blind, is necessary even if merely in order to motivate the act of writing. Any writing, however personal and subjective, can be considered an expression of a certain belief, to the extent that it implies a possible intention to communicate, and thus to take a position. In this sense, a radical disbelief expressed in writing is self-contradictory. In Can Xue's case, her attempt to radicalize disbelief in any possible personal or social tie not only fictionalizes the world of female subjectivity by situating it in a solipsistic world but also alienates a majority of a potentially sympathetic audience interested in gender issues.

As a result, her subversive voice remains largely unheard among potentially sympathetic listeners and has to a large extent been lost. The loss of this audience makes Can Xue's works more accessible to the newly established order of contemporary experimental fiction, which is indeed subversive but for all that no less patriarchal. Consequently, this order has reluctantly incorporated her fiction as a disturbed and disturbing element. Can Xue's originality, deliberately misunderstood and misrepresented as the outcome of the author's madness by the defenders of this order, risks turning into a somewhat embarrassing but nevertheless harmless decoration of one of its targets of subversion[43]—the myth of a masculine monopolization of language.

Can Xue herself appears aware of this danger. At a Shanghai conference organized in honor of two women writers, Can Xue and Wang Anyi, she delivered a speech, published as a postscript to her novel *Performance of Breaking out of Encirclement* (*Tuwei biaoyan*). Her speech, entitled "Aura of Dynamic Masculinity and the Good Period of Literary Criticism" ("Yanggang zhiqi yu wenxue piping de hao shiguang"), ridiculed the misogynistic discourse endorsed by most of her male colleagues.[44] From this point on, major Chinese literary journals, which once competed to publish her works, decided to reject all her manuscripts. Consequently, some of her recent stories were first published in Japanese or in English. In her speech, Can Xue jokingly called her own experimental writings the "art of putting on a stern facial expression" (*banlian yishu*) and attributed this art to the "masculine domain" in which she is mistakenly implicated.[45] A male colleague, whose voice unmistakably reminds us of that of Mo Yan, commented: "Those people in Shanghai are really blind. How could they invite you there? What could a woman speak on this subject [the art of putting a stern facial expression]? This problem can only be solved by men."[46]

At the same time, Can Xue uses the metaphor of an unpredictable cry for a woman's voice comparable to her own.[47] Thereby, she distances herself from the masculine order that her male colleagues tend to establish in the world of experimental fiction. Indeed, her disturbingly unpredictable cry radically disrupts the "dynamic masculinity" (*yanggang zhiqi*) of this literary form.

CHAPTER 4

Quest in Time and Space as a New History of Ancient and Modern Tibet

If Can Xue holds a minority status among Chinese experimental writers because of her gender, Zhaxi Dawa holds a similar position because of his nationality. Half-Tibetan and half-Chinese, Zhaxi Dawa expresses the sense of indeterminacy of his national identity in his writings. Even though Zhaxi Dawa writes about Tibet, the Tibet of his fictional world is not necessarily a positive entity. On the contrary, he has transformed it into an agglomeration of different value systems, such as Tibetan religion and tradition, Han culture, Communist ideology, and Western influences. Like the author's national identity, the Tibet of his fiction is indeterminable.

This indeterminacy may be considered more subversive than a direct challenge to the Communist ideological and Han cultural domination to the extent that it questions the basis and justification for such a domination: the concept of linear and teleological history. Since ancient times, Han culture has always tried to teach the "barbarians" (*fan*)—a name attributed to minorities in the ancient *Book of Rites* (*Liji*)—how to become civilized human beings. This has always meant adopting Han civilization. For its part, the Chinese Communist party pretends that the party leads all people, especially "backward" minorities, toward the final liberation—the Communist paradise. In this context, Zhaxi Dawa's denial of the concept of linear history amounts to debunking the cultural hierarchy, which privileges the Han culture, and the ideological domination established by the Communist party.

The characters in Zhaxi Dawa's fiction often embark on a quest, either religious (like Tabei in search of a place vaguely similar to the Buddhist paradise in "Souls Tied to the Knots of a Leather Rope" ["Jizai pishengzi shang de hun"])[1] or mundane (like Wu Jin in search of the descendant of his father's killer in "Brilliance of Wind and Horse" ["Fengma zhiyao"]).[2] These quests share a common characteristic: despite their convictions of the correctness of the search, the searchers do not truly understand its meaning. Paradoxically, their lack of understanding often motivates them to accomplish their search, because the action of searching itself becomes the end. After being discovered, the object of the search, if it exists, is often disappointing.[3] In this sense, the actual object serves more as an excuse for the action than as the goal. Or more precisely, the search aims at the discovery of the illusory nature of its object.

In these searches, time and space become transformable into each other, and they no longer perform the function of limiting the action. Zhaxi Dawa's heroes return to a historical past or move forward to an unknown future. They can be in Tibet in the morning and in Peru in the evening.[4] Since no event is irreversible, the reversibility of time makes tragedy impossible. As in the case of Wu Jin's execution and resurrection, death itself becomes an absurd comedy. Although Wu Jin does not really understand why he is supposed to kill a person he does not know and why he is to be executed for a murder he never committed, he does not need to worry about the consequences. During his execution, his murdered enemy comes to watch him. After being executed, Wu Jin talks to his murdered enemy on a disconnected phone and tells him that he would rather have a son than take revenge.[5]

Nevertheless, despite the absurdity, the searchers in Zhaxi Dawa's fiction seem to have lost something unknown. Whatever they find at the end of their searches does not recuperate their loss.

The irreducible sense of loss, which cannot even be portrayed as tragic, reveals a more tragic state—the loss of any possible value in truth. Tibet, which often stands for the object of search at a deeper level,[6] is tantamount to the value of a truth whose origin has been forever lost.

The characters' numerous quests in Zhaxi Dawa's fiction reveals the author's personal quest, which can be summed up by a fundamental question: What does it mean to be a contemporary Tibetan writer?

Agglomeration

In 1988, Zhaxi Dawa wrote a short story entitled "Invitation of the Century" ("Shiji zhiyao").[7] Sangjie, a young Tibetan doctor, invited to the wedding of his friend Jiayang Bandan, a historian, is journeying to Jiayang's home. After arriving at Jiayang's village, Sangjie joins other villagers in waiting for the groom, who for some strange reason has become a famous local lord. In addition, the powerful lord has just offended the central authorities and been condemned to prison for the rest of his life. After a long wait, one of the guardians brings out a baby, who continues to shrink until he returns to a woman's womb. The baby is actually the political prisoner, the lord, the groom, the historian, and Sangjie's friend. Sangjie, because of his friendship with the disappearing prisoner, is sent to the prison in his place, because the well-built bastille cannot remain empty.

The story starts with Sangjie's trip to his friend's wedding. Since the trip seems rather long, the hero regrets that he has not brought his bicycle.

> No matter what one might say, two wheels are much faster than two feet. He remembered that Jiayang Bandan was always thinking about one question: a thousand years ago, Tibetans had already connected the process of life and the turning of wheels, because life also consisted of an endless, perpetually rotating circle. Nevertheless, their ancestors never thought to use wheels as a means of trans-

portation. In 1907, the first vehicle to climb the Himalayas and to enter Tibet was an eight-horsepower Clairmont. People were, for the first time in their life, surprised to see a fast-moving mass of metal driven by four round wheels composed of steel rings, spokes, and rubber. "Why is this? Why?" Jiayang Bandan gazed at Sangjie with sorrowful eyes. He tried very hard to open his mouth, but was unable to formulate any answer. Jiayang Bandan never talked to Sangjie about history, but occasionally told him some juicy anecdotes. However, he still could not help asking "why" from time to time. Naturally, Sangjie could never answer him, because these questions had nothing to do with medicine. ("SJZY," p. 106)

Connecting the Buddhist notion of *samsara*, or more literally "turning of wheels" (*lunhui*), to an American car of 1907 is absurd in its contrast of the ancient and the modern, the abstract and the concrete, the religious and the mundane, the East and the West. In Zhaxi Dawa's writings, this absurdity always remains on the surface. Much like his character Sangjie, the author never seems to concern himself with any definitive answer to the same question: "Why is this? Why?" (*Zheshi wei shenmo wei shenmo*). Sangjie's position as a doctor in the short story in relation to the historian's question parallels the author's position as a writer of fiction in relation to history. Furthermore, Sangjie's position also parallels the author's position as a Tibetan storyteller in relation to the totalizing view of literature promoted by the Chinese Communist party under the label of "socialist realism." Unlike a historian, who attempts to support a vision of a rationalized history factually, Zhaxi Dawa, like a doctor, gives us visions of abnormalities as symptoms, by deconstructing any linear or teleological notion of history, one of the main bases of socialist-realist works. Sangjie's inability to articulate intelligible answers proves that he is outside the realm of historicity constructed in accordance with this allegedly realistic concept.

The failure to "historicize" the cultural, ideological, and historical situations of Tibet poses an unanswerable question. Unanswerable because the concept of history established by Communist China is predicated on an ideological and cultural domination that tends to reduce indigenous cultures to silence. Unanswerable because Tibetan culture cannot be preserved untouched in a museum in the contemporary world of change—as some advocates of pure Tibetan values would like. Unanswerable because cultural boundaries tend to become more and more fugitive, to the point that it is difficult to draw lines of demarcation among cultures. In a sense, Zhaxi Dawa's short story illustrates the coexistence of the traditional and the modern, of the indigenous culture, Chinese values, and Western influences. The connection between the wheels of an American car, which represent technology, modernity, and concreteness, and the wheels of life, with their religious, traditional, cultural, and philosophical connotations, is itself a metaphor of the world of agglomeration, the world of contemporary Tibet.

Through Sangjie's eyes, the author presents contemporary Tibet as an image of the grotesque agglomeration.

> Sangjie hurried, following his intuitive sense of direction. Deep in his heart he was still thinking about his kite that had flown away and disappeared in the distance. He had the impression that the boulevard, the coming-and-going cars, the foreign tourists with their hairy legs and heavy luggage, the wild dogs lying under trees on both sides of the street, the high buildings, and the lamas under their floral umbrellas, etc., in his eyes all resembled images reflected in a mirror—unreal and illusory. ("SJZY," p. 107)

Sangjie's lost kite becomes a guide for his life, and the story ends with the reunion of the hero and his kite in the most unexpected place, his prison cell. The kite leads him to complete the circle in his consciousness or semiconsciousness. We see the contemporary Tibetan city, Lhasa, in its mixture of contradictory values, from the point of view of Sangjie's dim consciousness. This point of view becomes more and more internalized and subjective. The absurdity of the combination of the lama with his floral umbrella becomes the unreal vision reflected in a deceptive mirror. Sangjie has become part of this mirror. The boundary between the objective and subjective worlds has been abolished. Sangjie's consciousness reflects contemporary Tibet in its agglomeration, confusion, and disorientation. To this extent, Sang-jie's trip to his friend's wedding can be considered a trip taken by Tibetan culture toward a timeless past, "free" from Chinese and Western influences.

The gap between the subjective and objective worlds, between the city and Sangjie's consciousness is further bridged by the Buddhist notion of the "mirror image" (*jingxiang*). The mirror image, turned into the point of departure for his journey to a timeless past, gives the journey a certain religious aura.

> He remembered that a friend had told him that if one put two mirrors together, face to face, one could see infinity. At present, he could experience the kind of loss that led toward infinity, resembling the feeling created by a position between two mirrors. As a result, the city disappeared behind him, suburbs and the country also disappeared behind him. . . . As if he had emerged from an atmosphere of fog and confusion, there were endless mountains and emptiness in front of him. The sun shining on top of the bright and blue sky extended the day so much that it became eternal. ("SJZY," p. 107)

In the endless process of reflections, the world and the self become identical. This identity, or loss of identity because of lack of differences, leads toward emptiness, or the world of nature, which is supposedly free of the cultural agglomeration of the contemporary world. In the natural world, the first thing that has disappeared is the division between the city and the country. The disappearance is to an extent incarnated by the hero, Sangjie, a country boy who has integrated himself fairly well into city life. The undifferentiated world of nature carries no human traces; even the path that leads Sangjie to the old village bears only the footprints of beasts. It forms a noticeable contrast to the crowdedness and diversity of the previous moment. By contrasting the modern world of agglomeration with the simple and natural past, is the narrator suggesting that a return to cultural origins through a somewhat religious path is a solution to the current situation in Tibet? If this is the case, his suggestion, however, is not devoid of irony. As Sangjie contemptuously calls the natural world of a primitive past a "wasteland" (*huangman*; "SJZY," p. 107) from which he would like to escape at any price, the author's skepticism is directed to the present and the future, as well as to the past. At the same time, the more the protagonist tends to escape from the past, the more he is haunted by it. Like the author of the "Invitation of the Century" who engages his modern characters in a hopeless quest for a forlorn origin, Sangjie cannot help experiencing life as a prisoner of the past despite his knowledge of modern science and his preference for the comforts of modern life.

On the one hand, Tibet as a cultural entity can exist only as a forlorn past in Zhaxi Dawa's world of fiction. On the other hand, the author cannot avoid projecting the values of Western liberalism, serving as a potential counterpart to the domination of communism, into the future of Tibet. Partly because of Zhaxi Dawa's ambivalent attitude toward the past and future, we can see in his writings an inescapable sense of playfulness in terms of temporality. In "Invitation of the Century," the trip to the past is indistinguishable from the trip to the future. Sangjie is invited to his friend's wedding, which turns into Jiayang Bandan's return to a woman's womb. In this case, marrying a woman in order to become a potential father is tantamount to marrying the mother's womb in order to go back to a forlorn origin. Moreover, the search for a past value, such as a religious and mythical origin, may often result in the discovery of a new value, as in the case of the old man on a donkey. Using an archaic folk tune, the old man praises the internationalism of the modern world to an audience in a remote village in ancient Tibet ("SJZY," p. 112). The past is hopelessly and comically mingled with the present and future. Whatever their efforts, the searchers in Zhaxi Dawa's fiction can find only an origin that is already a mixture.

Dislocation

In Zhaxi Dawa's "Souls Tied to the Knots of a Leather Cord," a young man, Tabei, embarks on a religious quest with a young woman, Qiong. The story is supposedly told by the Living Buddha Sangjie Dapu in a conversation with the narrator. The narrator, to his great surprise, finds that the Living Buddha, on his deathbed, is reciting one of the narrator's unpublished short stories. After rereading his own story—"his beloved castaways" (*ke'ai de qi'er*)—as he calls them, the narrator decides to look for his characters on the Kalong Mountains. When he finally finds them, Tabei is dying in Qiong's arms. After Tabei's death, the narrator, followed by Qiong, takes the place of the hero and continues the same quest.

In this narrative framework, Zhaxi Dawa mixes fiction writing and the Buddha's divine words. This framework is reminiscent of Gabriel García Marquez's *One Hundred Years of Solitude*, which supposedly has strongly influenced the Tibetan writer.[8] Indeed, the Columbian novel has a similar supernatural framework: Melquiades's parchments.[9] In both cases, everything is predicted in supernatural writing, and the plot itself equals the act of reading. However, this similarity does not make Zhaxi Dawa less interesting, since he provides the same framework with a fresh context, Tibetan Buddhism. Melquiades is a Gypsy and thus an outsider, who symbolizes mobility and opening toward the outside world in a Columbian village confined by mountains, whereas the Living Buddha is the earthly representative of Tibetan religion. Logically speaking, the same subject in Zhaxi Dawa's writing should be treated more solemnly than in Marquez's. Paradoxically, Zhaxi Dawa's account is much more lighthearted and playful. Aureliano, the last descendant of the family, deciphers the parchments completely only in the last moment of his life, which is experienced as the act of reading.

> He began to decipher the instant that he was living, deciphering it as he lived it, prophesying himself in the act of deciphering the last page of the parchments, as if he were looking into a speaking mirror. Before reaching the final line, however, he had already understood that he would never leave that room, for it was foreseen that the city of mirrors (or mirages) would be wiped out by the wind and exiled from the memory of men at the precise moment when Aureliano Babilonia would finish deciphering the parchments, and

that everything written on them was unrepeatable since time im-
memorial and forever more, because races condemned to one hundred years of solitude did not have a second opportunity on earth.[10]

Writing is the "speaking mirror" of the hero's life. Moreover,
the mirror determines the past, the present, and the future of
every minute of his life. Thus, the title of "speaking mirror" dig-
nifies the novel. This dignity is further reinforced by the unique-
ness of the story—since it is unrepeatable. Although many epi-
sodes in the novel are circular and repetitive, this ending provides
the supernatural framework with a sense of linearity that prede-
termines the otherwise dispersed plots.

Zhaxi Dawa's narrator, however, appears much less sure of
himself than the mysterious narrative voice in the Columbian
novel, even though his text is miraculously recited by the Living
Buddha. After he finds his characters, he tries hard to dissuade
Tabei from dying. Although he respectfully calls him "prophet,"
Tabei categorically refuses to listen to his creator, who, at this
very moment, is regretting what he has done to his "creature."

> Not until this very moment do I discover, belatedly, the truth about
> my "beloved castaways": They have all been endowed with life and
> will. Once characters are created, their every move becomes an ob-
> jective fact. In letting Tabei and Qiong come out of that numbered
> manila envelope, I have clearly made an irreparable mistake. And
> why is it that to this day I have not been able to give shape to "people
> of a new type"? This is yet another mistake. If someone demands
> to know why, in this great and heroic era, I still allow characters like
> Tabei and Qiong to exist, how shall I answer?   (*Spring Bamboo*, pp.
> 165–66)

Unlike the indifferent and confident Gypsy Melquiades, the
narrator of "Souls Tied to the Knots of a Leather Rope" is deeply
attached to his characters and uncertain about what he should do
with them. In the end, he literally identifies himself with the hero
in order to embark on an apparently aimless quest. The Living
Buddha's voice, instead of endorsing that of Zhaxi Dawa's narrator with a seeming dignity, compromises the authority or certainty of Buddhism by questioning the reliability of its spokes-

man—the Living Buddha, who speaks in his voice. At the same time, this flexibility provides the narrator's "beloved castaways" with lives of their own. The characters' independence and the narrator's lightheartedness reveal a deeply concealed problem, the lack of any commonly accepted cultural authority, or an ideological vacuum, that neither the native religion nor a Westernized modernization can overcome. The author's uncertainty despite the supernatural framework may be explained by the fact that his Tibetan origin in this case is overshadowed by his disillusionment with any collective belief. This deeply rooted disillusionment characterizes post–Cultural Revolution Chinese experimental fiction writers. By contrast, the Columbian novelist is much more ideologically engaged as an overtly left-wing intellectual, whose fictional world in the final analysis remains eschatological.[11] In the same vein, the Latin American author has more faith in native religions than the Tibetan writer does in Buddhism, since for him supernatural elements can be taken as another "form of knowing and understanding." It is his belief "that the writer has as much of a responsibility towards such forms of knowledge as towards the revelations of a more purely analytical inquiry."[12] In other words, the supernatural elements in Marquez's novel have gained the status of knowledge and need to be treated seriously as a kind of representative of the Third World culture,[13] whereas in Zhaxi Dawa's story, knowledge becomes supernatural in a fairly absurd sense. To a certain extent, the difference between the Columbian magical-realist author and the Tibetan experimental fiction writer is analogous to the difference between the May Fourth writers and their descendants at the end of the century. The Columbian writer, like Lu Xun, has rebelled for a cause, whereas Zhaxi Dawa and his colleagues are rebels without a cause, since they have no faith in any collective value system.

On the one hand, Zhaxi Dawa's "beloved castaways" challenge communism by means of their radical difference from the stereotype of "people of a new type" (*xinren*) in socialist-realist literature. On the other hand, being "endowed with life and will" (*bei fuyu le shengming he yizhi de*), they escape from the control of their narrator as well as from his spokesman—the Living Buddha, who recites the story on his deathbed. Despite their beliefs, the characters' connections to Buddhism do not seem to be taken seriously by the narrative voice, which gently but constantly mocks at their old-fashioned ideas. Although Buddhism allows Zhaxi Dawa's characters to distance themselves from Communist ideology, which is represented in socialist-realist literature by "people of a new type," it does not provide a positive voice with which its believers can truly identify. Like other elements in his fiction, religion is often subject to the author's playful treatment. Buddhism becomes a serious matter only as a counterpart to communism.

As the bondsman attempts to "evade the blockade of his own desire by projecting its reason into the external repression of the lord,"[14] Buddhism in Zhaxi Dawa's fiction gains its identity by negating the cultural and ideological domination of Communist China. Buddhist believers, like Tabei and Qiong, are believers only to the extent that they express their "creator's" disbelief in communism. Therefore, the negation of Communist ideology in Zhaxi Dawa's world of fiction becomes the raison d'être for the positive existence of Buddhism.

As a Tibetan writer in Chinese and someone schooled in an educational system dominated by the Han culture, Zhaxi Dawa is not necessarily an insider of Tibetan culture. However, because of the cultural and ideological domination of Communist China over Tibet, Zhaxi Dawa has chosen to identify with Tibetan culture, of which Buddhism is one of the most significant expressions, in order to assert his subversive position. This identification, limited to a negative function, comes into being thanks to the oppression of Communist ideology. Lacking a deep understanding of and faith in Buddhism, his identification cannot avoid being superficial. Nevertheless, this superficial identification distinguishes Zhaxi Dawa from the quasi nihilism of other contemporary experimental writers. His "negative" belief makes his writings, if not more optimistic, at least more playful. Since he must play two powerful ideological systems against one another, everything else can easily be reduced to the status of plaything in his world of agglomeration. On various occasions, Buddhism as a negative force even becomes identical to what it intends to negate, communism, in a faithless laughter of confusion (or cynicism).

During his trip, Tabei meets an old man. Although the traveler himself ignores his own destination, the old man tries to figure out the mystical nature of Tabei's journey by comparing it with journeys of previous pilgrims.

> We set up a commune here, and everyone was talking about taking the communist road. At the time few people could rightly say what communism was, we only knew it was one of the heavens. But nobody knew where it was. We'd asked travelers who came from the south, from the east, from the north, but none of them had ever seen it. That left only the Kalong mountains. So a few people sold all their belongings, slung their tsampa bags across their shoulders and set out to cross the Kalongs. They said they were going to communism. But they never came back. After that, not a single person from the village ever headed out there again, no matter how hard the times got. (*Spring Bamboo*, p. 157)

Tabei's unknown destination is also the place of hope for earlier pilgrims. His predecessors have never been able to return from their destination. Like his predecessors, Tabei is determined to brave any danger, even if he does not know exactly where to go and why he is going. This blind faith seems to equate Tabei in his relationship with Buddhism and his predecessors in theirs with communism.

Before his death, Tabei's faith is again ridiculed for his misunderstanding of the modern world.

> "What is it saying, Prophet? I can't understand it. Please tell me, quickly, you must have understood it, I beg of you." He turns around and prostrates himself at my feet.
>
> His ears catch the signals long before mine do. It is not until several minutes later that Qiong and I hear a sound, a very real sound, coming from the sky. We listen intently.
>
> "It's brass bells ringing on a temple roof!" Qiong cries excitedly.

"It's the chiming of church bells," I correct her.

"It's an avalanche! It's frightening!"

"No, this is the majestic sound of horns and drums and a multitude of voices singing," I correct her again. Qiong gives me a bewildered look.

"God is beginning to speak," Tabei proclaims solemnly.

This time I dare not correct anyone, even though the sound is the amplified voice of a man speaking in English. How can I tell Tabei that this is the grand opening ceremony of the Twenty-third Olympics being held in Los Angeles, U.S.A., and that, by means of satellites in space, television and radio networks are beaming their live coverage of this historic occasion to every corner of the earth?

"This is not a sign from God, my child. It is the sound of chimes and trumpets and a vast choir, signifying mankind's challenge to the world." It is the only thing I can think of to tell him. (*Spring Bamboo*, pp. 167–68)

Three people have three different interpretations for the same sound they are hearing on top of the Kalongs. Tabei is excited because he believes he hears a heavenly voice for which he decides to die. Qiong is scared because she thinks she hears the destructive sound of nature. The narrator feels condescending toward his characters because he knows both of them are mistaken. In short, each one's reaction is determined by his/her ideological makeup. Tabei is religious although he does not know exactly where Buddhism leads. Qiong often follows her "natural" tendency in her sexual longing and her desire for a more comfortable life-style. Moreover, like most female characters in Zhaxi Dawa's writing, she is basically passive and submissive, accepting as natural whatever is imposed on her. The narrator himself is revealed as being a believer in modernization, like Sangjie in "Invitation of the Century," who believes that Tibet's future may lie in the hands of a few "modernized" people able to end its isolation ("SJZY," p. 117).

Ironically, Tabei, a devout Buddhist, calls the narrator, a strange modernist, "prophet" (*xianzhi*). This irony is double-edged. On the one hand, Buddhism has little to do with "mankind's challenge to the world" (*ren xiang shijie tiaozhan*). The English voice that announces the opening of the Olympics is one of the most mundane sounds a Buddhist adherent may hear. First, it challenges the basis of ancient religion because it is founded on the value of human physical strength. Second, Buddhism regards desire to outshine others as vanity blocking the way to enlightenment, whereas the Olympics is based on this very vanity. On the other hand, the narrator's belief in modernization or Westernization coincides with the Chinese Communist ideology of the 1980's. Communism considers religion the "spiritual opiate of the people" (*duhai renmin de jingshen yapian*)—backward, stupid, and irrational. In contrast, technology, the major component of modernization, is the product of scientificity and rationalism, which are often in conflict with mysticism.

Thirty years ago, some pilgrims went to the Kalongs to look for communism. In 1985, Tabei follows their footsteps in search of Buddhist salvation. After Tabei's death, his creator, the narrator of this story, continues the quest with his protagonist's former lover. All of them follow the same road for different reasons. The believers in communism are forever lost in an unknown world, and Tabei dies enfolded in his misconception of the world. What about the narrator, who understands English and wears a Seiko watch and sunglasses? How can we be certain that he will not repeat the same journey as his predecessors? Is the voice he hears necessarily the sound of an American radio station? If his characters can be mistaken in their interpretations of this sound, why not he? The only proof that the narrator uses as a point of reference for the "objective" world is his Seiko watch—unreliable as it is.

Unlike Márquez, who ends his book by emphasizing that his story is unrepeatable, Zhaxi Dawa seems to tell us that everything in his story is bound to be repeated—hopelessly. What is the future then, besides this meaningless repetition? If Buddhism gains its value in the negation of communism, modernization or Westernization prevails because it serves as a negative value for both ancient Tibet and the current ideology of modern China. It goes without saying that this negative force, shapeless and chaotic as it is, cannot be captured in a positive light.

Individualized Time or Temporal Disorder

Sangjie's return to the timeless past is unfortunate, since it ends in his imprisonment for life. His historian friend, however, literally transforms his scholarly task into personal destiny. Instead of finding the origins of human society in a historical narrative, Jiayang Bandan returns to the womb after gradually regressing to a newborn baby. In fact, this return saves him from the fate of becoming a political prisoner. In other words, the womb, or the original world, is still, if not a safer place, at least a place with more room for hope. To this extent, the unknown situation is much better than political imprisonment, which symbolizes the present situation in Tibet under the rule of the Chinese Communist party.

This return to origins coincides with a chronological disorder in which the notion of time becomes meaningless. While the honorable Lord Jiayang Bandan is visibly shrinking into a little baby, the waiting crowd is aging rapidly. The girl who is supposed to be his potential mother remains unchangeably youthful ("SJZY," p. 111). Each character has a subjectified time according to his or her needs and narrative function. The girl with a black mole must keep her body youthful in order to receive the shrunken Jiayang Bandan in her womb. In order to recoup the form of fetus, Jiayang Bandan needs to retreat in time. The villagers' rapid aging symbolizes the endless process of waiting. In normal life, time functions as an objective standard tying each individual to an external reality. Transformed into personal properties in Zhaxi Dawa's fiction, time varies in accordance with its owner. Time is no longer an abstract measurement but a concrete entity that varies according to psychological, personal, and social elements. By depriving time of its normally objective quality, the narrator of the story creates a confusion in which everyone seems to lose contact with a unified reality.

The dissolution of time questions the official notion of history by means of which the current regime justifies China's occupation of Tibet—the Communist party liberated Tibet and brought about progress. Since time is individualized, progress may from different perspectives be interpreted as regression or stopping. Time, as the measurement of history, is itself constituted by subjective interpretations, depending on each individual's relation to what she or he perceives as reality. Official history, emphasizing the progress that was brought to Tibet by the Communist party, is only one of the subjective interpretations of time, and its imposed central position in Tibet results more from cultural, political, and ideological domination than from any objective reality.

The abolition of time as an objective measurement of history is highly politicized and paralleled by the absence of authorities. In "Invitation of the Century," Sangjie fails to communicate with the inhabitants of the timeless village precisely because of his notion of authorities and temporality.

"What is this place?" he asked the old man.

"This is the Jiayang Manor. During your trip, did you see some people coming in this direction?"

"Where is your party's secretary?" he mumbled.

The old man looked at him, puzzled.

"I mean the director of the village, where is he? You still do not understand. Well, how about the director of safety, or the chief of the people's militia?"

"I do not understand what you are saying." After quite a while, the old man replied slowly: "If you are looking for chiefs, here the only one is the chief of the village. There aren't any higher officials. But he's not here, he went to another post to welcome the young master." . . .

"In what year is this goddamn thing happening?" he shouted, reddened with anger.

"Indeed, you will soon see the young master here."

"What year is this?" He asked in a low voice.

"What year?" The old man replied after thinking for a little while: "We countrymen never pay attention to what year it is. The only important thing is to be able to count how many sheep we have and how much cereal we harvest." ("SJZY," pp. 108–9)

In Zhaxi Dawa's story, temporality and political hierarchy are two systems of differentiation by which modernity is measured.

Modern life is characterized by the refinement of its systems of differentiation. The encounter between the old man, a villager in good old Tibet, and the youngster, a citizen of modern Lhasa, emphasizes the difference between ancient and modern Tibet in terms of differentiation. For the old man, time and political hierarchy are equally superfluous. According to him, a farmer does not need to know the identity of his numerous chiefs or the year in which he is living, as long as he can provide his family with enough food.

The old man's terse answers to Sangjie's anxious questions ridicule the complications of modern life. What use are the numerous cadres' titles without which a modern Tibetan like Sangjie does not know how to behave in a new environment? The year, as a marker of a historical period, is important for Sangjie, since in his eyes Tibet differs in accordance with historical period. For the old man, however, the division of time by years is superfluous as the titles of Sangjie's numerous cadres. Since food is his main, if not only, concern in life, historical changes do not have a substantial impact on him. Unlike Sangjie, who lives in the modern world, the farmer of ancient times does not wish to improve his world.

Both political hierarchy and the refined measurement of time imply efforts to reorganize society and human relations to nature according to certain human aspirations. One is synchronic, and the other, diachronic—to borrow Ferdinand de Saussure's expressions; or one is more political, centered on social structure, and the other, more scientific, centered on technology and relations between society and nature. Political hierarchy suggests an effort to restructure the world, and the refined measurement of time implies an attempt to control the future.

To a large extent, the process of reorganization is also the process of modernization. The old man's indifference toward political hierarchy and the measurement of time casts an ironical light on the effectiveness of efforts at reorganization. Like Sangjie's kite, which, having traveled through centuries by the end of the story, returns to the point of departure, namely, his hand, the old man views Tibet as unchangeable despite its vicissitudes at a more superficial level. Just as all the pilgrims in "Souls Tied to the Knots of a Leather Rope"—be they Buddhist, Communist, or modernist—must go to the Kalong Mountains to search for their paradise, the people of different generations repeat the same action under the cover of different names. One thing remains essential for the old farmer in "Invitation of the Century": food, which sums up the most basic economic needs.

To a certain extent, the old man's irony does sound delusive, because despite his indifference he cannot escape from time or from political hierarchy. Like the other villagers, he ages and must silently endure the messengers' oppression. The difference between him and a modernist like Sangjie is that he feels peaceful because he is not concerned with changing the status quo, whereas Sangjie is frustrated by his desire to improve life. In other words, one is serenely passive, and the other, ineffectively active. In Zhaxi Dawa's story, however, Sangjie's desire is subjected to irony because the very notion of improvement appears questionable. Change never means a linear movement of progress in a certain direction. In most of his stories, it appears to be a chaotic movement toward different directions, which often leads toward the point of departure disguised by a new name. Coincidentally, the four stories by Zhaxi Dawa analyzed in this chapter all end at the point where they begin.[15] Narration is primarily a cyclical movement.

However, irony directed at the present situation is a double-edged weapon. If refined differentiation in modern times may be perceived as ineffective and useless, especially in the eyes of an ancient Tibetan farmer, the isolation of the old farmer's ancient village does not necessarily appear less absurd for a modern reader of "Invitation of the Century."

While Sangjie returns to a remote past represented by this village, a nameless old man on a donkey passes by, journeying toward modern time. The old man uses his body as a kind of world map by designating different parts of it as geographical areas. Although he is mocked by the villagers for his eccentricity, the narrator still wishes that the end of the village's isolation will bring some hope.

[Sangjie] thought about the girl with a black mole on her chin, and remembered that she had gone in the same direction as the eccentric old man. He truly hoped that the old man was still waiting for her on the road. He had said that his donkey could carry two people. One day, she would have to come back, and at that time, she would display a beautiful map of the world on her eternally youthful body. At that time, villagers might have become able to understand and to read it—Sangjie had confidence.   ("SJZY," p. 117)

Sangjie, as the spokesman for the narrator, vaguely hopes to find a better future for Tibet in modernization, which is symbolized by the world map on the old man's body. However, according to Sangjie, the modernization of Tibet by means of an unattractive male body fails because no one is truly interested in this body, which is burdened with its own history. Through his protagonist's voice, Zhaxi Dawa suggests another alternative: replacing the old, undesirable male body by that of a beautiful female. Furthermore, the youthful body belongs to a virgin mother, in whose womb the fetus of a modern historian, Jiayang Bandan, finds its origin. Immaculate and sacred, the youthful body of the virgin mother sustains male desire by forever postponing gratification. Desirable and untouchable, this body becomes a perfect vehicle for representation, since it provokes desire that cannot be consummated. Her body becomes the location for a possible birth of a new history, which will eventually channel unconsummated and sublimated desire toward a better future. In other words, the desire for her body will become the desire for successful Tibetan modernization.

If the old man on a donkey, thanks to his age and experience, represents ancient Tibet subject to modernization, the girl represents the Tibetan origin by means of her pregnancy. Since he himself has chosen his body as a vehicle of modernization, the old man's representational power is mainly subjective. Chosen as the vehicle of modernization because of her reproductive function, the girl's representational power is in contrast mainly objective. Moreover, the female body, devoid of any personal history, is also a better signifier thanks to its emptiness. Nevertheless, the question remains open: If the old man's version of modernization fails to attract attention from the Tibetans of the ancient village, can an unsuccessfully modernized Tibet be rescued through the embellishment and eroticization of the means of representation? Or to phrase the question differently: Can Westernization, which, as the girl's body, represents a more attractive version of modernization, save Tibet from an unsuccessful and destructive modernization, which, symbolized by the old man's body, is imposed by the dominance of communism and Han culture?

"Perhaps the villagers might understand" (*cunliren xingxu neng lijie*) ("SJZY," p. 117). By minimizing the possibility of such a successful modernization through the use of both the modal adverb "perhaps" (*xingxu*) and the modal verb "might" (*neng*), the author underlines his own skepticism. Despite his deep nostalgia, Zhaxi Dawa realizes that Tibet as a pure cultural entity can no longer be found, even through a trip to the timeless past. Ironically, modernity, which has been introduced to ancient Tibet in such a destructive way, presents the only possible way out for the author of "Invitation of the Century."

This dilemma may partly explain Zhaxi Dawa's ambivalent attitude toward the concept of temporality and historicity. In his stories, present-day Tibet is a mixture of contradictory values. Ancient Tibet, as a pure origin, has been forever lost. Even if this origin might be recovered through some strange quests, ancient culture can no longer survive in the modern world. The future appears even more threatening to Tibet's cultural and political identity. Nevertheless, since the author, despite the efforts of his various characters, has never truly found an "authentic" cultural identity as a firm ground on which to stand, he cannot even be serious about his loss, which is transformed into the loss of a fantasized origin. Consequently, his ambivalent attitude toward history and time is necessarily playful. Everything is transformed into a game, including the potential rebirth of the historian Jiayang Bandan as the symbol of the future Tibet, "a more beautiful world" (*shijie hui bian de meili yixie*) in "a time without an aristocracy" (*meiyou guizu de shidai*; "SJZY," p. 115), through the body of a virgin mother.

Women as Numbers

Zhaxi Dawa's *Tibet: Mysterious Years* (*Xizang yinmi suiyue*) closely resembles Márquez's *One Hundred Years of Solitude*. The story is about four generations of a Tibetan family that, after years of living in the mountains, moves to the city. At the end of the story, a woman doctor from Lhasa named Ciren Jiemu enters a grotto atop a mountain, where she encounters a mysterious old man who appears in turn as a skeleton and as a living being. The name of the woman doctor, "Ciren Jiemu," is shared by women of different generations in this story. She holds a Buddhist rosary, which a moment ago had miraculously appeared behind her. The old man speaks to her while waving his hands:

> "Ciren Jiemu, count the number of pearls in the rosary."
> "There are one hundred and eight," Ciren Jiemu replies promptly.
> "Each one of them is one period of time," he utters. "Each one is Ciren Jiemu; Ciren Jiemu is every woman." The old man opens his eyes, and for a while gazes at her solemnly. Finally, in a few words he reveals this ultimate truth yet unknown to the common people.[16]

Through the voice of the hermit who transcends the boundaries between life and death by being at the same time a skeleton and a living person, this long family history teaches us the "ultimate truth" (*zhenti*). *Zhenti* in Buddhism means the "true essence," which is emptiness. In Zhaxi Dawa's story, however, it refers specifically to women. Women are identical to the pearls in the Buddhist rosary miraculously emerging behind Ciren Jiemu, the woman doctor. Women are identical to the years disappearing one after another. Women are mysteries or, more precisely, the representations of mysteries. Like numbers, they are abstract entities that have no "essence" or substance in themselves. Due to their lack of any individuality, they can be used as counters, symbols, and indices for something that is otherwise unrepresentable, the "ultimate truth" (*zhenti*).

By identifying women with the "ultimate truth"—the emptiness left by an ideological vacuum—Zhaxi Dawa uses women not only as abstract and neutral numbers but also as a magical medicine that sutures male subjecthood. By covering up the emptiness of this "ultimate truth," women mystify the sense of disorientation in the male subject, as if there were certain deep religious implications behind it. By means of the emptiness of women as a representation of the "ultimate truth," Zhaxi Dawa turns the male subject's trauma caused by the ideological vacuum into a simulacrum of religious faith. Female bodies, like the pearls of the Buddhist rosary in *Tibet: Mysterious Years*, which are devoid of any individuality, function as representations of what cannot be represented or, more precisely, as a covering up of what must remain unrepresentable—nothingness in its radically mundane sense.

It goes without saying that this function of women deprives Zhaxi Dawa's female characters of any subject position and voice. One of the numerous women called Ciren Jiemu in *Tibet: Mysterious Years* functions purely as currency. After Dalang, the patriarch of one of the last two families in the mountains, saves a rich merchant's life, the latter asks him if he can pay back his benefactor by means of money. Dalang refuses money but suggests that a woman would be a better form of payment. The next day, the merchant brings him a woman named Ciren Jiemu. From this point on, she serves as the wife of Dalang's three robust sons. Interestingly, this woman reminds Dalang of his beloved Ciren Jiemu, Mima's daughter, who devotes her life to supplying food and drink to a Buddhist hermit in a secret grotto. In this case, women are like money, not only exchangeable but also indistinguishable one from another.

The hermit in the secret grotto depends on the devotion of women of different generations. Mima, the ancestor of the last family in the mountains, commits a sinful act against Buddha. In order to make restitution for his sin, his wife Chaxiang has to devote her life to providing food and drink for the sacred man. Ciren Jiemu, their only daughter, is born simply for the sake of continuing her mother's career. As we saw at the beginning of this section, the narrator implies that at the end of the story, another Ciren Jiemu, the woman doctor from Lhasa, will continue the same job after the death of Mima's daughter.

Who is the mysterious and anonymous old man for whom generations of women sacrifice their happiness, desire, and life? Why does he deserve such unconditional worship? The only two scenes in which a reader may learn something about the hidden god are the dream of Ciren Jiemu, Mima's daughter, and the final dialogue between the old man and the woman doctor.

In Ciren Jiemu's dream, the hermit is identified with her potential lover, Dalang. Before her devotions to the hermit began, Dalang claimed her as a belonging and insisted on touching her body. He comes to her door to claim his food carrying the same bag and teapot that, like her mother, Ciren Jiemu uses to bring food and drink to the invisible hermit. At that point, to her great surprise, Ciren Jiemu realizes in her dream that the sacred man to whom her family has made offerings for generations is nobody else but her potential lover. Once she wakes up, she realizes that Dalang was right in the dream—she has indeed forgotten to send food to the hermit in time.

The connection between Dalang and the mysterious hermit is interesting, because the former is apparently presented as the opposite of the latter. As the father of three robust sons, Dalang daringly and independently indulges in food, sex, and other of life's pleasures. In short, in a mundane sense he can be taken as an emblem of masculinity. He has had an intense desire to possess Ciren Jiemu, Mima's daughter, since her birth, and only agrees to give her up for religious reasons. His successor, the sacred man, becomes in Ciren Jiemu's dream Dalang's own double. In other words, Dalang's physical self gives up the woman to his religious self, but only in order to make Ciren Jiemu more completely devoted to her male god. To this extent, the connection between the august hermit and the mundane father transcends the symbol of masculinity based on a common trait between them: both religious faith and masculine power are established on the basis of women's sacrifice and submission.

In her dream, Ciren Jiemu sadly complains to Dalang, who is also the hermit:

"When I was very little, you held me in your arms, asking me to become your wife once I grew up. If at that time I could have spoken, I would have told you that I was scared. After I had just grown up, you always stretched your hands from the side of the brook and deeply disturbed me with your caresses. While leaving Kuokang, you took several sheep from my household. After this I thought I would be able to overcome my sexual longing. But every night, I constantly have sinful and shameful dreams. Like a demon you consistently hide yourself in my head. You climbed on the top of the mountain, not because you wanted to leave me alone, but because you wanted to conquer me and to dominate me from on high. You have even laid the Jela Mountains on me to the point that I feel almost suffocated by their weight. Aren't you ceaselessly manipulating me?" she says while crying bitterly. (*XZ*, p. 173)

In Zhaxi Dawa's story, a man's relationship to a woman is like a god's relationship to a human being. Ciren Jiemu exists merely as Dalang's plaything, exactly replicating her relationship to the invisible hermit. Her resistance is useless and expressed only in the form of powerless tears. The tears do not even inspire any compassion in the heart of her potential lover, who is also in this dream her god. Logically, one should not expect such a powerful god to love his believer, who serves only as the object on which he exercises his divine power. Even sexual desire is turned into a pure desire for power, which may well destroy the object of desire, woman. The existence of this masculine power, symbolized in the weight of the Jela Mountains on Ciren Jiemu's back, may be proved only by the woman's suffering. Similarly, the hermit's religious power is manifested only in his Buddhist token, the rosary, of which each pearl is identical to a woman. Without women's suffering, the mountain as a phallic symbol would be empty and weightless. Without women's suffering, the Buddhist hermit would be a common old man.

As a mark of differentiation, woman's lack of any subject position, expressed in the form of total submission to the religious and/or masculine world, is used to prove man's ontological and metaphysical existence. Therefore, a clear-cut sexual hierarchy is necessary in Zhaxi Dawa's writings in order to prevent his world from falling apart completely. Nevertheless, this hierarchy is not

enough to provide Zhaxi Dawa's world of fiction or male subjectivity with a meaningful existence, precisely because a complete negation of female subjectivity, which the author attempts
to do, cannot function in a supposedly open-ended world.

The objectified hierarchy justifies another hierarchy personified by the living-dead hermit in the grotto, who requires complete obedience from human beings—male or female. This hierarchy may be perceived either as religious—the representation
of the Buddhist tradition—or as political—the incarnation of the
party. Furthermore, the desperate gesture of reducing women to
objects and signs that support the male subject position reveals a
castration complex, since the aggressiveness of this gesture results from an invincible fear—fear of the disappearance of difference. Without violence and power, which maintain political and
sexual hierarchies, the differences are likely to disappear. For
Zhaxi Dawa and a number of Chinese writers of his generation,
sexual difference, uncertain as it is, is taken as the basis of meaning
in a world where political, cultural, and ideological values have
become nonsensical. It is as if they could save themselves from
either irreducible confusion or from irreducible violence as long
as they can justify sexual hierarchy as natural. By unconditionally
participating in the misogynistic discourse that prevails among
contemporary Chinese experimental writers, Zhaxi Dawa at a
deeper level renounces his Tibetan identity. He situates himself in
a center that equally relinquishes gendered and ethnic minorities
to the bottom of the ladder. Because of the lack of resistance, his
marginality mainly serves as a decoration for the Chinese cultural
center. This decorative marginality barely distinguishes him
from other searchers of masculinity in their longing for a firm
ground in a world of ideological vacuum.

CHAPTER 5

• ⟶

Femininity and Masculinity
in Su Tong's Trilogy

> What *counts* as the sexual is, as we shall see, variable and itself
> political. The exact, contingent space of indeterminacy—
> the place of shifting over time—of the mutual boundaries
> between the political and the sexual is, in fact, the most fer-
> tile space of ideological formation. This is true because ideo-
> logical formation, like sexuality, depends on retroactive
> change in the naming or labelling of the subject.
>
> —Sedgwick, *Between Men*

In *Between Men: English Literature and Male Homosocial Desire*,
Eve Kosofsky Sedgwick explains that patriarchy is established on
the basis of "male bonding" or the "male homosocial relationship." The homosocial relationship differs from homosexuality
by the absence or, rather, repression of any erotic desire. In order
to protect the relationship from the danger of eroticism, it is mediated by the traffic in women in heterosexual relations. This traffic allows men to channel the threatening eroticism between them
to safely differentiated sexual objects—women. Consequently, in
modern Europe, more specifically in eighteenth-century En-
gland, the patriarchal order generally sustains itself through both
homophobia and misogyny. Homophobia confirms the existence
of a discontinuum between homosocial and homosexual desire,
and misogyny reinforces the difference between men and their
subordinate sexual partners.[1]

Sedgwick, however, cautions against the historicity and cultural specificity of her approach. As she mentions in her book, in some cases, such as in ancient Greece, tolerance of a special kind of homosexuality (namely, the master and his disciple) might be based on a complete dismissal of women (the equation of women with slaves).[2] This was the case in traditional China, where Confucius compared women to inferior men.[3] For example, Ximen Qing, the protagonist of the sixteenth-century Chinese novel *Golden Lotus* (*Jin Ping Mei*), despite his numerous affairs and six marriages with women of different social classes, occasionally sleeps with men. However, his greatest crime against Confucian morality has nothing to do with his sexual orientation but lies mainly in the excessive nature of his desire.[4] In a highly hierarchical society, homoeroticism does not necessarily threaten homosocial bonding. The stable distribution of power, knowledge, wealth, and social privilege are sufficient to distinguish the master from his slave. The inferior sexual partner is already feminized by his powerlessness or lack of knowledge; this was the case in both traditional China and ancient Greece.

At the same time, homophobia may co-exist with an apparent absence of misogyny. This was the case in Communist China. The government used women's representational power—as the oppressed sex—to make a statement on its progressive stance. Nevertheless, women's emancipation in a superficial mode did not prevent the emergence of an extreme form of homophobia. Before the 1980's, homosexual practices could easily lead to capital punishment. This severity can be explained by the puritanical undertone of communism. In most cases, puritanism characterizes any ideology with strong religious implications, including communism. Eroticism, because of its emphasis on personal pleasure, threatens to disrupt the monolithic structure of this kind of dominant ideology, and thus to weaken its authority. Homosexuality cannot be justified by a reproductive function. Lacking a utilitarian purpose, it is perceived as all the more disruptive and as needing to be repressed at any price. However, the repression of homosexuality also reveals the superficiality of the women's emancipation movement in contemporary China. First, the Communist party is afraid of gay men's indeterminacy, which was traditionally associated with femininity. Second, the party is more interested in emancipating certain useful virtues in women that were traditionally defined as masculine, such as courage and endurance, which make women good fighters and workers for the Communist cause.[5] In other words, men must remain "manly," and women must become similar to men—or at least be judged by "manly" standards. Both men and women must become useful "instruments of the Communist party"[6] by unconditionally submitting to the party line. In this context, homophobia in Communist China reveals the superficiality of the women's emancipation movement to the extent that it represses "femininity" in both women and men.

More than a decade of economic reform has had a great impact on social structure of contemporary China. As in most East European countries, the agony of communism has left an ideological vacuum in an economically more pluralistic China. The superficial equality gained by the women's emancipation movement has implicitly or explicitly been taken as the source of the current disorder and thus as an excuse for a misogynistic discourse.[7] However, the disorder prevailing in contemporary Chinese society has to a degree lifted the complete ban on homosexuality. Although Chinese society remains highly homophobic, the repression of homosexuality is no longer total, because the central power has been substantially weakened and decentralized by the practices of the market economy. Only in this specific context does the homosocial relationship, as described by Sedgwick, need to sustain itself through both misogyny and homophobia. The misogynistic discourse objectifies women and legitimizes their position as goods in the traffic between men. The homophobic discourse creates a certain illusion of stability within homosocial bonding.

In socialist China before the 1980's, the notion of revolutionary heroism was accompanied by a strict puritanism, and the women's emancipation movement was combined with desexualization of the body. To gain the title "revolutionary," one had to renounce any personal interest, including sexual desire. Very often, sexuality outside marriage could be as damaging as counterrevolutionary activities. A man who had an extramarital affair was labeled a "rascal" (*liumeng*), and a woman, a "whore" (*poxie*). Both rascal and whore were considered "bad elements" (*huai fenzi*)—one of the five types of class enemies in socialist China. Since the transgression is often determined by the object of transgression, during the post–Cultural Revolution era, one of the subversive gestures among contemporary Chinese writers has been to approach sexuality daringly and openly, especially in terms of illicit sexual acts. In this context, the sexual is more than ever political.

As Yue Mingbao argues in "Gendering the Origin of Modern Chinese Fiction," the masculinist vision of May Fourth intellectuals damaged their revolutionary potential, since their subversion was limited by its roots in gender-biased patriarchal discourse.[8] Confined by patriarchy, revolution has in the end become a transition of masculine power from one generation to the other within a family. The apparent discontinuity hides a deeper continuity between the authoritarian father and the disobedient son as well as their disheartening resemblance. By the same token, Chinese experimental writers of the 1980's limited their subversion by the instrumental use of the female body and the misogynistic portrayal of women. Their search for individual emancipation by means of sexual liberation was hindered by their own sexism. The inherent contradiction reveals legacies from both the Communist and pre-Communist Chinese traditions. Moreover, since the subversive position has already been occupied by the Communist father, subverting the subversion may mean a return to the misogyny of the Confucian grandfather. As I explained in Chapter 2 on Mo Yan's *Red Sorghum*, female desirability in contemporary China cannot be completely dissociated from the sense of independence gained by women through their massive participation in various professions. At the same time, a woman's independence must be subsumed under a dependency to her sexual partner in order to confirm the belief in his male superiority, a

belief deeply rooted in the cultural tradition—and more implicitly, in the patriarchal ideology of the Communist party.

It is not an easy task to balance the simulacrum of independence, inseparable from female desirability, and the absence of a
female subject voice, which may threaten male superiority, in the
portrayal of women. Mo Yan succeeded in creating such a balance
in *Red Sorghum* thanks to a naively utopian version of supermas-
culinity, which is personified by Grandpa Yu Zhan'ao. He kills
anyone less masculine than himself in order to preserve the total
dependency of his independent lover, Grandma, for himself.[9] Because of the disillusionment with any idealistic vision of the
world, however, this utopian harmony unavoidably collapses in
more recent and sophisticated works, such as in Su Tong's trilogy,
The Exodus of 1934 (*Yijiusansinian de taowang*), *The Family of the
Opium Poppy* (*Yingsu zhijia*), and *Crowd of Wives and Concubines*
(*Qiqie chengqun*).[10]

Su Tong's trilogy can be considered an exploration of sexuality, mainly centered on men. In most cases the female characters, onto whom the male characters project their sexual fan-
tasies, are constructed as whimsical and self-contradictory. Moreover, they serve as objects of the traffic in women, which sustains
relationships among men. Although the *Crowd of Wives and Concubines* is occasionally narrated from the perspective of a woman,
Songlian, her narration focuses on her own desirability in relation
to her aged husband. At the end of the story, Songlian completely
loses her perspective and becomes demented. As a rule, women
are assessed by their desirability and reproductivity—which
means that they are mainly instrumental in the world of male sexuality. The exploration of sexuality thus becomes a search for
masculinity in sexual relations. Interestingly, to the extent that
women exist mainly as objects of male desire in Su Tong's trilogy,
their instrumental and animal-like nature problematizes the notion of masculinity. Apparently men cannot desire women without their irrational and animal-like shortcomings, which serve as
marks of sexual difference. Women's debasement is contagious
and may infect their superior sexual partners, men. In order to

avoid this contamination, some male characters choose homosexuality. This alternative, however, does not necessarily make
their search for masculinity more successful. Despite the association of femininity with animality in Su Tong's fiction, masculinity still can be preserved only by a contrast to the beastly
femininity.

Femme Fatale

Su Tong's novella *Crowd of Wives and Concubines* is about life
in a large household of a rich landlord in his fifties, Chen Zuoqian. The story centers primarily on a young woman, Songlian,
the landlord's fourth wife. Before reaching the age of nineteen,
Songlian marries the old man. After entering his large mansion,
she struggles to keep her position as the favorite wife in the household. Whimsical, intelligent, and seductive, Songlian can be considered a femme fatale. However, once she loses Chen's favor, her
situation gradually deteriorates. At the end of the story she becomes completely mad after witnessing the murder of the third
concubine, Meishan, another femme fatale.

Luce Irigaray writes: "Femininity lends itself: borrow all that
one attributes to it, imposes. Is this nothing but a location of substitution in between? Surrogate, hiding-place or cloth, vacant for
productions and reproductions. It can simulate—fortune. But it
returns to a machine constructed by the iron hands of necessity."[11]
Apparently, Songlian is the protagonist in *Crowd of Wives and
Concubines*. But in fact, as a symbol of femininity in the story, her
personality is an empty space onto which the male fantasy (male
characters', the writer's, and/or the reader's?) can be freely projected. Her whimsicality, which may on the surface be interpreted
as a sign of independence, is symptomatic of the lack of consistency in her subjective world. The lack negatively proves the
completeness or consistency of her male partner, for whom
Songlian is only a plaything—under the control of Chen Zuoqian's "iron hands of necessity."

When Songlian first enters Chen Zuoqian's household, his third wife, Meishan, refuses to see the new concubine out of jealousy.

> Among Chen's three previous wives, Meishan lived closest to Songlian's apartment, but she was also the last one Songlian met. Songlian had heard long before that Meishan was a femme fatale and wanted very badly to see her. Chen Zuoqian was unwilling to introduce her and said, "It's so close, go there yourself." Songlian replied: "I already went there. The maid told me she was sick and didn't let me in." Chen gave a snort of contempt: "She claims to be sick whenever she's not happy. She wants to prevail over me." Songlian asked: "Do you let her?" Chen waved his hands: "She dreams! Women can never prevail over men." (QQCQ, pp. 164–65)

To a large extent, Meishan can be perceived as Songlian's mirror image. Both of them first see each other by peeping at the other through a window curtain. As a former student, Songlian is educated, and as a former traditional opera singer, Meishan has artistic talent. Both have tried to "prevail over" Chen Zuoqian, their aged husband, and both have failed to do so. Both have tragic endings. Indeed, women can never prevail over men, even if they are, like Songlian and Meishan, femmes fatales. They are allowed to have limited freedom as long as their freedom produces a certain aesthetic effect as marker of their femininity or sexual difference. In other words, their freedom is also instrumental in enhancing their desirability in the eyes of their masters. They can "simulate fortune"—to use Irigaray's words, as long as the simulacrum of fortune is in the end under the control of man's "iron hands."[12] Their fatal beauty is deadly only for themselves. If they go beyond the allowance of freedom granted to an aesthetic object, they bring about their own destruction. The threatened master will certainly pronounce their death sentence, since "women can never prevail over men" (*nüren yongyuan pabudao nanren de toushang lai*).

Songlian's fate is closely related to two objects, her bamboo flute and an unused well in Chen Zuoqian's garden. According to

Songlian's version, the flute was left to Songlian by her father after his suicide. She keeps it at the bottom of her trunk. Chen Zuoqian discovers the flute and believes it to be a gift from a former young lover. Unbeknown to Songlian, he destroys the flute out of jealousy. The unused well is situated in a remote corner of Chen Zuoqian's back garden. Songlian has heard from different sources that two women of the preceding generation in the family, very likely concubines like herself, were killed in this well. At the end of the story, Songlian witnesses the killing of the third wife, Meishan: led by her husband, a group of servants throw the adulterous concubine in the unused well.

In Chinese "bamboo flute" (*xiao*) also means phallus.[13] Songlian's flute never appears diegetically as present; rather, it is only mentioned *in absentia*. Songlian is reminded of the flute after the friendly and handsome young master Feipu, surrounded by male servants, plays his flute. In this case, the flute has obvious erotic undertones. In order to desire a man, Songlian needs to find support in the phallic symbol. If she fails to do so, she can be only a desired object, but never a desiring subject.

Songlian's awareness of the loss of the flute marks her decline. First, her desire for Feipu can never be fulfilled, since the young master is mentally castrated by his invincible fear of the opposite sex, even though he feels attracted to Songlian. One may say that Songlian is attracted to him because his lack mirrors her own. But since the lack is the basis of their mutual attraction, their friendship is necessarily sterile within a heterosexual economy. Second, since she is so stubbornly upset by the loss of the flute allegedly left to her by her father, Songlian also loses the old master's favor. At the same time, Chen Zuoqian himself loses his potency. This means that he has to avoid his seductive young wives and to move closer to the less demanding and more complaisant older ones. Third, Songlian, suspecting that her maid, Yan'er, has hidden her flute, inadvertently discovers that Yan'er has been trying to curse her by black magic. Her severe physical punishment, brought about by Songlian's uncontrollable anger, leads to

Yan'er's death and is considered her mistress's worst crime by Chen Zuoqian and the family.

The fictional presence of the flute in Songlian's mind seems to hold together her subjective world. Until she realizes the loss of the phallic symbol (as the name of the father in Lacanian terms? or as the object of desire?), Songlian keeps everything under control: her husband's favor, the seduction of her potential lover, and her authority within her private corner, her apartment. The symbolic loss of the phallic flute destroys her subjective world, as if the loss of the flute were paralleled by Songlian's loss of self-control, since her world of self is emptied by this loss. Songlian's behavior becomes meaningless, as if she were cut off from the symbolic order through the loss of contact with the phallus. Meishan tries to justify her friend's nonsensical behavior by attributing it to pregnancy. As an imaginary sign of man or a sign of fantasy, the flute must be replaced by the metaphorical image of man or the symbolic act, the act of reproduction. The only logical explanation for a woman's disruption of the symbolic order is her reproductive function, since a mother participates in the symbolic order as the carrier of the husband's image. Unfortunately, Songlian is not pregnant. As a result, she is doomed by her unjustified anger—or her disruption of the symbolic order.

If the flute, as a phallic symbol, represents power and control, the unused well, as a metaphor for a sterile womb, indicates dissemination and death. Although the only raison d'être of the well is to execute women in the family when the master judges this to be necessary, the killer and its victims metonymically become identical.

After entering Chen Zuoqian's household, Songlian becomes fascinated by the unused well.

> There was a purple vine trellis, in the corner of the back garden. From summer to autumn, the vine always bloomed murkily. Songlian saw, from her window, those purple cottonlike flowers wave in the autumnal wind, becoming more and more delicate everyday. She noticed under the trellis there was a well, surrounded by a stone

table and chairs. It was a leisurely, comfortable place, but there were no visitors—the path leading to the place was covered by weeds. Butterflies flew around, and cicadas sang on the trellis. This reminded Songlian of the same time last year, when she was reading books under the purple vine trellis at school, as if everything were in a dream. Songlian slowly walked in that direction. She lifted her dress, carefully avoiding touching the weeds and insects. Slowly she moved several branches of leaves with her hands and saw that the stone table and chairs were covered by a layer of dust. She walked to the well, the walls of which were covered by moss. Songlian bent forward to look inside the well. The water was dark blue. Old leaves floated on the surface. Songlian saw her own visage glimmer in the water and heard her own breath absorbed and amplified by the well, sounding oppressive and weak. A gust of wind came and blew her dress so that it looked like a flying bird. At this moment, Songlian felt a sensation of cold, which, like stone, slowly knocked on her body.   (QQCQ, p. 169)

From the very beginning, Songlian is identified with this well. As a student, her favorite spot at school was under a purple vine trellis, located in a spot analogous to the site of the unused well in Chen Zuoqian's garden. The world of the well is also a metaphor for her subjective world: morbid, lonely, friendless, and, at the same time, mysterious and seductive. Like herself, the purple vine silently blooms in the forsaken spot. The stone table and chairs invite visitors, who never come. Like Songlian's intense sexual drive and sensuality, they remain unused—"covered by a layer of dust" (*jile yiceng huichen*). The water of the well is also covered by old leaves—a sign of neglect by the human world. Songlian's face is reflected in the water, and her breath is echoed by the water. There is almost a fatal attraction between the well and the female protagonist. Songlian bends forward, as if driven to merge with the well.

Songlian's decline coincides with another encounter with the well (QQCQ, p. 193). The loss of her flute marks the starting point of Songlian's decline, and the well stands as an omen of her final destruction. Consequently the symbol of masculinity, be it imaginary or real, is the source of her prosperity, whereas the symbol of femininity is related to self-destruction. Femininity is attractive as long as it is determined by male desire and supported by the token of masculinity (the flute). As soon as it is detached from the phallus, femininity becomes a dangerous trap and a bottomless hole, like the bewitched unused well—sterile and deadly.

As we might expect, the well is exclusively related to women. Songlian and Meishan claim that they are the well. When people talk about the well, they refer to "female family members" (*nü-juan*). Songlian and Meishan are the only people fascinated by the well; most of the time the rest of the family seems to ignore it. Meishen's life ends in the well—pushed by Chen Zuoqian's servants—as the punishment for her adultery. Songlian becomes part of the well—after her madness, she can no longer separate herself from the dangerous trap despite her fear.

In this sense, the well is a symbol not only of femininity, but also of femmes fatales—since both Songlian and Meishan are described as such in Su Tong's story. As Mary Anne Doane explains in her *Femmes Fatales*: "The femme fatale is situated as evil and is frequently punished or killed. Her textual eradication involves a desperate reassertion of control on the part of the threatened male subject. Hence, it would be a mistake to see her as some kind of heroine of modernity. She is not the subject of feminism but a symptom of male fears about feminism."[14]

The well is a dangerous sign, the symbol of death. It is deep—no one can really measure it. It is mysterious—no one seems to understand it. It inspires fear, because this symbol represents excess and uncontrollable female sexuality. The point is that a man does not need to control his sexuality, as long as he is rich and powerful. But uncontrollable female desire is infinitely dangerous. In the linguistic system of patriarchy, there is no room for female sexuality—since a woman supposedly cannot be a desiring subject. Instead, her desire must be integrated into the system of male desire—no matter how self-contradictory the male desire is. As an excessive sign with no place in the patriarchy, the femme fatale must be punished by death—as in Meishan's case—

or by the loss of reason—as in Songlian's case—in order to reassert the masculine mastery of the symbolic order.

By making the well an exclusive sign of dangerous femininity, Su Tong succeeds in exorcising the threat presented by independent women. What does woman want according to the author? It is the flute—or the phallus—since that is the only way for her to acquire limited freedom and an identity. Without the phallic symbol, her desire becomes senseless, like the bewitched well, since it exceeds the symbolic order and the system of male desire. This excessive sign can be extremely dangerous in its senselessness. Fortunately, the danger is only directed at the carrier of the excessive sign herself—the femme fatale—as long as man stays away from her or acts as her absolute master. Ironically, the excessive symbol of femininity is also the killer of excessive women, as in the case of the unused well.

Animality and Femininity

In Su Tong's stories, femininity is often related to animality. Animality may be attributed to a highly seductive woman, whose essence is in most cases represented by cats. In his short story "Blue and White Dyehouse" ("Lan bai ranfang") and the second novella in his trilogy, *The Family of the Opium Poppy*, the most seductive female characters have symbiotic relationships with cats. But unlike the femme fatale, whose attractiveness results from her overflowing sexuality, these "cat women" seduce men thanks to their animal-like indifference and aloofness. *The Family of the Opium Poppy* is about the rise and decline of a rich landlord, Liu Laoxia, who specializes in the opium trade. The family includes Liu Laoxia; his wife, Cuihuahua; Liu Yanyi, an idiotic son; Liu Chencao, presumably the illegitimate child of Cuihuahua and her husband's servant, Chen Mao; as well as Liu Suzi, the daughter of Liu's first wife. This family is as decadent as its symbol, the opium poppy. Cuihuahua, who was the concubine of Liu Laoxia's late father, supposedly murdered Liu Suzi's mother. Liu

Chencao inadvertently kills his idiotic brother, Liu Yanyi, out of self-defense. Liu Laoxia enriches the family by planting opium and loses all his fortune when the Communist party takes over.

In *The Family of the Opium Poppy*, Liu Suzi is a cat woman, with a cat eternally resting on her knees. She seems uninterested in anything, including the fact that her father trades her for a large piece of land to her future husband, a hunchback in his fifties, who is in addition impotent. Liu Suzi is completely unconcerned about her great impact on the opposite sex. This impact can bring about disasters, either to other people or most likely to herself, as in the case of the femme fatale. Her lack of concern strangely resembles total independence, because she will do whatever she wants regardless of the consequences. Furthermore, her decisions cannot be explained in terms of "common sense," meaning the sense shared by most of the male characters in the story: her father, her husband, and her rapists. Precisely because she is in this sense beyond their logic, she has become a mystified object of male desire—outside their system of symbolization.

Her mother drowns in a bathtub, while Liu Suzi, as a baby, survives in the water by floating on top of her mother's corpse. To this extent, she becomes identical with the symbol of femininity in traditional Chinese culture, water—changeable, shapeless, unpredictable, and elusive. Men can dispose of her body against her will, but their power is in a sense powerless from Liu Suzi's perspective, because it does not seem to have a real psychological impact on her. Paradoxically, she succeeds in turning the power exercised on her body into a psychological weapon against her supposed master.

After her marriage, she spends most of her time at her father's house.

> Liu Suzi never cut her brown-black long braid, and she sat on her bamboo bed. Whenever her father came in, she held the yellow cat in her hands and said: "Twenty hectares of land." Only the father and the daughter could understand what the "twenty hectares of land" meant. Liu Laoxia had married his daughter to the hunchback

merchant in exchange for twenty hectares of land. Liu Laoxia replies: "My daughter, if you don't want to leave, you can stay at
home. But twenty hectares is not a mark of shame but rather one
of our glory. Your father hasn't raised you in vain." Liu Suzi laugh-
ingly tossed her long braid around her neck and said: "Father, this
twenty hectares of land will be inundated, thunderstruck, and will
sink in your hands. Just wait and see. That also is fate." (QQCQ,
p. 101)

The narrator says that only the father and the daughter understand what the "twenty hectares of land" (*sanbai mu di*) means.
Actually, this piece of land has completely different meanings for
them. For the father, its only real value is economic. For example,
in the middle of the story, a bandit chief called Jiang Long robs
Liu's household. Jiang demands that one of Liu Laoxia's descendants follow the bandits into the mountains—either Chencao will
become a bandit, or Liu Suzi will sleep with him for three days
and nights (QQCQ, pp. 115–16). Liu Laoxia, without hesitation,
chooses to give up his daughter, even though he knows perfectly
well that Liu Chencao is his son only in name. Cuihuahua, Liu
Laoxia's present wife, who was previously married to his own father, gave birth to the child after an affair with his long-term hired
hand, Chen Mao. Liu Laoxia knows even if they do not truly have
a blood tie, a son is always more useful than a daughter, because
a son will be able to take over the father's keys and perform the
function of master of the household. As for a daughter, if she can
bring twenty hectares of land to her father regardless of what
kind of devil she is married to, Liu Suzi is already doing surprisingly well. In other words, Liu Laoxia measures everything and
everyone strictly in terms of economic value, including his own
offspring.

In many respects, Liu Suzi's world is diametrically opposite
to that of her father's. If the twenty hectares of land represents a
flattering price for her body in the eyes of the landlord, Liu Suzi
considers the same land as a token of his crime—for which Liu
Laoxia will be punished. As she states, "Father, this twenty hectares of land will be inundated, thunderstruck, and will sink in

your hands." In other words, she predicts that the price for her body will destroy her father's patriarchal economy. For her, her body is all she values in the world, although she does not have the freedom to dispose of it in accordance with her will. Her suicide is a gesture of a radical rebellion. By destroying herself physically, she frees her body from any law that tries to subject it to a specific value—sexual, ideological, or political. In this sense, her body becomes a sublime object—to use Žižek's expression[15]—priceless because it is intangible and unapproachable and always escapes from the iron law of ownership in the patriarchal economy. As a sublime object, her body remains agelessly young and beautiful. Even her father must acknowledge her sublime value after her death: "Even men cannot be compared to you" (*nanren dou buru ni*). This may be considered the highest praise for a daughter by a father who personifies the patriarchal economy. Following Liu Laoxia's logic, his daughter becomes more valuable than men through her suicide. Furthermore, following the example of his daughter, Liu Laoxia commits suicide with his wife in the Shuaicao Pavilion, which symbolizes the phallus in the novella. In fact, the father and daughter never understand the meaning of the twenty hectares of land from the same perspective. The father regards his daughter highly because her death makes her equal to his loss of land, whereas his daughter dies because she does not acknowledge any value other than her own body. Her body is valuable to her father only because it becomes the metaphor for his land; her suicide, which acquires metaphorical value from her father, is ironically utterly narcissistic—rejecting any external value system, be it private ownership or communism.

Liu Suzi represents femininity or desirability in Su Tong's story because she is outside the male system of desire. She desires nothing but her own body. The inseparable yellow cat is her double, in which her seductiveness is intensified and animalized. Chen Mao feels irresistibly attracted to her from the moment he sees the trace of a cat's paw on her neck, like a plum blossom. This

passion ruins him. By raping her, he risked his career as a revolutionary and his life at the hands of his illegitimate son, Chencao.

In this case, the cat or the trace left by the cat on the female
body becomes the essence of seduction. It incarnates femininity
in its deceptive depth and mysterious animality. The trace of animality separates Liu Suzi even further from the world of men.
She can never be mistaken for a man, even when cross-dressed as
in her first meeting with Lu Fang, the regional leader of the Communists and a former fellow student and close friend of Chencao
(QQCQ, p. 128). Her femininity associated with animality is the
secret of Liu Suzi's seductiveness. Her indifference to the opposite
sex makes her a perfect object of desire—which is further objectified by her narcissism. She desires her own body as men supposedly do. She will never be a subject whose desire will contradict that of a man. At the same time, her desire for her own body
makes her a rival to the men who desire her. Because of their
power, they are always momentary winners in their struggles
against the narcissistic girl—either by selling her body or by raping her. However, Liu Suzi always takes revenge in the end by
situating herself beyond their system of desire and of exchange.
Her final victory is also her self-destruction, which leads to the
murder of her rapist, the death of her father and her stepmother,
and the execution of her brother. In other words, she is equal to
the twenty hectares of land that results in the Liu family's destruction—as she predicted from the outset.

Paradoxically, the most desirable woman in Su Tong's trilogy
is characterized by the absence of desire. The absence, symbolized
by the image of the cat, becomes an indelible mark of sexual difference—a proof of the *manhood* of her sexual partners. As a result, any equal sexual relationship with her is impossible. Making
love to her means either making her a prostitute—as in her marriage—or raping her—as in the two other cases. In this sense, the
cat woman in Su Tong's works is not only a mark of sexual difference but also a symptom of the impossibility of sexual relations—except in violence. Preserving sexual difference in Su
Tong's story requires putting women in a demeaning position.

Any tenderness becomes a threat to difference, because it may suggest a certain equality between the male subject and the female object of desire. As a result, masculinity is kept intact at the price of female animality, and sexual intercourse means male conquest and the reinforcement of female suffering.

Male Bonding: Impossible Substitute for an Impossible Relationship

Every sexual relationship between men and women in Su Tong's trilogy seems to lead to a dead-end: the suffering of women and the degradation of men. Women, who are beastly in any case, drive their sexual partners into animality, which entails violence against women. Logically speaking, sexuality and tenderness can co-exist only in male-male relations, from which the "weak sex" is completely excluded. Indeed, the only traces of humanity in Su Tong's trilogy can be found in the two characters, Liu Chencao in *The Family of the Opium Poppy* and Chen Feipu in *Crowd of Wives and Concubines*. Both are characterized by the absence of desire for the female body and the presence of a highly intense relationship with another man. Furthermore, in the trilogy, Chencao and Feipu are the only men from whom women in their families obtain support and friendship, since their interest in women is safely desexualized.

Liu Chencao has an interesting given name. "Chen," the first Chinese character of his given name, reveals his implicit descent from his biological father, the hired hand Chen Mao, by implicating the latter's family name. Moreover, "Chencao" in Chinese means "sinking herb," which corresponds to the name of the pavilion, "withered herb" (*shuaicao*).[16] The first characters in the pavilion's and the hero's given names combine nicely as *shuaichen*, which means "decline." The Shuaicao Pavilion, in which Liu Laoxia, Chencao's legal father, has had numerous sexual encounters with different women, stands as "the symbol of masculinity" (*nanxing xiangzheng*) for the men in the village (QQCQ, pp. 93–94). Chencao's name inevitably connects the hero with the pavilion, the phallic symbol, of which the narrator did not feel comfortable enough to specify the "peculiar shapes" (*teshu de zaoxing lunkuo*). However, this connection is based on the "decline" (*shuaichen*) of masculinity, since Chencao, due to his sheer difference, marks the end of the family line.

Chencao, as a former high school student, still keeps some traces of idealism. He is not completely integrated into the patriarchal economy his father represents. The only way for him to become part of this system is by becoming addicted to opium— the source of the Liu family's wealth. But opium only provides him with the illusion of being integrated—he still remains much closer to the feminine world represented by his sister. Like the women in the story, Chencao is basically a passive instrument. However, he is an instrument not only in his father's patriarchal economy but also in his sister's world of femininity—he will pay with his life for killing the second rapist of his sister, Chen Mao. Chen Mao has become a leader in the campaign to confiscate the Lius' land after the arrival of the Communist army. Unbeknown to Chencao, Chen Mao is also his biological father. When Chen Mao asks Chencao why he wants to kill him, Chencao replies: "They have asked me to kill you" (*tamen rangwo bani shale*) (QQCQ, p. 154). In other words, he is only a passive agent. Who are "they"? His legal father and sister. Chencao has no fixed identity. His identity as the heir of *The Family of the Opium Poppy* is misconstructed as a result of his opium addiction. His blood ties him to the enemy of his legal father, Chen Mao, whom he murders in order to fulfill the demand of his alleged family. His education ties him to Lu Fang, who, as the regional Communist leader, has to execute him at the end of the story. His marginality in the Liu family ties him to his mysterious sister, who often represents the value system opposite to that he is supposed to assume as the only male descendant of the family. Interestingly, he dies in a big opium jar, which symbolizes his misconstructed identity. In short, Chencao is a sign of indeterminacy par excellence—vacillating among Liu Laoxia's world of patriarchy, Liu Suzi's domain of femininity, and Lu Fang's realm of Communist ideology.

Like the platinum keys, the women in the Liu family are passed from one generation to the next. Chencao's mother was previously the wife of his legal grandfather. To this extent, Chencao's indifference toward the opposite sex can be considered a passive denial of Liu Laoxia's heritage. His attachment to his fellow student, Lu Fang, is symbolized by a tennis ball, which is very likely a farewell gift from Lu to Chencao. Before he follows Liu Laoxia to the poppy farm after his graduation, Chencao loses the tennis ball. The narrator gives this description: "He felt that this afternoon something had escaped from him, just like the gray tennis ball. At each step, Chencao looked back three times. He heard his father shouting at him: 'Chencao, what are you looking at? Let's go home.' Chencao said: 'The ball has disappeared'" (QQCQ, p. 91).

Chencao never found this ball, but neither did he forget it. His nostalgia for the ball leads to his killing his idiot brother, Liu Yanyi, in self-defense. After his return from school, Chencao asks the maid to make him a ball of cloth and cotton to substitute the lost tennis ball, but she misunderstands his request and believes that the young master "wants to play with a doll" (*wan'er bu wawa*) (QQCQ, p. 97). Since the substitute for the tennis ball is mistaken for a doll, a girl's toy, the ball is clearly connected to femininity. Chencao wants to play with his brother, Yanyi, whose only concern is his voracious hunger. The hunger, which is explained by the narrator as a mark of masculinity in the Liu family, has never been experienced by Chencao (QQCQ, p. 94). Yanyi takes Chencao's substitute tennis ball as a piece of steamed bread. When he finds out that it is not edible, Yanyi tries to kill his brother but provokes his own death. Later, Chencao in tears asks: "I wanted to play tennis with him, why did I kill him?" (*Wo xiang genta daqiu zenmo bata shale*) (QQCQ, p. 99).

Like his attachment to his classmate, the tennis ball, a symbol of male bonding, cannot be replaced. The desire to replace it by the fake brotherhood between Chencao and Yanyi leads to crime and death. In this action the brothers reverse personalities. Chencao has no trace of the killer in his personality, whereas Yanyi has always shouted at people: "I will kill you" (*wo shale ni*). This role reversal confirms Chencao's status as heir of the Liu family; it is as if Chencao must be disguised in the personality of his brutal brother in order to usurp this role.

Later on, while following his legal father into the mountains in search of the bandits, Chencao picks up a dead person's eye, yet another substitute for the tennis ball. "He always grasped the eye tightly, thinking that perhaps the tennis ball had rolled here. Then, the eye appeared at the moment of the disappearance of the ball, which made him feel that there was a kind of trap for this reason, I[17] must grasp the eye tightly" (*QQCQ*, p. 140). The second substitute leads to the murder of his biological father, Chen Mao. Chencao shoots at one of his eyes and penis. The eye rolls toward his feet. When he picks it up, it sticks to his fingers, like the one he picked up in the mountains.

After five years of separation, Chencao again encounters Lu Fang, who has meanwhile become the local Communist leader in charge of the land reform movement. As the owner of the majority of the land in the village, Liu Chencao becomes his class enemy. However, Lu Fang still looks for traces of their intimate friendship by reminding Chencao of their tennis game, while Chencao is having hallucinations about the lost ball. The ball is definitively lost. Despite their good intentions, neither his legal father, whom Chencao addresses in the dream, nor his former intimate friend, whom Chencao addresses while awake, can help him find it.

> Suddenly, Lu Fang heard Chencao call his name: "Lu Fang, give me a hand!" Lu Fang stretched out his hand and grasped Chencao's cold sweaty hand. Lu Fang remembered their past friendship when they often held each other's hands. In the shadow of the storage room, they both saw a large fresh green lawn, on which the sun at dusk cast golden spots. They played tennis, and the ball rolled on the lawn. Lu Fang said: "Chencao, let's play tennis." These words shook Chencao's entire body. His eyes shone for one moment and again darkened. Chencao lifted his hand and wiped his eyes; his whole body smelled of opium: "The ball fell and disappeared."

Chencao sighed. Lu Fang quickly threw off Chencao's feeble hand and also said: "It fell and disappeared; I also can do nothing." (QQCQ, p. 132)

If the phallic symbol, the Shuaicao Pavilion, is emptied by Chencao's alleged father's excessive sexuality, the symbol of the male bond, the tennis ball, has forever disappeared and can survive only in the two intimate male friends' memories, however romanticized the reminiscence might be. Although the two one-time friends can never regain the same kind of intimacy because of political and social changes, the picturesque image of reminiscence shared by them at the moment of their reunion is no doubt the most—or more precisely, the only—tender moment in the entire story. Even the light and colors become soft and fresh, suggesting happiness and hope. However, this hope is merely a false one, and the happiness is only a dream, because no one can again find the ball, which represents the last link in their relationship. The ball has disappeared, since there is no room for such a relationship either in Liu Laoxia's patriarchal economy or in Lu Fang's Communist ideology. The symbol of the male bond can be replaced by the semblance of a piece of bread, as an object of a voracious desire that marks masculinity in the Liu family, and by a dead person's eye, indicating war and masculine violence. At the same time, the substitutes, as bad omens, unavoidably lead to the violent destruction of one of his closest male family members by the protagonist.

Chencao's passivity is a logical outcome of his lack of a subject position.[18] He does not have a subject voice either in the family or in society. His function is mainly instrumental. Nevertheless, in his denial of his own body, Chencao's disheartening passivity may also be interpreted as resistance to the patriarchal order. Chencao tries to assert a degree of freedom by denying his physical desire for his male friend, who has become the representative of Communist power. In fact, his physical desire for Lu Fang is already a form of resistance, a refusal of the reproductive function implied in heterosexual relations. This function is central to the heir of his legal father's patriarchal economy. To this extent, the denial of his homosexuality can be interpreted as a double negative, which reconnects him to the Liu family. The negation is essentially internalized in Chencao's case, since what is actually negated twice is his body or bodily desire. His body is turned into an empty space of negation where social, economic, and ideological conflicts cancel each other out in the form of sexuality without truly confronting each other. In this sense, his reconnection with the Liu family, like the phallic symbol, the Shuaicao Pavilion, is "emptied" (*kongkong dangdang*)—meaningless, because his body is already an empty or emptied signifier, which may take any available meanings without truly taking a position.

By denying his physical desire, Liu Chencao creates an illusory freedom vis-à-vis his father's patriarchal order and his former friend's bond to communism. But the price of freedom is his "disembodiment"—to borrow Judith Butler's words: "The pursuit of disembodiment is necessarily deceived because the body can never really be denied; its denial becomes the condition of its emergence in alien form. Disembodiment becomes a way of existing with one's body in the mode of denial. And the denial of the body—as Hegel's dialectic of master and slave—reveals itself as nothing other than the embodiment of denial."[19] "The embodiment of denial" in Chencao's case is expressed in the form of opium addiction, which, in the end, completely destroys his body and mind.

In *The Family of the Opium Poppy*, Chencao's repressed homosexual desire, embodied by the lost tennis ball, can be considered a failed attempt to search for male subjectivity. But what does Chen Feipu's explicit homosexual relationship with Young Master Xu, the son of a rich merchant, in *Crowd of Wives and Concubines* "embody" in Su Tong's map of reconstructing male subjectivity? In fact, the term *homosexual* used in this Chinese context may be misleading, since a clear-cut dichotomy between heterosexuality and homosexuality did not exist in traditional China.[20]

With regard to Rock Hudson's body as viewed by American women spectators during the 1950's, Richard Meyer explains that

Hudson's "erotic neutrality toward women" "promises straight women a space of sexual safety."[21] For the same reason, from the young concubine to the maid in the story, female desire also seems to converge on Chen Feipu's body.

Like Chencao's father, Liu Laoxia, Feipu's father, Chen Zuoqian, is an accomplished womanizer. At the age of fifty, he marries the nineteen-year-old high school student, Songlian, who is even much younger than his oldest son, Feipu. Perhaps because they are the only educated people in the household, Feipu and Songlian feel a strange attraction to each other at first sight. Songlian strikes Feipu as "different" (*bu yiyang*), and Feipu impresses Songlian as "surprisingly handsome and youthful" (*chuhu yiliao de yingjun nianqing*) as well as "very clever" (*henyou xinji*) (QQCQ, p. 173). As a frustrated young concubine, Songlian invests erotic desire in the young master of the household, the only interesting man she has occasion to encounter, whereas his attraction to her remains mainly narcissistic. On her birthday he says to Songlian: "Without you, I wouldn't be able to find anyone to talk to in the family" (QQCQ, p. 220). When Songlian expresses her desire, Feipu fails to respond.

Feipu raised his head and looked into Songlian's passionate eyes. His body, especially his legs, became totally motionless. He remained immobile. Songlian closed her eyes and heard two kinds of breath, one was harsh, the other, soft. She pressed her legs even more tightly against his, waiting for something to happen. As if many years had passed, Feipu withdrew his knees, leaning obliquely against the chair, and in a hoarse voice said, "This is not good." Songlian acted as if awakened from a deep sleep and murmured, "What is not good?" Slowly Feipu lifted his hands, folded them, and bowed, "I can't, I am still afraid." While saying this, his face was twisted with pain, "I am still afraid of women; women are too frightening." She said, "I don't understand what you mean." He rubbed his face, "Songlian, I like you. I truly mean it." She replied, "How could you treat me like this if you like me?" He almost sobbed, always avoiding her eyes. "I can't change. Heaven has punished me. Men in the Chen family from generation to generation enjoy women. But as for me, I am impotent. Since my childhood,

I have found women frightening. I am afraid of women, especially
of women in my family. You are the only one I'm not afraid of. But
I'm still impotent. Do you understand?" Songlian was already in
tears. She hid her face and said softly, "I understand; you don't need
to explain any more. Now, I don't blame you at all, really, not at
all." (QQCQ, pp. 222–23)

Feipu is uninterested in women—or interested in men—because his fear of the opposite sex makes him impotent in heterosexual encounters. Like the semblance of bread or the eye in relation to the lost tennis ball for Chencao in *The Family of the
Opium Poppy*, Feipu's explicit homosexual relationship with
Young Master Xu becomes a substitute for his failed heterosexuality. However, as in the case of Chencao's lost tennis ball, which
he tries to replace by either a cotton ball or a human eye, in Su
Tong's world of fiction substitutes cannot truly replace the original, even when it has been forever lost.

In reading this passage, we have to bear in mind that Su Tong
was one of the first contemporary writers in mainland China to
explore the subject of homosexuality. If the Chinese Communist
party initiated a women's emancipation movement for its political
interests, it has also reinforced homophobia in Chinese society.
Even during the 1970's in China, sodomy, as a crime, might easily
lead to capital punishment. In this context, Su Tong's attempt to
explore the topic of homosexuality, however naive and homophobic the experiment may appear (since it is centered on heterosexuality), can be perceived as subversive.

Since homosexuality in this context—*faute de mieux*—becomes the supplement of heterosexuality, it should not surprise
us to see the narrator's ambivalence toward this subject. The two
men in the trilogy who show some signs of humanity, Chencao
and Feipu, are not interested in heterosexual relations; it is as if
sex with women corrupted humanity in men. Nevertheless, as
we see in Songlian's failed seduction scene, Feipu chooses not to
have sex with women, not because he enjoys homosexual relations more but because his fear of the opposite sex castrates him
and makes him impotent in heterosexual relations. In other

words, he is portrayed as more manly without the contamination of beastly women, and at the same time less than a man, incapable of penetrating—thus dominating—the opposite sex. In this case, the male subject is trapped in a double-bind situation.

As Eve Kosofsky Sedgwick observes, "Only women have the power to make men less than men within this world. At the same time, to be fully a man requires having obtained the instrumental use of a woman, having *risked* transformation by her."[22] Feipu's sexual orientation is a gesture of resistance to the name of the father in Lacanian terms, the obscene and powerful Chen Zuoqian, by refusing, as heir of the family, the instrumental reproductive function. But his gesture itself is necessarily impotent, since it is associated with femininity—as he himself explains to Songlian concerning his "feminized weakness" (*nüren cai xihuan*) for sweets (QQCQ, p. 190). Nevertheless, both the father's corruption and the son's impotence must be blamed on others, namely, women. If Chen Zuoqian indulges in excessive sexual activities, this is because "all women are interested in rich men" (*nüren dou xiang gen youqianren*)—as the father explains to Songlian, who married him for his money (QQCQ, p. 175). If Chen Feipu renounces his manhood, this is because "women are too frightening" (*nüren tai kepa*)—as the son explains to Songlian while she is trying to seduce him (QQCQ, p. 222).

In the patriarchal economy, women are left out of the traffic in their bodies. At the same time, Su Tong nevertheless holds them responsible for the fall of the father and son, who negotiate the values of these sexual objects. In both *The Family of the Opium Poppy* and *Crowd of Wives and Concubines*, financial power is literally transacted through the body of the woman who has or tries to have sexual intercourse with both the father and son.

In *The Family of the Opium Poppy*, Liu Laoxia marries Cuihuahua, the concubine of his own father. In *Crowd of Wives and Concubines*, Songlian, as the youngest wife of Chen Zuoqian, is attracted to his oldest son, Feipu, and invites him to her bed. To this extent, Feipu's refusal of Songlian's body can be considered a symbolic refusal of his father's financial power: he is not good for women as well as "useless in business" (*nali shi zuo shengyi de liaozi*) (QQCQ, p. 220). At the same time, woman, as the symbol of the financial transaction, causes the failure of this transaction. In *The Family of the Opium Poppy*, both women and the source of the Liu family's riches, opium, corrupt men physically and mentally. In fact, they are on various occasions interchangeable and cause the downfall of the Liu family—as Liu Suzi predicts in terms of the price of her own body (QQCQ, p. 101). In *Crowd of Wives and Concubines*, Feipu justifies his impotence by his fear of women. His fear is further justified by his father's corruption. Women, as symbols of financial transaction, corrupt even the objects they symbolize, financial power and the name of the father. If in Su Tong's trilogy men are caught between the corruption of their masculinity by the female body and the failure to manifest their manhood by means of the instrumental use of the same body, women are caught in a worse dilemma. They are not empowered to speak about the traffic in their own bodies because of their inner deficiencies, "superficiality" (*qianbo*) (QQCQ, p. 102) and "ridicule" (*kexiao*) (QQCQ, p. 201). At the same time, the reasons for their disempowerment, their inner deficiencies, make them responsible for men's failure. Since the goods that have been traded are corrupt by nature, how can one assume a normal transaction between a father and son? Their deficiencies make the father's authority powerless and the son's rebellion impotent.

Among the writers I study in this book, Su Tong is the most interested in sexuality. His portrayal of sexuality, however, is strangely asymmetrical, as if women at best could only play purely instrumental roles in their relations to men. Sexuality in absence of any female desire is itself both instrumental and impossible; instrumental to the extent that it serves mainly as the search for a reconfirmation of a lost masculine identity, and impossible because of the lack of minimum equality between the male subject and the female object. The inferiority of the female body that is indispensable for a reconfirmation of masculine identity cannot avoid contaminating the superiority of the masculine order.

CHAPTER 6

• ⤳

Violence and Cultural Nihilism

Political power comes from the barrel of a gun.
—Mao Zedong

The misogynistic discourse common among most contemporary Chinese experimental fiction writers results in part from a subversive intent against the failed women's emancipation movement promoted by May Fourth radicals and the Communist party. By contrast, these writers also present certain remarkable resemblances to their predecessors, especially in one aspect, cultural nihilism. This aspect has characterized the May Fourth movement as well as the socialist revolution led by Mao Zedong and his party.

As an American historian of modern China, Maurice Meisner, explains in his *Mao's China and After*:

> Destruction, not inheritance—and not yet construction—was the Maoist injunction when the Great Proletarian Cultural Revolution was launched in 1966, just as it had been the injunction of the pre-Marxian Ch'en Tu-hsiu when he had launched the New Culture Movement half a century before. If the Cultural Revolution was a "utopian" movement, it was (unlike the Great Leap) marked by a strangely negative utopianism, its author far more preoccupied with the weight of the past than with any positive vision of the future.[1]

To a large extent, negative utopianism has been transformed into a form of destructive violence, which cost numerous lives during the Cultural Revolution. Moreover, the Cultural Revolution was not an isolated incident. For more than a century, modern Chinese history has been permeated with violent revolutions. As Mao Zedong stated, "There is no construction without destruction" (_bupo buli_); construction of a better future is thus perceived as predicated on destruction of the past. In addition, destruction has never been truly limited by vague notions of the past. Often the past serves merely as an excuse for extensive and blind violence. Before the Cultural Revolution, the socialist revolution, which was largely based on a negative utopian vision, was directly or indirectly responsible for a heavy toll on human lives among both its proponents and its enemies.[2] After ten years of post–Cultural Revolution economic construction, the bloody crackdown on the student demonstrators in Tian'anmen Square served as a reminder that Communist leaders, following Mao's example, were still more "preoccupied with the weight of the past than with any positive vision of the future." Instead of negotiating a constructive solution, they chose the destruction of discontented popular forces they perceived as "enemies of the regime." Paradoxically in official discourse, the Chinese youth were connected to a past of which they had no direct knowledge.[3] Once again, a fictional connection with a vague notion of the past served as an excuse for extensive violence.

Negative utopianism is aimed mainly at destruction of the past, as if a wonderful future would necessarily be generated by this destruction. The destruction, however, is mainly symbolic—it is intended to annihilate the symbolic texture through which the Chinese cultural past has been constituted.[4] Because of the destroyed symbolic network surrounding this past, one can no longer define it simply in terms of its historicity. Paradoxically, a past that has lost its origins has become a non-historical place to which each generation of radical intellectuals has referred as a point of subversion. This past represents Confucianism, authoritarianism, and everything that needs to be changed in the process of Chinese modernization or democratization. Precisely because of its unsymbolizable nature, however, this past can also be used as a subversive weapon against communism, which has already subverted the same past from a different angle. Nevertheless, this past is by no means an empty signifier. It is a point at which the modernist (male) subject fails to constitute itself as well as a point that the same subject cannot avoid in the process of its own subjectivization. Since the May Fourth movement, Chinese intellectuals have continued to speak about traditional society. At the same time, "tradition" (*chuantong*), like "fiction" (*xiaoshuo*), has never been clearly defined.

Thanks to radical cultural nihilism, destruction itself has assumed a full teleological dimension as the most important, if not the only, goal of radical revolution. The teleological vision of destruction is subtended by a cultural nihilism, the dominant mode of thinking among radical intellectuals in twentieth-century China. Since they have held China's cultural past responsible for the economic and political failures of the twentieth century, a radical elimination of this past appears to be a logical solution to China's problems. This apparently logical solution has, however, never truly solved China's problems. Ironically, instead of problematizing the practice of violence motivated by cultural nihilism, every generation of radical intellectuals has tended to blame the failure of the preceding attempt at changing China on their predecessors' lack of radicalism vis-à-vis their cultural heritage. In order to "compensate" for the mistakes of the previous generation, radical intellectuals tend, from different perspectives, to go one step further in their radical departure from China's past.

Mao Zedong can be considered the undisputed champion of the practice of this kind of radicalism. As Maurice Meisner writes:

Mao Zedong, by declaring the Chinese people "blank," was driven by a utopian impulse to escape history and by an iconoclastic desire to wipe the historical-cultural slate clean. Having rejected the traditional Chinese cultural heritage, Mao attempted to fill the emotional void by an even more iconoclastic proclamation of the nonexistence of the past in the present. A new culture, Mao seemed to believe, could be fashioned *ex nihilo* on a fresh canvas, on a "clean sheet of paper" unmarred by historical blemishes. In his iconoclasm and in his belief in the power of human consciousness to mold history, Mao's concept of cultural revolution owed far more to the modern Chinese intellectual tradition of the May Fourth era than to Marxist-Leninist traditions.[5]

As the political leader and ideological founder of Communist China, each of Mao's words, at the height of his personality cult, was carefully and respectfully recorded. Mao's declaration of the death of the cultural past was no exception. This declaration had a strong impact on the socio-symbolic network. Although this past may very well survive in the collective (un)conscious, at a symbolic level the Chinese people have become disconnected from their past. Thanks to Mao, breaking with the past has become one of the tasks of a revolutionary, the most honorable (or profitable?) title for a citizen in socialist China. Indeed, it is a requirement.

Nevertheless the question remains: Can any new culture be fashioned *ex nihilo* on a fresh canvas, especially if this canvas has also been the locus of five millennia of history of a (destroyed?) civilization? However solemn it may be, in the final analysis Mao's declaration functions only at a symbolic level. It marked the symbolic death of the tradition—to use Slavoj Žižek's expression—as a sentence pronounced by the Great Leader of the Chinese Communist party. Žižek posits two kinds of death: natural death—the death of the natural body—and symbolic death— the death of "the symbolic texture through which so-called reality is constituted."[6]

In many aspects, Mao's proclamation of the death of tradition did not substantially affect the deep roots of the thousands of years of Chinese civilization. On the contrary, by denying its roots, the Chinese socialist revolution has granted the unnamable past the status of a "sublime body."[7] Tradition, whose natural body survives despite Mao's proclamation of its death, has become the locus of the difference between natural death and its symbolization, or, to use another of Žižek's expressions, the real-traumatic kernel in the midst of symbolic order.

Paradoxically, the Chinese past, denied the right to be named, has become a non-historical entity. This entity, which is taken as one of the ideological roots of the Communist party and the society it has created, is constantly referred to as a determining factor in History, although it may carry different names. This past cannot truly be eliminated. Even without a name, it continues to haunt contemporary Chinese ideological, political, and social structures. Since it has not disappeared but only been denied or repressed by the dominant ideology at a symbolic level, the past cannot be digested by the process of modernization. All Chinese modernists or even "postmodernists" (as some literary critics would like to call themselves) are in one way or another governed by this unsymbolizable and indigestible locus, the Confucian past, from which they claim to be separated by a clear-cut line of demarcation. Mao Zedong, the most radical advocate of destruction of the past, for example, turned the People's Republic into a hierarchical and authoritarian empire, a copy of the traditional structure of political power, which Mao's violent revolution intended to destroy. As I have tried to demonstrate in this book, most experimental fiction writers and critics, despite their desire to cut themselves off from tradition, be it Confucian or Communist, have joined the traditional patriarchy by reviving its misogynistic discourse. The past that several generations of Chinese iconoclasts have been determined to destroy by depriving it of a clear definition has become the "non-historical kernel around which the symbolic network is articulated."[8]

For Lu Xun's generation, this past was represented by its oppression. Women, as the oppressed, played a major role in this representation. Ironically, several decades later, some intellectuals are again using women to represent an evil (this time, Communist) past, seemingly to subvert this past. In reality they are formulating a misogynistic discourse. In both cases, women are used to represent a past of which they are taken as either perfect victims or official voices. In neither case are women granted truly subject voices, due to their representational functions in the patriarchal order. To a degree, women are indeed connected to the past, a past that not only burdens the present but also influences the future. As the most significant minority in terms of power distribution in the Chinese patriarchy (both Confucian and Communist), women's social position can serve as a measure to assess society's willingness to accept difference and thus to deal with its own past.

Nevertheless, the effort to listen to voices different from those of the authoritarian father and the iconoclastic heir cannot result from a destruction of the past; rather, it must come from a maturation of Chinese society. This maturity will allow China to accept its past, just as an adult accepts his or her childhood by respecting the differences between it and the present. As we have seen, throughout modern Chinese history, the destruction of the past has offered no alternative but an eternally recurring childhood. This childhood, because of its lack of maturity and refusal to accept difference, engenders further violence.

Yu Hua, a highly acclaimed contemporary Chinese writer, excels in describing the logic of violence. This expertise may partly explain the fascination of his works for Chinese literary critics. On the eve of the Tian'anmen Incident, the literary journal *Beijing Literature* devoted a special issue to his fiction.[9] In his stories, Yu Hua has succeeded in recreating an impeccable logic of violence. In this chapter, I raise the following questions: Does Yu's parody of Communist ideology subvert its basis, namely the logic of violence, by demonstrating the absurdity inherent in this logic? Or does it perpetuate violence by suggesting that nothing can be outside the circle of violence, thus further ruling out the possibility for fundamental change in the current power structure? I shall base my analysis mainly on two stories written by Yu Hua, a novella written before the Tian'anmen Incident, *Life in the World Resembles Smoke (Shishi ruyan)*,[10] and a short story written after the incident, "An Accident" ("Ouran shijian").[11]

The Universal Father

Life in the World Resembles Smoke, published in 1988, is an account of a group of nameless people who live on the margins of life and death. The characters are designated in four ways: by a

number (from 2 to 7, with the exception of 5); by their relationship to a number (for example, 6's daughter); by their profession
(the driver, the fortuneteller); or by a certain trait (the woman in
gray, the blind man). The characters encounter each other by
chance as strangers, or live as neighbors who hardly know each
other. A central figure, the fortuneteller, ties them loosely together; each at a crucial moment in his or her life addresses a question to this figure.

The fortuneteller is a ninety-year-old patriarch. As the father
of five children, he has absorbed the essence of his children's lives
in order to prolong his own. Endowed with magical power, the
fortuneteller is able to use the years of life allotted to his prematurely dead children as his own. Moreover, in the middle of each
month, the old man lures a girl of twelve or thirteen from the
street to his house with candies and then rapes her. Sexual intercourse with immature virgins is his other magical resource for
longevity. As his name tells us, the fortuneteller can predict the
future. Occasionally, he even helps a customer avoid the future
of which he or she is most afraid, provided that the change ben-
efits him personally. Nevertheless, the prescribed change always
has a fatal side-effect, which is worse for the customer than the
feared and avoided future.

The fortuneteller is not only the father of his own five children but also the father of any other children who need to be "fa-
thered." He adopts two children after the death of his fifth son;
one is 3's unborn baby, which was sired by 3's grandson. 3 tells
the fortuneteller that her chief problem is that she does not know
if she should consider her baby her son or her great-grandson
(*SSRY*, p. 199). Incest, like death, is no longer a transgression of
taboo, but simply and literally a transgression of naming. Later
on, the fortuneteller also adopts 7's five-year-old son, who is supposedly the cause of his biological father's illness. Since, according to the Chinese calendar, 7 was born in the year of the lamb
and his son in the year of the tiger, the existence of the tiger in
the same family threatens the life of the lamb (*SSRY*, p. 203). By
adopting 3's incestuous and 7's symbolically patricidal children,

the fortuneteller is transformed into the universal father. But what does it take to *act* as a father in Yu Hua's fiction? What does he have to do in order to fulfill the function of a father? The fortuneteller's behavior provides a disturbing answer: the aged father nourishes himself on the blood of his youthful but doomed children in order to perpetuate his own life. The world of Yu Hua's fiction is as doomed as the young people in it—it is a world without a future. Furthermore, on different levels, each father in this story repeats the action of the fortuneteller.

6 has seven daughters, and one by one he sells the first six to a trader in women who marries them off. His seventh daughter commits suicide when she learns that her father is on the verge of selling her. After a difficult negotiation, 6 succeeds in selling his daughter's corpse at a very good price. Even in death, the daughter cannot escape from the fate of being a commodity assigned by her greedy father (*SSRY*, p. 208). In order to save his life, 7 hands his five-year-old son over to the fortuneteller, although 7 knows that his son will soon share the fate of the fortuneteller's own offspring. The shorter the child's life, the more profitable it is for the old man:

> His fifth son's death endangers the outcome of the fortuneteller's past efforts. He feels that the years of life left by his first four children have already been used up. Now he is using the years left by his fifth son. His own death will follow. He believes that his fifth son's life can allow him to live only a few years longer, because this son's life was too long—indeed, he was already fifty-five years old at his death. The fortuneteller feels strongly that his own body is withering.   (*SSRY*, p. 198)

The stronger the father, the greater his ability to shorten his children's lives in order to preserve his own. The father-son relationship allows the aged father to absorb the blood of the young son. As in Lu Xun's "Madman's Diary," in Yu Hua's story cannibalism is used as a metaphor for social relations in China. In Lu Xun's story, the protagonist's rage against the cannibalistic society literally drives him mad.[12] In *Life in the World Resembles Smoke*, however, we can no longer detect any trace of the same kind of rage or even of mild anger. In Yu Hua's story, cannibalism is not only a daily practice but also an indispensable plus for a qualified father. 7's life is threatened by his son's, not because he is a better father than the fortuneteller, but because he is not strong enough to squeeze the life out of his son. 7 must concede the name "father" to the fortuneteller, the highly qualified universal father. To be a father to a child in this context means to be a vampire who nourishes himself on the blood of the child's life. A father who cannot do this will lose not only his name but also possibly his life. Following this logic, the fortuneteller becomes the most capable and dutiful father, whom the failed parents entrust with their children.

4 suffers from severe somniloquy. Her father takes her to the fortuneteller. The fortuneteller suggests to the father that they "take the devil out of her womb" (*cong yinxue li bagui wa chulai*). Her father not only agrees, but also, by holding her body tightly, helps the old man rape his own daughter (*SSRY*, p. 201). Once again, the symbolic father, the fortuneteller, assisted by the biological father, is able to prolong his life thanks to his ability to absorb the youthful blood of his offspring. The longevity of the old man will be paid for by the death of the young girl (4 commits suicide at the end of the story).

In one other respect, the fortuneteller represents the perfect father as the symbol of cultural, social, and political authority. He is omniscient. Like the Chinese Communist government, controlled by a number of octogenarians, the fortuneteller seems to control the life of each citizen. Like the aged cultural tradition, the fortuneteller seems able to permeate the roots of each individual and family. His authority, which has never been challenged, is based on his unshakable knowledge. At the same time, the knowledge results not only from his ability to "predict" the future but also from his power to create the future by forcing people to submit to his orders. In this case, the fortuneteller's power depends largely on the people's belief in the existence of such a power. The belief forces them to submit to his power unconditionally. Their unconditional submission thus creates a future in accordance with the fortuneteller's prediction. This future again helps him reinforce the people's belief. In this sense, the fortuneteller, like the Communist party, represents the people since his morbid power is "entrusted" to him by the people. Paradoxically, the dependency of his power on the people's perception of him as powerful makes him all the more powerful, since the people's voices can be heard only through their sole representative, the octogenarian magician. Slaves of their own perception, the people become voiceless.

In a sense, the fortuneteller is death incarnate, since his life belongs no longer to him but to his prematurely dead children. As a living corpse, the fortuneteller personifies the law, which is composed of dead letters. The law also contributes to the creation of the future. This future means the survival of the aged father at the price of his children's lives and a degenerated repetition of the past. This future belongs to the agonized patriarch who has eliminated all his children. This future is necessarily illusory because a world without descendants is also a world without a future. This future is tantamount to a prolonged agony—a prolonged process of death.

Women as Products of Male Fantasy

If the boys must die in the place of their aged fathers in Yu Hua's story, what happens to the girls? In addition to the similar duty of dying in place of their fathers, the daughters' bodies are also used either as merchandise for their greedy fathers' financial gain or as sexual instruments to prolong their fathers' lives through black magic. There are two daughters in the story, 4 and 6's daughter. The descriptions of male reactions to their voices and appearance suggest that both of them, especially 4, are highly desirable. In this sense, they are not only, like their brothers, disposable properties of their fathers, but also objects of highly commodified value in which male erotic desire is invested. However, only the fathers have the right to dispose of the daughters' bodies. For other, younger men, their brothers, the highly desirable female bodies are forbidden fruit. The brothers' desire only enhances the commodified value of the sisters' forbidden bodies. At the same time, the lack of physical contact does not make the relationship less difficult. The repressed and thus intensified male desire plunges the coveted objects into an uncomfortable atmosphere in which 4 and 6's daughter feel constantly watched or on the verge of being touched.

Because of her "name," 4 plays a more important role than 6's daughter in the network of male desire. Other children in the story are designated by their parent's number; 4 is the only child with her own number. Her relative independence in terms of naming can be justified by the fact that most male characters are to a degree attracted to 4, either by her voice or by her appearance. Her neighbor, 7, hears her talking in her sleep the night he falls ill. The voice in her dream, "like the wind touching the surface of the water" (*xiang yizhenzhen cong jiangmian shang chui guo de feng*) "greatly warms 7's heart" (*shi qi de neixin gandao shifen wennuan*; *SSRY*, p. 172). The driver, a young bachelor, finds her "extraordinarily beautiful" (*yichang meili*). Even the incestuous adolescent, 3's grandson, cannot help noticing the driver's attraction to 4, thus becoming indirectly attracted to his object of desire (*SSRY*, p. 175). After 3 leaves her grandson at home alone to deliver their baby elsewhere, her depressed grandson watches 4's door every day. It is as if his longing for his grandmother were displaced into the desire for his beautiful adolescent neighbor (*SSRY*, p. 204). After hearing a short utterance by 4 as she passes by, the blind man sits in the same place for years waiting to hear 4 again (*SSRY*, p. 176). In short, 4 becomes an abstract emblem of male desire on which men's sexual drives converge, regardless of their concrete sexual objects.

4's body is composed of visual and acoustic impressions left to the male characters, as if she existed only as a substantiation of male desire. Thus she is "seen" from the perspective of the blind man:

> The blind man sits on the humid sidewalk. The uninterrupted rain makes him as humid as the sidewalk. More than twenty years ago, he was abandoned in a place called "in the middle of the road."

More than twenty years have passed, and now he is sitting in this place. Nearby, there is a high school. The blind man sits here because he can hear the attractive voices of the girl students. Their voices make him feel as if a limpid spring floated in his heart. The blind man shares a room with an idiot and a drunkard. The drunkard has told the blind man all his youthful adventures. He said that the sensation of touching a woman's skin was similar to the sensation of touching flour. That is why the blind man has come to this place. However, at the beginning, he did not come here every day. Only after having once heard 4's voice did he begin to sit here every day. This seems a long time ago. At that time, several girls' voices floated by. It was the first time he had heard 4's voice among them. She pronounced only a single, ordinary sentence, but her voice, like the wind, permeated the blind man's heart. The voice was as fresh and sweet as a fruit, as if it came to the blind man with several drops of dew. 4's unforgettable voice has left an unerasable scar on the blind man's heart. Since then, the blind man has come here every day. Each time he hears 4's voice, his heart cannot help quivering. (*SSRY*, pp. 175–76)

In the past, the blind man was abandoned "in the middle of the road" (*banlu*). Presently, the sidewalk where he sits everyday becomes the end of the road, or his life's destination. The entire life of the blind man seems to focus on a single aim, to hear 4's voice. This voice is objectified in a motionless sonic picture, which is separated from any visual images—"as sweet and fresh as a fruit" (*xiang shuiguo yiyang ganmei*) with "several drops of dew" (*dixia le jige shuizhu*). Objectively, the blind man cannot see the object of his desire. Subjectively, his blindness frees him from any restrictions based on 4's physical appearance. A floating voice is the point of departure for a subjective reconstruction of the desired object. "The flour" (*mianfen*), "the spring" (*quanshui*), "the fruit" (*shuiguo*), and "the wind" (*feng*), metaphors for 4's voice, become materials for the blind man's reconstruction of a visual image of the female body. 4's body is highly desirable precisely because it exists as a metaphorical product of male fantasy. In other words, the blind man desires 4's body as a metaphorical construction of his own desire, which is triggered by the drunkard's description of the sensation of touching a woman's skin.

Paradoxically, loving a girl becomes the privilege of the blind man, because his blindness enables him to love her as a pure product of his fantasy.

Because her attractiveness is measured largely by her function as an empty space or as a playground for male fantasy, the weaker her identity, the more desirable the girl becomes. Since 4 is the object of the most intense male desire, she cannot have an identity of her own. As we see in her relationship to the blind man, her voice is a pure signifier of her body. The meaning of "a single, ordinary sentence" (*shifen pingchang*) does not have the slightest bearing for the blind man. It is, rather, the objective *quality* of her voice that attracts him so much that he follows this voice at the price of his life. In the same vein, although 4 never pronounces any meaningful words, almost every male member of her neighborhood has heard her voice because of her somniloquy. The words she pronounces in her dreams are pure sonic images. The blind man compares the voice of 4's "single, ordinary" sentence to the wind; 7 also describes her dream speech as "the wind touching the surface of the water" (*ru feng chuizhou shuimian*; *SSRY*, p. 172). The sounds of the wind belong to nature and need no reference or interpretation. In this sense, the sounds of the wind may be perceived as pure form, as 4's may also be. One can hardly trace the origin of this voice, since it exists mainly as the sensations it provokes in other people. 4's voice is perfectly objective or objectified to the extent that it is completely free of any intentional or subjective trace.

At the end of the story, 4 drowns herself in the river. Even her death is transformed into a pictorial sequence of a striptease.

> As 4 walks toward the river, her right hand unbuttons her jacket. Her movements are very cautious and extremely graceful. After this, her body appears oblique like the branch of a tree. Little by little, she begins to push away the jacket. Then, with her right hand she holds one corner of the jacket, which is dragging on the ground. After walking a little while, she lets go of the jacket, which quickly lies down on the street—silently. Subsequently, still appearing very beautiful, she unbuttons her dark blue sweater. The sweater, after

falling on the ground, resembles a person dying peacefully. Later, she unbuttons her white blouse. Just at this moment, a breeze blows it and it moves mischievously. The blouse falls slowly, as if it were a sheet of white paper.   (*SSRY*, pp. 210–11)

4 repeats one single gesture: unbuttoning her clothes. By qualifying her movement as "cautious" (*xiaoxin yiyi*) and "extremely graceful" (*shifen youmei*), the narrator transforms her body into a moving sculpture—senseless, emotionless, and speechless. Her clothes, by contrast, are animated. Her jacket that "drags" (*chuiluo*), her sweater that "resembles a dying person" (*xiang yige ren zhengzai pingjing de siqu*), and her blouse that "moves mischievously" (*tiaopi de piaodong*) are much more alive than 4 herself. She is walking, and her clothes keep falling from her body to reveal her beauty. The action of walking is no longer important, since it changes only her geographical location but not the posture of her body. At the same time, the movements of her clothes bring changes in their own situation. Her shirt, for example, can be as "mischievous" as a lively child, whereas she herself is compared to "the branch of a tree" (*yige shuzhi*). In this scene, since 4 is more objectified than the surrounding objects and it is the clothes that are subjectified, we may ask whose subjectivity is at stake. A Chinese critic, Dai Jinhua, provides an answer to the question: Yu Hua's "narrative language is like a visual caress from a man, saturated with exuberance and desire."[13] 4's clothes are subjectified by a language that is saturated with male desire, and they are substitutes for the male author (reader), who fantasizes enjoying the sensual experiences of touching, teasing, and caressing 4's youthful body. In the image of dying beauty, a destructive drive is manifested as the apogee of sensuality to the point that sensual experience requires the destruction of the object of desire, the female body.

Like the bright pink peach blossoms always blooming at the riverside when a young girl drowns herself, beauty can hardly be separated from death in Yu Hua's story.[14] If anything may appear beautiful in his shockingly disgusting world, it is the death of a young girl. Because 4 is young and beautiful, her death fulfills several allegorical functions. The process of her death amounts to an erotic experience for the narrator—through the anthropomorphized clothes' actions of touching and caressing her dying body and the blind man who will blindly follow her voice to death. Her death sums up the transitory quality of life and beauty—the girl who epitomizes male desire must die in the prime of life. By eliminating her from the world, the narrator emphasizes even more the gloomy atmosphere of life—everything left in the world is hopelessly ugly. In fact, it is the very ugliness of life, summed up by 4's rape by the omniscient octogenarian fortuneteller with the help of her biological father, that is the direct cause of her suicide. Like the body of the other young girl in the story, 6's daughter, who is sold by her biological father to a trader in women to obtain a maximum financial profit, 4's dying body is used by her creator, the author of the story, to extract the maximum profit in terms of narrative functions. Since 4 is free of any personal desire and individual identity, her emptiness allows her body to allegorize fully the different values in Yu Hua's world of fiction. She is a perfect number because of her abstractness. Her function equals the currency that guarantees different circulations in a market economy—a market centered on male erotic desire, or the death drive.

To a large extent, the exploitation of the female body by various male characters as well as by their author duplicates the relationship between the fortuneteller and other people. Women do not exist except as the materials of male fantasy. Similarly, human lives have no value unless they are useful to subtend the agonizing existence of the octogenarian vampire. Both relationships are based on a logic of naked power, or a logic of violence. At a deeper level, the exploitation of the woman's voiceless and expressionless body justifies the fortuneteller's unlimited power over young people's passive lives. Young men, such as the blind man and the driver, cannot complain. Since in their world of fantasy women exist only as pure objects, voiceless and lifeless, why couldn't the fortuneteller dispose of his sons' lives in exactly the same way the sons take advantage of women's bodies? Like son, like father, in this case. The son's behavior in this context justifies that of the father, since the victim of the ruthless father repeats the same ruthless logic in victimizing his sister. Since a voice can be heard only by displaying power, the son loses his voice in front of his father just as the woman loses her voice in front of the male subject. Everyone seems to have a fair share, except for the woman who is situated at the bottom of the hierarchy.

Writing and Violence

In January 1990, the Chinese literary journal *Great Wall* (*Changcheng*) published Yu Hua's "An Accident." The duration of narrative time in the story is approximately three months, from September 5 to December 3, 1987. "An Accident" begins with a murder in a cafe. At the end, the same scene repeats itself in the same place. This time, the murder is performed by two people who, three months earlier, had witnessed the opening scene. Except for the brief descriptions of the murders at the beginning and at the end, most of the text consists of the correspondence between the two witnesses of the first murder, who are also the two actors in the second. Five days after the first incident, one witness, Chen He, sends the other, Jiang Piao, his identification card, which a policeman had mistakenly exchanged for Chen's card when returning them to the two witnesses. At that point the two do not know each other. Chen He is extremely interested in discussing the motivations of the murderer with Jiang Piao. Chen firmly believes that a woman was the cause of the murder. In response to his letters, Jiang Piao expresses disagreement over many details. They speculate and argue about various psychological stages experienced by the murderer and question each other's speculations and arguments, intertwining these elements with their respective lives. Finally, after gradually helping Chen make the initial version more "logical" through constant questioning,

Jiang Piao accepts Chen He's interpretation. The two decide that the murderer was sentimentally attached to his wife, a promiscuous woman. After being abandoned by his wife, the murderer can no longer bear his lonely and boring life. He decides to end his life by killing one of her lovers. The fact that this womanizer might be only one of her lovers or might not even have known her no longer matters to the murderer; he will be satisfied as long as he can find an outlet for his anger. Then, the two correspondents decide to meet at the same cafe, where Chen He repeats word for word, gesture for gesture, what the first murderer had done three months previously.

The initial murder is turned into the basis for a play the two witnesses begin to write. The content of this play, however, derives mainly from the authors' nearly diametrically opposed personal life-styles: Chen He is a cuckolded, dull husband, and Jiang Piao is a cynical, hedonist womanizer. Furthermore, Chen He and Jiang Piao are not only the playwrights but also the actors. From the outset, Chen He identifies with the sexually frustrated killer and forces Jiang Piao to enter into the mind of the light-hearted victim. They finish writing their play and acting in it at the price of their own lives. By means of their letters, the two spectators of the murder succeed in identifying with its two fictionalized actors—the murderer and his victim. If to witness violence leads to violent actions, violence is contagious—mediated by writing. As a result, violence in life and in writing are intertwined, and writing itself is an exercise of power.

According to this strict logic, in order to avoid being victimized by violence, one must victimize other people as an outlet for frustration and anger. Built on this logic, the world of Yu Hua's story may appear simple and transparent. However, the transparency is necessarily momentary. The simplicity of the order itself engenders disorder—everyone wants to be in the position of master; no one really wants to stay in the position of slave. In order to become the master, one must first master the logic of violence.

The Logic of Violence

As we can see, "An Accident" is not accidental. On the contrary, it is the outcome of rigorous logic: the logic of domination and violence. In accordance with this logic, everyone must play an assigned role in a violent power struggle, either as the usurper of the other's wife, or as the usurper of the other's life. At the same time, one is both a benefactor and a victim of violence, because everyone plays the role of logician and is also played on by the logic of violence. At the beginning of the story, Chen He, as a cuckolded husband, is a victim of Jiang Piao's violation of his property, his wife. However, by successfully using the logic of violence in his letters, Chen He invites Jiang Piao to join his logical game. By convincing him to identify with the dead victim, Chen He succeeds in reversing their roles. Armed with his pen and knife, in the final scene he becomes the master of violence, and Jiang Piao, its victim.

Interestingly, this story was written right after the Tian'anmen Square Incident of June 4, 1989, in which numerous demonstrators and bystanders were killed by the Chinese Communist army's tanks and automatic weapons. Situated in its historical context, Yu Hua's fascination with the logic of violence is not accidental. The text itself exists as a question mark in relation to violence and its mimetic effect. As Mao Zedong declared: "Political power comes from the barrel of a gun" (*qiangganzi limian chu zhengquan*). The power of the Communist party was established on violent revolutions. In 1989, some Chinese Communist leaders used this argument to justify the crackdown on the peaceful student demonstrators: in order to defend a political power that originated in violence, the Chinese government needed to use violence to crush the opposition.[15]

Nevertheless, violence may appear egalitarian to the extent that it abolishes differences in its final goal: death. Despite their completely different life-styles, the two playwrights, Chen He and Jiang Piao, can easily identify with each other in many respects, because they adhere to the same logic of violence and because both are its victims. As the inadvertent exchange of their identification cards by the policeman implies, their personalities are interchangeable. Furthermore, their names can be perceived as two puns, "sinking into the river" (*chenhe*) and "floating on the river" (*jiangpiao*). The puns suggest the contrasting traits of the two protagonists: Chen He's dullness and Jiang Piao's lightheartedness. Despite their apparent opposition, however, the two characters are equally related to the water; they are both objects that "accidentally" fall into the river of life.

The world governed by the logic of violence excludes any possible feelings that may be shared by individuals. More than six decades ago, Lu Xun complained about the high wall dividing the Chinese people:

> The wall isolates us and makes communication impossible. This is because our intelligent ancestors, called sages, divided people into ten different categories, each of which was classified in a hierarchical structure presumably in accordance with its degree of superiority. Nowadays, although we no longer use the same titles, the ghost of the hierarchy is still alive. Moreover, the isolation has developed further so that it has even extended to the different parts of the human body so that the hands even become contemptuous of the feet. The creator of human beings was already ingenious enough to make us insensitive to others' physical pain. Our sages and their disciples even further perfected creation by making us insensitive to others' emotional pain.[16]

The domination of communism has even further transformed this sad phenomenon into a marker of masculinity for the descendants of Lu Xun's generation, such as Yu Hua and his colleagues. The point Lu Xun tried to make several decades ago is that a hierarchical society made people insensitive to each other's suffering, leading to the dissociation of the "hands and feet" (*shouzu*)—a Chinese metaphor for brothers. Yu Hua's story seems to suggest that only insensitivity can preserve a gender hierarchy that may serve as a firm ground for masculinity—or male superiority. Chen He's lack of masculinity is attested by his failed attempt to share his feelings with his promiscuous wife.

Chen He has a lingering sense of attachment to his wife. But in the story Chen He's attachment reveals his weakness because his feeling results more from a misunderstanding than from any kind of deep understanding of femininity—which in Yu Hua's story is embodied by Chen's wife. Jiang Piao, by contrast, understands her much better, even though his understanding is based only on her cuckolded husband's fragmentary description. Paradoxically, Chen He does not understand women precisely because he tries to understand them and to treat them seriously, whereas Jiang Piao understands women because he knows that women do not need to be understood or to be treated seriously. To treat them seriously is itself a violation of the logic of violence, which will sooner or later induce punishment to the male subject. In order to extort loyalty and obedience from a woman, a man need only know how to apply the logic of violence. This is the sole principle that both men and women in Yu Hua's story must obey. Men, however, can play both the roles of victim and victimizer, whereas women, because of their weaker nature, are capable only of complaisantly subjecting themselves to their own victimization. In this logic, attachment to a woman reveals Chen's lack of masculinity, which causes his attempts at sexual conquest to fail. Jiang Piao feels that Chen's ignorance of the opposite sex is responsible for his wife's sexual frustration and thus indirectly responsible for her unfaithfulness. Without knowing who Chen He's wife is, Jiang Piao says to himself while making love to her, "Her husband must be a fool." Jiang means that Chen's ignorance of the opposite sex makes him incapable of pleasing women ("ORSJ," p. 35). Later, following Jiang Piao's implicit advice, Chen even tries to flirt with other women, and again his ignorance makes him unattractive.

Chen He's sentimental attachment to a woman becomes the cause of his sexual impotency. Furthermore, because he can neither win his wife's devotion nor take revenge on her for what she has done to him nor find an outlet in other women, Chen He is doomed to commit an even greater act of violence—transgression of the logic of violence. He must kill someone who is not even necessarily responsible for his misery in order to find an outlet for his frustration and anger. Sentiment is not only an illusion but also the first step toward blind destruction. To this extent, sentiment itself is discounted as one of the elements in the logic of violence—an impurity that stupidly and vainly disturbs the impeccable structure of violence.

As in the first murder, Chen He's attachment to his wife becomes an empty excuse that serves as the basis on which the two male protagonists build their story. Chen He's wife is the implicit tie that binds the two men, her forsaken husband and her frivolous lover, since her body becomes a battlefield on which the two men's conflicting values converge in the form of sexuality. On the surface, the two men are related by having witnessed the murder. In fact, the scene of the first murder is meaningful to them precisely because it illustrates the relationship between Chen He and Jiang Piao by their connections with the same promiscuous and nameless woman, Chen He's wife. Without Chen He's wife, the two male characters could not successfully identify with the actors of the first murder. Without this process of identification, they could not perform the second murder. In this sense, Chen He's wife plays an instrumental role in the murder.

Both Chen He and Jiang Piao live in a completely isolated world. Chen He's failed marriage only underlines his loneliness, whereas Jiang Piao's successive affairs with married women confine him even more in his solitude. Their only passion in life is to write the letters in which they try to solve the mystery of the murder, or the mystery of their own deaths. Their writings are concerned with the question of how to reason according to a logic of violence in a world of naked power. This world is desperately logical and transparent to the extent that the rigorous logic of violence leaves no room for small pleasures. Sex is a matter of technique for both the good and bad technicians, Jiang Piao and Chen He. Family is a burden that a clever person like Jiang Piao avoids at any price and that leads an idiot like Chen He to death. Sentiment is a disguised form of violence, a disharmony in communication. In this case, one can derive pleasure only from a serious game in which one's life is at stake, because life is the only thing one owns and can play with. Therefore, Chen He and Jiang Piao must play as seriously and rigorously as possible, as if the game were a mathematical equation—as does the author in regard to his reader. Writing itself becomes violence, which finally "destroys" the writer's "subversive intent"—to borrow Susan Rubin Suleiman's book title[17]—in accordance with the impeccable logic of violence. Without doubt, Yu Hua's exploration of the logic of violence is subversive to the extent that it casts an ironical light on the basis that structures official discourse in China. In a sense, it can be considered more subversive than any previous attempt to explore the same subject of violence, because Yu Hua's story pushes the notion of transgression to its limits.

Georges Bataille writes that eroticism cannot be separated from violence—both transgress the most important taboo: death.[18] Since transgression defines itself in opposition to social norms or prohibitions,[19] it is, to a large extent, shaped by the objects of transgression, taboos. The most subversive element in Yu Hua's writing is that violence becomes an order—as rigorous and logical as the order that governs official discourse. In many cases, the orders in Yu Hua's fiction and in contemporary China become identical since they are engendered by the same logic of violence. In other words, transgression is not only shaped by social norms or prohibitions but also transformed into a perverse mirror image of social norms. By drawing a disturbingly similar picture of the official order in his world of fiction, Yu Hua succeeds in denouncing the logic of naked violence in the current political order. But at the same time, transgression itself becomes impossible in the final analysis, because the distance between order and violence, between prohibitions and transgressions, has completely disappeared.

By identifying violence with the official order, Yu Hua pushes subversion to its limits and radically denies the existence of the taboo in a process of identification with it. If the Chinese government decides to sustain its power by use of the threat of death—by offering the choice of obedience to the political power or death—as in the case of the Tian'anmen Incident in June 1989, Yu Hua chooses to present death in a fictionalized order of violence. In this representation, death is no longer a taboo, but rather a norm or a convention. By conventionalizing death, Yu Hua's order of violence may be considered a radical transgression of the taboo. This radical transgression is tantamount to the destruction of any transgressive momentum, however, precisely because it is unable to "maintain" the taboo "in order to benefit by it."[20] Interestingly, in order to achieve the identification with the violent core that structures official discourse, Yu Hua must exclude any women—except as an instrumental role in male-male relationships—even in a story that is supposedly about a crime of passion. Moreover, in Yu Hua's world of violence eroticism is no longer possible—since transgression itself is turned into an order that abolishes prohibitions and limits and consequently any possible pleasure in transgressing them.

The abolition of the distance between taboo and transgression in Yu Hua's works objectifies the order of violence inherent in the dominant ideology in China. The objectified logic of violence also represents an extreme form of cultural nihilism to the extent that in Yu Hua's world any value system is destroyed by the system of naked power. In this sense, one may say that Yu's fiction reaches the degree zero of culture. At the beginning of the twentieth century, Lu Xun and his generation of radical intellectuals searched for an alternative to Chinese culture, which they perceived as devoid of any positive value. That search to a large extent laid the intellectual foundation for the Chinese Communist party. At that time many radical intellectuals considered the party the only dissident organization powerful enough to negate traditional Chinese society by means of revolution. At the end of the century, Yu Hua and his generation of experimental writers have also tried to depict violence as a sign of the nullity of any cultural value. Violence in Yu's stories, despite his initially subversive intent, contributes to consolidating the logic of the dominant ideology indirectly, through a process of identification. In his world of naked power, any resistance to the logic of violence becomes an "impurity" that disturbs its impeccable structure. This structure of power is also the structure of the Communist state or of the dictatorship of the proletariat.

However, it is not enough to draw an accurate portrait of the current political structure in order to deconstruct it. How could one even hope to shake such a structure, if its subversion merely depicts its invincibility? To a large extent, the invincibility is attested by means of the murder of the young as well as the rape, torture, and fragmentation of the female body. The only one who seems to benefit from this structure is the past, which is personified by the octogenarian fortuneteller in *Life in the World Resembles Smoke*. The fortuneteller is also the vampire who lives on the blood of the young. The old man represents the returned past par excellence, a past that different generations of radical intellectuals in China have tried to deny and to destroy. This unsymbolizable past haunts Yu Hua's works by multiplying its faces, either as a murderer of the young, a rapist of women, or an unscrupulous trader in women and even in their corpses. In this world of naked violence, no subject voice can truly be formulated *against* power. If there is a subject voice in Yu Hua's fiction, this voice, as in the case of 4's stripteasing prelude to death, tends to identify with the nameless and undefinable past by means either of the fetishization of naked power or of the misogynistic exploitation of the female body.

As we have seen, Yu Hua's world is desperately logical, and the only functioning logic is that of violence. Consequently, the subject can articulate his voice only according to this logic. Even the writing process itself, as in the case of the two writer-criminal protagonists in "An Accident," must also submit to the same logic of violence. In a sense, both Lu Xun's search for a cultural alternative and Yu Hua's deliberate violation of any possible cultural value lead to the same conclusion: cultural nihilism can offer no viable solution. It is only a dead-end for modern China as well as for its literature and arts. The difference is that Lu Xun reached this conclusion by means of a stoic but fruitless resistance to the power structure, whereas Yu Hua, by means of a clever cynicism, complaisantly identifies with the same structure.

Conclusion

According to Frederick Engels, gender oppression is rooted in an economic structure, private ownership.[1] This notion, widely accepted by different Marxist schools, has also prevailed in previously socialist countries such as China. In fact, in the history of human civilization, the gender hierarchy has repeatedly been justified and reinforced by labor divisions based on private ownership that often regard women as property. In traditional China, for example, women, as part of the property of patriarchal families, rarely had access to independent professions as individuals. Partly due to the theoretical emphasis in the Marxist tradition on the economic structure as the only source of women's oppression, the women's emancipation movement in socialist countries was basically limited to changes in the division of labor.[2] However, several decades after a rather superficial women's emancipation movement in terms of the division of labor, Chinese women are still oppressed, despite their theoretically independent financial status. Although women's lack of financial independence was one of the reasons for their oppression, this was certainly not the only reason. The persistent oppression proves that patriarchy has its roots not only in the economy but also in ideology. It is much more difficult to uproot patriarchal ideology than to change the economic structure, because the ruling party itself is deeply rooted in the same ideology.

Although women's participation as individual workers has to a certain extent improved their economic status, the failure of women's emancipation at the ideological level has forced both Chinese men and women into a double-bind situation. Having lost a secure position as the only legitimate provider for his family, a contemporary Chinese man encounters many more difficulties in proving his superior power vis-à-vis his sexual partner than did his ancestors. At the same time, his power is preserved almost intact in the collective imaginary, which is largely determined by the traditional as well as the Communist patriarchal ideologies. In order to meet what is expected of the superior sex, he must find means to substantialize his own image of power. A Chinese woman, by contrast, is torn between two contradictory demands—to compete with men in the public sector and to remain inferior to men in private spaces. The Communist party encourages a woman to become as "useful" as men in her career. The traditional patriarchy, which still insists on equating femininity with submission, imposes a no less powerful demand on Chinese women—especially in the realm of the family.

In the past, both men and women were required to believe in the party and the revolutionary cause and to sacrifice for their belief. The collective belief was to a large extent objectified and transformed into different rules that controlled people's behavior even in everyday life. A Chinese, despite her or his disbelief in this collective ideology, had to behave as if she or he believed in it, by following the rules of a faithful believer. This behavior is not difficult to understand, since one's political life, economic interests, social position, and even personal relations depended largely on how much one could fake a belief in communism. Under the circumstances, the double-bind gender situation that burdened both men and women could easily be counted as one of the numerous sacrifices required by their beliefs. Nevertheless, this form of objectified belief was eroded by constant political struggles within the party, which intensified during the Cultural Revolution. Later, the objectified belief was further undermined and destroyed by the economic reforms, which tended to replace the transcendent signifier, the party, by an apparently much more egalitarian signifier, money. Since the party line came to be decentralized by money, the painful process of make-believe is no longer required of a Chinese citizen. As a result, the previously repressed double-bind situation has emerged on the surface, since the disappearance of the transcendent signifier makes apparent the meaninglessness of any sacrifice.

As I have pointed out, the women's emancipation movement in China was limited mainly to changes in the division of labor. Sociologically speaking, these changes were more quantitative than qualitative. Almost all women participate in production, whereas men, despite their threatened sense of superiority, still occupy the most important political, economic, intellectual, and social positions. At the same time, the large number of Chinese women in the workplace has indeed brought certain qualitative changes, not so much in the collective area of power distribution as in the individual abilities of women to face challenges. In order to deal with the double-bind situation the old and new patriarchies have imposed upon them, women have no choice but to become stronger. Women's competence threatens the traditional image of masculine superiority even more, since it risks destabilizing institutional power, which is still essentially gendered as masculine. Only by denying women's strength can the current patriarchal ideology justify the masculine institutional power and recreate an image of undebatable masculine superiority. This need is made more urgent by the fact that in the collective unconscious the traditional gender hierarchy is still unshakable. At the same time, women's strength, which is required by their daily life, is a no less powerful reality. The more difficult it is to deny this reality, the more aggressive the attempt at denial becomes. The aggressiveness may partly explain the misogynistic tendency prevailing in contemporary society as well as in literature, as we have witnessed in most works of experimental fiction writers.

Among experimental fiction writers, men in general seem to

endorse the misogynistic tendency in society without assuming a critical distance. Each of the four male contemporary writers studied in this book displays a personal trademark of uncritical endorsement. Mo Yan's narrator in *Red Sorghum* fetishizes the mutilated bound feet of his grandmother as the ultimate mark of female beauty. Zhaxi Dawa compares women to the pearls in a divine rosary that anonymously denote the transcendent truth. Su Tong associates female attractiveness with animality. In Yu Hua's writings, women are described as piles of senseless and voiceless meat. The only woman writer studied here, Can Xue, goes against the grain with courage and determination, qualities that have earned her a reputation as insane.

The prevailing misogyny of this subversive literary form may partly be explained by its subversive function vis-à-vis communism. Chinese experimental fiction, which emerged during the late 1980's, can be considered a relatively mature form that radically subverts the literary representation favored by Communist ideology, namely, socialist realism. In comparison with all previous post-Mao literary forms, such as the "literature of wounds" (*shanghen wenxue*), "root-searching literature" (*xungen wenxue*), and "literature of educated youth" (*zhiqing wenxue*), experimental fiction has broken much further away from the conventions of socialist realism in terms of language, narrative structure, and ideological complexity. However, its subversive role also reinforces the misogynistic mark carried by this literary form. Since the party in the past assumed the subversive role of the self-claimed spokesman of the oppressed against the Confucian tradition, it is even more difficult for would-be transgressors of Communist ideology to articulate their position. On the one hand, minority discourse is no longer readily available to the rebellious sons against their Communist fathers, who appropriated it as representative of their political stance against their Confucian grandfathers. On the other hand, opting for an oppositional discourse against this already oppositional ideology may very well lead to a dangerous identification with a conservative position previously occupied by the Confucian grandfathers.

At the same time, in this literary form, all conventional boundaries, such as those between good and evil, true and false, right and wrong, life and death, have been deconstructed, because of the writers' keen awareness of the lack of any recognizable transcendent signifier. In this world of floating signifiers, the gender hierarchy has become the only remaining fortification that may still be considered solid ground for male writers, however imaginary that ground may be. The imaginary ground remains the last territory on which male subjectivity may still constitute itself as a potential totality. Their desire for a solid ground in a world of uncertainty can be considered a longing for an objective social order against which a coherent self can be defined. This order will certainly differ from the Communist one, even though the fundamental hierarchical structure will not change. As Ernesto Laclau powerfully demonstrates, no objective social order exists.[3] Any claim of objectivity for a social order may be a dangerous path to totalitarianism, since this objectivity can result only from a reduction of different interest groups to the single voice of the dominant group. As in experimental fiction, the longing for a different objective order in which the male subject may eventually constitute itself as a coherent totality leads to a complete silencing of women's voices in their works as well as among women writers. The only exception is Can Xue, whose voice is perceived by most Chinese critics as a hysterical cry devoid of any objectivity and outside the symbolic system.

Women's fate both in the socialist revolution half a century ago and in the contemporary literary form most subversive of Communist ideology indicates the weakness of oppositional politics. One point in common exists between the Communist fathers and their rebellious sons: both generations have chosen an oppositional politics against the previous one. Being oppositional in this Chinese context implies rejecting the existing social order by assuming that it will be replaced by another, much more rational and objective one. The new social order, defined mainly as the negation of the old one, leaves little room for compromise. Because of this uncompromising opposition, the choices have virtually been limited to two poles. One pole is the Confucian tradition, a generalized term that includes everything in China's past. The other pole is defined against this past, as in the socialist revolution.

The oppositional pole often needs to find support from an outsider, the powerful West, represented either by Marxism or liberalism, as the counterpart of the traditional China. The West, however, functions as a powerful but no less empty signifier, which may represent diametrically opposite value systems. The representation of the West in terms of gender problem can be taken as a case in point. At the beginning of the century, the West, through its literature and arts, served to introduce the notion of gender equality to the May Fourth radicals. At the end of the century, the West provides experimental fiction writers an image of masculinity sustained by a debasement of women. To this extent, the West still remains mainly a cultural signifier of various value systems—albeit a signifier of authority—but not a cultural partner with whom China can conduct dialogues on an equal footing.

This unequal relationship between China and other cultures is a byproduct of the practice of oppositional politics, since an uncompromising oppositional politics makes it difficult, if not impossible, to accept difference, be it internal or external. The oppositional desire to distance oneself as far as possible from the pole against which the potential new social order is defined is likely to leave the various positions in between voiceless. Moreover, the oversimplified options of the two basic poles make it difficult, if not impossible, for the oppositional party to place itself in opposition to both poles, as in the case of experimental fiction. In order to overcome this inherent self-contradiction, the oppositional party may need to choose an Other in order to redefine its otherwise untenable and undefinable position. This Other may be internal or external. However, both internal or external others share one characteristic: they are reduced to oversimplified images that represent the polarized position of the oppositional party, as in the cases of Chinese women and Western culture. Consequently, the alternative representations of the two poles not only silence some minority groups and ritualize cultural exchanges but also often reduce these groups and other cultures to a position of an oversimplified Other against which the new social order is defined.

In the socialist revolution, Chinese women functioned as the objects of social oppression that negatively represented the evil old tradition. It was largely against this tradition that the Communist party justified its power. In the name of the oppressed, which often meant women, the party rose to power, although the ideology of salvation was itself no less patriarchal.[4] Women's negative representation as the object of social oppression in Communist ideology has several decades later become a positive identification with the party's gender politics. By means of this identification, women are attacked as a threat to male subjectivity in place of the party. In both cases, women's fate indicates that a straightforward oppositional politics is inherently contradictory to democracy because it virtually reduces diversified interest groups to a single position by means of a simplified representation.

As the largest minority group in terms of power, Chinese women have been used as a significant other that allows both the Communist party and its rebellious descendants to articulate oppositional discourses. On the one hand, this Other has made opposition possible. On the other hand, precisely because the opposition must be defined to the detriment of a silenced other, it cannot be considered truly democratic. If women, half of the Chinese population, must be virtually silenced and excluded in order to serve as a signifier of a masculine ideology, how could the other half of the population possibly enjoy democracy? In this sense, the need to use an other as the basis for oppositional discourse inevitably leads to the failure of oppositional politics. Since Chinese women are the largest minority group, their treatment can be used as a test case for democratization of China. In the repression of women's subject voices and in the denial to them of subject positions, the patriarchal structure of the past will continue to haunt the rebellious sons, who are desperately and vainly trying to break away from the past by means of a cultural nihilism that justifies destruction and violence.

Reference Matter

Notes

For complete author names, titles, and publication data for the works cited here in short form, see the Bibliography, pp. 207–13.

Introduction

1. Laclau, pp. 89–92.
2. Rey Chow, *Writing Diaspora*, pp. 99–119.
3. "What we must bear in mind here is the radical ontological status of symptom: symptom, conceived as *sinthome*, is literally our only substance, the only positive support of our being, the only point that gives consistency to the subject" (Žižek, *Sublime Object*, p. 75).
4. Delannoi, p. 24.
5. Ibid.
6. Rosemont, pp. 82–84.
7. A well-known biography of a military official is entitled *Cong nuli dao jiangjun* (From slave to general).
8. *Analects*, 17.23.
9. According to Laclau (p. 81), the social imaginary can claim universality only through a myth that at the same time resists the full achievement of this universality. If within a society, the social imaginary coincides with universality, mythical space is no longer necessary or possible. Totalitarian society in socialist countries is characterized by a spu-

rious correspondence of the social imaginary, the dominant ideology, and its mythical subjects, whose objective interests are transparently represented by their government.

10. Ding Ling, a writer of the May Fourth generation, had a stronger feminist awareness than most of her contemporary women writers—especially in her early works. In 1927, at the age of 23, Ding dealt with the issue of female sexual desire in "Sophie's Diary." In 1932, Ding joined the Communist party after the Nationalist government executed her husband, Hu Yeping, a Communist writer. The Communist party could not forgive this woman's outspokenness. In 1957, accused of being a rightist partly because of her feminist concerns, she was sent to the border province of Helongjiang, where she spent 22 years working as a farmer. Ironically, her life in this concentration camp eliminated her subject voice as a woman. After her return to Beijing, she became a spokeswoman of the party line. For critical discussions of Ding Ling as a woman writer, see Tani Barlow's introduction to a collection of Ding Ling's short stories in English translation (Ding Ling, pp. 1–45), and also Feuerwerker. For an insightful reading of the "Diary," see Rey Chow, *Woman and Chinese Modernity,* pp. 162–70.

11. Irigaray, *Je, tu, nous,* p. 14.

12. See Wolf, and the introduction to Lu Tonglin, *Gender and Sexuality.*

13. In 1986, a man using the pseudonym "Adam" published an essay entitled "Adam's Bewilderment" in the journal *Zhongguo funü* (Chinese women). After dividing professions according to gender, "Adam" added: "However, generally speaking, women are not as good as men even in their specialties. For example, singing songs to induce a baby in the cradle to sleep certainly belongs to the realm of female natural instincts, but until now the best lullabies have always been composed by men. One can provide numerous similar examples. Don't try to explain them merely in terms of differences imposed by cultural and social history. To a large extent, they are proofs of men's inner superiority." "Adam's" essay has been reprinted in Li Xiaojiang (see p. 222), which apparently claims to be a response to the bewildered "Adam."

14. For example, Li Xiaojiang, a Chinese feminist, has edited a series of women's studies since 1988. This series, which is intended to include 20 to 25 books on gender issues in various topics of the humanities, has been published by a relatively obscure press in Henan province, the Henan renmin chubanshe. See, e.g., Li Xiaojiang, as well as Meng and Dai. Li Xiaojiang is the general editor of both books. Dai Qing, another

notable woman's voice, wrote a series of reportage articles on women's oppression in current Chinese society; she came to the United States for one year of research following imprisonment for alleged counterrevolutionary activities during the student demonstrations. See, e.g., Dai Qing, "Chonghun zui" and the collection of reportage, which she edited, *Xing kaifang nüzi*.

15. Meng Yue, a feminist critic from mainland China, for instance, told me in a phone conversation that she could accept the misogyny manifested in the works of a great number of male experimental writers since this was simply a sign of their attempt "to overcorrect the wrongdoing (of the Communist party)."

16. "Only women and inferior men are difficult to deal with" (*wei nüzi yu xiaoren nan yang ye*; *Analects*, 17.23).

17. I borrow this comparison from Decker, p. 135.

18. In the context of this book, I use "great narrative" to designate official expressions of traditional Chinese cultural and social values, which are largely centered on Confucianism.

19. In classical Chinese, *ming* designates not only proper names but also words and titles.

20. Confucius's loyal disciple Zilu asked his master: "If the king relies on the master to govern the country, what will be your priorities?" (*jun dai zi er weizheng zi jiang xixian*). The master answered: "I must rectify names" (*bi ye zhengming hu*; *Analects*, 13.3).

21. Asked by the Prince Hui of Liang how to govern a country, Mencius replied: "Let the ruler be a ruler, subject be a subject, father be a father, son be a son" (*junjun, chenchen, fufu, zizi*; *Mencius*, 2.3).

22. Ji Yun, a Qing Confucian scholar, wrote: "Writing must carry the Dao to clarify its nature" (*wen yi zaidao ming qi dang ran*; quoted in Liu Xie, pp. 1–2).

23. "Great men" (*daren*) in classical Chinese means either virtuous men or powerful men.

24. Yan Shigu quotes Ruzhun in his comments on Ban Gu's explanation of writers of *xiaoshuo*: "*Baiguan* means low officials. . . . Tiny grains of rice are called *bai*. Gossip on the street is indeed a tedious type of speech. Since emperors wanted to learn about street customs, they established the title *baiguan* for collecting gossip" (Ban, p. 39). However, Ban's list of examples of *xiaoshuo* suggests that during his times this term meant "legend," which was categorized as a form of historical rather than literary writing. See Lu Xun, *Zhongguo xiaoshuo shilüe* (An abridged history of Chinese fiction), in Lu Xun, vol. 9.

25. Zheng Xuan, a Han commentator on the *Shijing* (Book of songs), wrote: "Poetry expresses ideals" (*shi yan zhi*) (Zheng, p. 9). Ban Gu (p. 7) quoted this passage in his comments on poetry in the "Yiwen zhi" of the *Hanshu*; Yan Shigu explained this passage as deriving from the *Shujing* (Book of documents).

26. In the "Yiwen zhi" in the *Tangshu* (Book of Tang: "Catalogue of artistic writings"), fictional works are included in chap. 2, "Miscellaneous History" ("Zashi"). One of the terms used to describe fiction is *yeshi* (Ouyang, p. 22).

27. In the "Yiwen zhi" of the *Hanshu*, Ban Gu (p. 13) explains historical writing in terms of *shiguan*: "In ancient times, kings had official historians who took notes of the king's every action. As a result, kings were cautious in their speeches and actions." See also the entry for *shiguan* in *Cihai* (1:734): "*Shiguan*, title of an official, established in the Shang dynasty [approximately 17th to 11th c. B.C.]. Initially *shiguan* was the title of a military officer on duty away from home. Later, it became the title of the official historian close to the prince. He was also called the bookmaker [*zuoce*]."

28. See Wang Yang-ming; and Tu.

29. See, e.g., Yü.

30. Li Zhi (1527–1602), a commentator on the novel and an eccentric intellectual, emphasized the naturalness of the human mind as the final standard of any morality in his "Tongxin pian" (On the childlike mind). Tang Xianzu (1550–1616), the playwright, suggested that reason must be subservient to sentiment in his "*Mudan ting* xu" (Preface to *The Peony Pavilion*). Feng Menglong (1574–1646), who edited a large number of vernacular stories, promoted vernacular language for its direct expression of sentiment in, for example, his "*Gujin xiaoshuo* xu" (Preface to *Stories Old and New*) and "*Xixiang ji* pingdian" (Comments on *The West Pavilion*). Jin Shengtan (1608–1661), a commentator on several important traditional Chinese novels, believed that vernacular literature was even superior to the Confucian classics. See his "*Shuihu* dufa" (Method of reading the *Water Margin*) and "*Xixiang* dufa" (Method of reading the *West Pavilion*).

31. *Nan'an wenshi ziliao*, p. 22.

32. Chow Tse-tsung, pp. 269–89.

33. Lu Xun, for example, suggested to young Chinese readers that they not read a single Chinese book, although he himself was well read in classical Chinese literature (Lu Xun, 3:12). Hu Shi (*Zhongguo gudian xiaoshuo*), who spent enormous amount of time doing "positivistic research" (*kaozheng*) on the traditional Chinese novel, apologized for his

fondness for this genre by stating how inferior it was to its Western counterpart.

34. See, e.g., Mao Dun.

35. See Eide, pp. 71–104.

36. Hu, "Yipusheng zhuyi."

37. "Two conditions are needed to develop individuality: individual freedom, and individual responsibility" (ibid., p. 504). Interestingly, Bill Clinton's acceptance speech at the Democratic party convention in 1992 echoed the Chinese scholar, who had imported these values from America more than half a century earlier.

38. "It's better to worship Darwin and Ibsen than Confucius and Guan Kong" (Lu Xun, 1: 333).

39. Ibid., 1: 159.

40. See Witke, pp. 7–13.

41. See note 13 to this chapter.

42. Gu Yanwu, a Qing Confucian (1613–1682), in his essay entitled "Zhuzi wannian dinglun" (Zhuzi's views in his old age), criticized Wang's attempt to devalue Zhu Xi, the Song Neo-Confucian scholar, whose writings, according to Gu, Wang had shrewdly manipulated. Gu considered Wang's disciples, such as He Xinyin and Li Zhi, as "plagues on the world" (*yishi zhi huan*), causes of destruction of a dynasty (Gu, pp. 27–28).

43. Chow Tse-tsung, p. 103.   44. Dirlik, pp. 43–52.

45. Ibid., pp. 57–145.   46. See, e.g., Liu Xiaopo.

47. Li Tuo (p. 13) praises experimental fiction for its "subversion of Maoist discourse (*Mao wenti*)."

48. One of the important crimes of which his opponents accused Li Zhi was sexual misconduct, which was imitated by his disciples. His disciples, according to Li's accusor, even raped women (*Shenzong shilu*, vol. 369, cited in Zhang Jianye, p. 241; see also Gu, p. 31).

49. See my introduction to *Gender and Sexuality*; and Yue.

50. See, e.g., the comic account of this concept of revolution in A Q's daydreaming (Lu Xun, 1: 515).

51. See, e.g., Salisbury.   52. Laclau and Mouffe.

53. Ibid., p. 1.   54. Ibid., p. 167.

55. Laclau, pp. 89–92.   56. Laclau and Mouffe, p. 175.

57. Laclau and Mouffe (p. 131) use Gramsci's term *organic crisis* to designate the unstable situation of a society in which antagonisms proliferate.

58. Laclau and Mouffe (p. 160) use the term *equalitarian imaginary* to describe the Western radical tradition since the French Revolution.

59. Yue.

60. For example, Huang Ziping, Li Tuo, Liu Zaifu, and other important literary critics are among the Chinese intellectuals in exile in the United States following the crackdown on the student demonstrations.

61. Lauretis, p. 5.

62. Minorities and peasants are often used as fields of projection by contemporary fiction writers. See, e.g., Zhu Hong. Concerning the attitude of the students toward workers, see Rosemont, pp. 21–23.

63. Tocqueville, p. 109.

Chapter 1

1. "Destruction of the Four Olds" was an early campaign during the Cultural Revolution; its aim was the destruction of old thought, old culture, old customs, and the old routine.

2. See, e.g., Su Xiaokang's television program, "*River Elegy*: TV Politic," in Barmé and Jaivin, pp. 138–64.

3. See Meisner, p. 16.

4. Mao Zedong, "Qingyuan chun: xue" (Snow), in *Shici*.

5. "Die on the battlefield" (*zhansi shachang*), a proverb, expresses the lofty aspirations of a loyal warrior in traditional China.

6. Yue Fei, the legendary hero of the Southern Song dynasty, was executed by the order of the Song emperor.

7. Qu Yuan (ca. 340–278 B.C.), a great poet and high official of the Chu kingdom. Having failed to realize his political ideal, unification of China by his king, Qu Yuan drowned himself in the river. He has been remembered as the great patriot in China, and the anniversary of his death is a special holiday (Duanwu jie) and commemorated with a special kind of food (*zongzi*) which is made for his wandering soul.

8. On the benevolent sexism of certain radical writers, including Lu Xun, see Yue.

9. Simon Ley, the Belgian sinologist, for example, constantly expresses in his writings a desire to preserve an intact traditional culture, as if China would be better off turning into an immense museum of its precious past.

10. Arif Dirlik (p. 12) states: "The laying of the foundations of 1920 meant for the Communists the reorganization of the May Fourth legacy." At the same time, the Nationalist government in Taiwan blamed the May Fourth movement for loss of the mainland, since it strengthened the influence of the Communist party (Peng, p. 65).

11. Meisner, p. 14.

12. Ibid., p. 16.

13. Mao Dun (1896–1981) is the author of *Ziye* (Midnight; 1933) and other literary and critical works. Rou Shi (1901–31), author of *Zaochun eryue* (February; 1929) and other stories, was executed by the Nationalists in Longhua with four other writers and some party members. Ding Ling (1907–86) published "Shafei nüshi riji" (Miss Sophia's diary; 1927), *Taiyang zhaozai Sanggan heshang* (The sun shines over the Sanggan River; 1949), and other works. Xiao Jun (1908–) wrote *Bayue de xiangcun* (Village in August; 1942) among other works.

14. Mao Zedong, "Zai Yan'an wenyi zuotanhui shang de jianghua" (Talk at the Yan'an Forum on literature and the arts), *Xuanji*, pp. 833–34.

15. Lu Xun, 2:195.

16. Ibid., p. 196.

17. Ibid.

18. Lu Xun (3:12) wrote to young Chinese readers: "I believe that you should read very few, if not no, Chinese books, and read many more foreign books."

19. See Mencius's notion of the "human relationships" (*renlun*; *Mencius*, 10.3). I use the masculine singular third-person pronoun instead of both masculine and feminine to refer to the individual either in the Confucian or the May Fourth context. Although, unlike the misogynistic defender of the patriarchal order Confucius, Lu Xun and his generation of radical intellectuals were the benevolent advocates of women's emancipation, women in their works had not truly gained subject voices. As in the case of the women's emancipation promoted by the Communist party, women were the *objects* not the *subjects* of this movement. Concerning this problem, see Yue.

20. Reiss.

21. At the end of his short story "Sinking," Yu Dafu's protagonist blames the weakness of China for his own failure in sexual relationships ("Sinking," in Lau et al., p. 141).

22. Lu Xun, 1:422.   23. Ibid., 11:20–21.

24. Ibid., 1:435.   25. Ibid., p. 485.

26. Vance, pp. 51–85.   27. Lu Xun, 7:81.

28. Anderson, "Morality of Forms," p. 41.

29. Lu Xun, 2:7.   30. Ibid., 1:158–65.

31. Wolf.   32. Lu Xun, 2:112.

33. Ibid., p. 113.   34. Ibid., p. 127.

35. Ibid., p. 110.

36. Wang Shifu of the Yuan dynasty is the author of *Xixiang ji*. His

writing was largely influenced by a previous version, *Dong Xixiang*, supposedly compiled by Dong Jieyuan of the Jin dynasty.

37. See Lu Tonglin, "How Do You Tell a Girl from a Boy?" pp. 63–74.

Chapter 2

1. Mo Yan, *Hong gaoliang*, in Dong et al.; hereinafter cited in the text as *HGL*. All translations are mine.

2. See, e.g., Zhang Zhizhong.

3. The "Fifth Generation" of filmmakers generally refers to the 1983 graduating class of the Institute of Cinema at Beijing, the first class after the Cultural Revolution. Most of them are in their early forties and late thirties and spent their formative years in the countryside, army, or factories. Some of them did not actually attend the same class, such as Huang Jianxin and Zhang Junzhao, but they also belong to the same age group. Their films are characterized by an emphasis on individual expression, formalistic experiments, and subjective approaches.

4. For a good description of the connections between the novella and the film, see the article by the woman director Zhang Nuanxin.

5. See Zhang Zhizhong's introduction.

6. The Chinese critic Li Tuo describes Mo Yan's style in the preface to a collection of the latter's short stories: "Life-style and characters in his fiction are after all lively reflections of realistic life in our countryside" (Mo, *Touming de hongluobo*, p. 2).

7. See Wang Xiaoming, "Bu xiangxin de," p. 25.

8. For an interesting analysis of this subject in contemporary Chinese literature, see Cai.

9. Yang.

10. Liang.

11. Luo and Yang.

12. Yuan.

13. Feng.

14. Ibid., pp. 37–38.

15. The "three submissions" prescribed that a woman submit to her father before marriage, to her husband after marriage, and to her son after her husband's death. The "four virtues" were woman's probity, speech, appearance, and skill.

16. Feng, p. 119.

17. Mao Zedong, "Qingyuan chun: xue" (Snow), in *Shici*.

18. Yang, pp. 567–68.

19. Liang, pp. 376–82.

20. Yang, pp. 355–64.

21. In Mo's "Dry River," for example, a boy from the same family

background is beaten to death by his family members. The story ends on a narcissistic note: "By the time people found him he was already dead. His parents stared blankly, their eyes like those of fishes. . . . Folks with faces as bleak as the desert gazed upon his sun-drenched buttocks . . . as if looking at a beautiful and radiant face, as if looking at me myself" (Tai, p. 227). Mo Yan's short story entitled "The Transparent Red Radish" talks about a child of the same social origin who tries to create a solipsistically magical world to protect himself from daily mistreatment and torture.

22. Mao Zedong, "Zenyang fenxi nongcun jieji" (How to analyze rural classes), in *Xuanji*, p. 114.

23. Ibid., p. 817.

24. On this subject, see the comments on "root-searching literature" by Guo; and Fan.

25. Žižek, *Sublime Object*, p. 133.

26. Can, *Tuwei biaoyan*, pp. 347–48.

Chapter 3

1. Legge, pp. 263–64.

2. Li Disheng, p. 506.

3. "Writing must carry principle" (*wen yi zaidao*), Ji Yun, in Liu Xie, pp. 1–2.

4. Li Tuo, p. 6. All translations of Chinese critics in this chapter are my own.

5. During the 1980's, a number of important literary journals, such as *Beijing wenxue* (Beijing literature), *Shanghai wenxue* (Shanghai literature), *Zhongshan*, and *Shouhuo* (Harvest), at least for a period, were to a large extent controlled, if not monopolized, by this group of avant-garde literary critics.

6. Liu Suola may arguably be considered the only other woman writer who has gained a similar reputation, even though her works are much more traditional than Can Xue's.

7. Cheng Yongxin, p. 370. 8. Cheng Depei, p. 71.

9. Cheng Yongxin, p. 266. 10. Li Xiaojiang, p. 222.

11. Yu Hua, for example, constantly refers to Li Tuo as his master in his collections and interviews; see his preface to *Shibasui*.

12. In her "Three Women's Texts and a Critique of Imperialism," for example, Gayatri Spivak explains how gender boundaries are deconstructed and reconstituted by the racial policy of Western imperialism.

13. Irigaray, *Speculum*, p. 237.

14. "A Mei zai yige taiyang tianli de chousi" (A Mei's melancholy thoughts on a sunny day), and "Kuangye li" (In the wilderness), in Wu Liang et al., *Huangdan pai xiaoshuo*, pp. 301–5, 319–23; hereinafter cited as *HDPXS* in the text. "Wo zai nage shijie de shiqing—gei youren" (What happened to me in that world—to a friend), in Cheng Yongxin, pp. 366–70; hereinafter cited as "WZNS" in the text.

15. All three stories have been translated by Ronald R. Janssen and Jian Zhang in their beautiful selection of Can Xue's stories entitled *Dialogues in Paradise*. However, because of the need for close textual analysis, I have decided to use my own translations.

16. Sima Xiangru (179–117 B.C.)wrote: "One relies on the elegant lute to change the tone; / Music of melancholy longing should not last long" (*Yuan yachin yi biandiao*, / *zou chousi bu kechang*).

17. A socialist-realist novel written by Hao Ran during the 1960's, for example, is entitled *Yanyang tian* (Bright sunny day).

18. "The red sun" (*hong taiyang*) appeared in a song entitled "The East Is Red" (*Dongfang hong*). During the Cultural Revolution, it was a daily ritual to sing this song in order to express loyalty to Chairman Mao.

19. "The reddest, reddest sun in our heart" (*women xinzhong zuihong zuihong de hong taiyang*) is an expression used by Lin Biao, the vice-president of the Communist party at the beginning of the Cultural Revolution, who excelled at flattering Mao Zedong. His expression, used in a speech he delivered on Tian'anmen Gate in 1966, was repeated by several million Red Guards and Chinese people during the Cultural Revolution. His skill at flattery, however, did not spare him from a tragic end. Politically dishonored, he died in a mysterious airplane crash in Mongolia in 1969.

20. Paul Valéry, "La Jeune Parque."

21. The Chinese character *xiong* designates not only the chest but also the breast.

22. See Wilhelm.

23. Irigaray, *Speculum*, pp. 227–40.

24. Ibid., p. 227.

25. See Irigaray's two books, *The Speculum* and *This Sex*.

26. Irigaray, *Amante marine*.

27. Irigaray, *Speculum*, pp. 243–364.

28. Irigaray, *Je, tu, nous*.

29. Irigaray, *This Sex*, pp. 23–33.

30. Irigaray, *Je, tu, nous*, p. 24.

31. See Zhu Ling.

32. Irigaray, *Speculum*, p. 238.

33. "The name of the father"—a Lacanian notion—is used by Irigaray to refer to the law or central authority of a patriarchal order, especially in the context of Christianity. See Irigaray, "Return to the Name of the Father," in *Speculum*, pp. 346–53.

34. Irigaray, *Speculum*, p. 238.   35. Irigaray, *This Sex*, p. 30.

36. Irigaray, *Speculum*, p. 200.   37. Irigaray, *This Sex*, p. 79.

38. In his essay, Li Tuo (p. 10) chose Yu Hua as the best model for experimental fiction. He also mentions several other experimental writers, such as Ye Zhaoyan, Ge Fei, and Sun Ganlu—all of them men.

39. Engels, p. 129.

40. For a conceptualization of the relationship between gender hierarchy and other social inequalities, see Lauretis, p. 5.

41. Irigaray, *Je, tu, nous*, p. 34.

42. Ibid., p. 34.

43. Wang Xiaoming ("Pibeide xinling," p. 73) uses Can Xue as an example of the limitations of women's works. In Wang's opinion, Can Xue cannot write true masterpieces because she is too radically individualistic. Given that individualism is a highly valued ideology among Chinese intellectuals of the post-Mao era, this criticism sounds surprisingly out of touch—especially coming from an avant-garde critic. However, there is a certain truth in Wang's comment, since Can Xue's solipsism indeed imposes limitations upon her works—but not exactly in the sense of Wang's interpretation. Instead of writing as a man, as this male critic expects of a woman writer, Can Xue probably needs to acknowledge her specificity as a woman writer more publicly in order to overcome the limitations imposed by the solipsistic nature of her writings.

44. Can Xue, *Tuwei biaoyan*, pp. 332–51.

45. Ibid., p. 333.

46. Ibid., p. 336.

47. Ibid., p. 340.

Chapter 4

1. Zhaxi Dawa, "Jizai pishengzi shang de hun" (Souls tied to the knots of a leather rope), in Tai; hereinafter cited as *Spring Bamboo* in the text.

2. Zhaxi Dawa, "Fengma zhiyao" (Brilliance of wind and horse), in Huang and Li, *Zhongguo xiaoshuo yijiubaqi*.

3. For example, Tabei, the hero of "Souls Tied to the Knots of a Leather Rope," dies with the delusion that he has found the heavenly voice, which, according to the narrator, is actually the voice of American radio announcing the opening of the Olympic Games.

4. "Brilliance of Wind and Horse."

5. Ibid.

6. Wu Jin's intent to murder in "Brilliance of Wind and Horse" embraces archaic Tibetan cultural values in terms of family revenge, Tabei in "Souls Tied to the Knots of a Leather Rope" searches for the religious Tibet of the past, and Sangjie in "Invitation of the Century" journeys to a historical Tibet.

7. Zhaxi Dawa, "Shiji zhiyao" (Invitation of the century), in Lu Fang; hereinafter cited as *SJZY* in the text.

8. Márquez.   9. Ibid., p. 381.

10. Ibid., p. 383.   11. González Echevarría, p. 26.

12. Minta, p. 37.   13. Ibid., p. 64.

14. Žižek, "Beyond Discourse-Analysis," p. 252.

15. The narrator in "Souls Tied to the Knots of a Leather Rope" ends the story by identifying with the protagonist in order to repeat the same journey. Sangjie's kite in "Invitation of the Century" returns to his hand at the end of the story. Wu Jin in "Brilliance of Wind and Horse" is deciding what he will do with his life at the end of the story, exactly as he was at the beginning. *Tibet: Mysterious Years* starts with the settlement of Ciren Jiemu's family on top of the mountains because of her required devotion to the hermit and ends in another Ciren Jiemu's suggested devotion to the same hermit.

16. Zhaxi Dawa, *Xizang: yinmi de suiyue* (Tibet: mysterious years), in Wu Liang et al., *Mohuan xianshi zhuyi xiaoshuo*; hereinafter cited as *XZ* in the text.

Chapter 5

EPIGRAPH: Sedgwick, p. 15.   1. Ibid., p. 20.

2. Ibid., p. 4.   3. *Analects*, 17.23.

4. The *Jin Ping Mei* (Golden lotus) was compiled by Lanling Xiaoxiaosheng at the end of the sixteenth century. Ximen Qing, the lewd hero, makes love to his six wives and numerous female as well as several male servants. In the *Honglou meng* (Dream of the red chamber), a novel written by Cao Xueqin in the eighteenth century, Jia Baoyu, the adolescent hero, is the only male member in his family's garden, where his female cousins and maids live. He is famous for his tender attachment to girls in the family. At the same time, the only sexual bonds he has outside the family are with male friends. See my *Rose and Lotus*.

5. One of Mao Zedong's poems praises militiawomen for "preferring military uniforms to feminine dresses" (*bu'ai hongzhuang ai wuzhuang*).

6. Liu Shaoqi.

7. See my essay "How Do You Tell a Girl from a Boy?"

8. See Yue.

9. See Zhu Ling.

10. All three novellas are included in Su Tong; hereinafter cited as QQCQ.

11. "La féminité s'y prête: emprunte tout ce qu'on lui attribue, impose. N'est rien qu'un lieu de substitution entre? Suppléance, cache ou toile vacants pour productions et reproductions. Peut feindre—le hasard. Mais revient à une machine construite des mains de fer de la nécessité" (Irigaray, *Amante marine*, p. 119).

12. Ibid., p. 119.

13. Oral sex was called "playing the flute" (*chuixiao*) in traditional China.

14. Doane, pp. 2–3.

15. Žižek, *The Sublime Object*.

16. *Shuai* was originally read as *sai*. But in modern times, people commonly identify this character with *shuai*, which means decline, waning, or withering.

17. The narrator often changes pronouns for no apparent reason.

18. I borrow this word from Žižek ("Beyond Discourse-Analysis," p. 251), who describes Laclau's notion of the subject position in terms of the Lacanian concept of "the empty space" "in its confrontation with the antagonism, the subject which isn't covering up the traumatic dimension of social antagonism." In other words, Chencao has no subject position because he refuses to position himself in any antagonism either against his legal father's patriarchal economy or against his former friend's Communist ideology. As a result, he will never be in a position of thinking about "achieving an identity with (him)self"—according to Žižek's logic.

19. Butler, p. 133.   20. See note 4 to this chapter.

21. Meyer, p. 282.   22. Sedgwick, p. 40.

Chapter 6

1. Meisner, p. 317.

2. In the White Terror of 1927–30 initiated by the Nationalist government against the Communist party, hundreds of thousands were killed (ibid., p. 27). During the first three years of the People's Republic of China, two million so-called class enemies were executed, according to the estimate of many relatively impartial observers (ibid., p. 81). Hun-

dreds of thousands of innocent people died during the Cultural Revolution and the Tian'anmen Square Incident.

3. See the article by the Department of Propaganda of the Beijing Municipal Party Committee (Beijing shiwei xuanchuan bu), which called the activists of this movement mainly "criminals who were released from prison without being completely reformed, members of political rascal clans, and the remnants of the Gang of Four, a tiny number of bad elements, and dregs of society."

4. Žižek, *Sublime Object*, p. 132.

5. Meisner, pp. 316–17.

6. Žižek, *Sublime Object*, p. 132.

7. Ibid., p. 134.

8. Ibid., p. 135.

9. See *Beijing wenxue* 1989, no. 6.

10. Yu, *Shishi ruyan* (Life in the world resembles smoke), in Huang and Li, *Zhongguo xiaoshuo yijiubaba*, pp. 172–212; hereinafter cited as *SSRY*.

11. Yu, "Ouran shijian" (An accident); hereinafter cited as "ORSJ" in the text.

12. Written from the perspective of the madman, who feels a strong threat to his life from traditional society, Lu Xun's story is much more subjective and hopeful than that of his contemporary follower (Yu Hua told me that Lu Xun is his favorite modern Chinese writer). Despite the threatening atmosphere, "The Diary" ends on an optimistic note: "Please save the children" (Lu Xun, 1:433).

13. Dai Jinhua, p. 29.

14. In *Life in the World Resembles Smoke*, three young girls (*shaonü*) die. At the beginning and the end, the narrator repeats the same sentence: "At the riverside, the bright pink blossoms are blooming" (*SSRY*, pp. 173, 212). Dressed in a bright red sweater, 6's daughter, who has also drowned herself in the river, lies dead under a peach tree at the riverside (p. 207).

15. Li Ruihuan, the Chinese vice-premier, for example, supported his argument for military intervention by emphasizing the price they had paid to gain political power.

16. Lu Xun, 7:81.

17. Suleiman.

18. Bataille, p. 42.

19. "If we observe the taboo, if we submit to it, we are no longer conscious of it. But in the act of violating it we feel the anguish of mind without which the taboo could not exist: that is the experience of sin. That experience leads to the completed transgression, the successful

transgression which, in maintaining the prohibition, maintains it in order to benefit from it" (ibid., p. 38).

20. Ibid., p. 39.

Conclusion

1. Engels.
2. On this subject, see Funk and Mueller.
3. Laclau, pp. 89–92.
4. Concerning the problem of salvation, see my introduction to *Gender and Sexuality*.

Bibliography

Anderson, Marston. *The Limits of Realism: Chinese Fiction in the Revolutionary Period*. Berkeley: University of California Press, 1990.

———. "The Morality of Form: Lu Xun and the Modern Chinese Short Story." In Leo Ou-fan Lee, ed., *Lu Xun and His Legacy*. Berkeley: University of California Press, 1985.

Ban Gu, ed. *Hanshu yiwen zhi* (History of the Former Han: treatise on writings). Hong Kong: Taiping shuju, 1963.

Barmé, Geremie, and Linda Jaivin, eds. *New Ghosts, Old Dreams: Chinese Rebel Voices*. New York: Random House, 1992.

Bataille, Georges. *Eroticism: Death and Sensuality*. San Francisco: City Lights, 1986.

Beijing shiwei xuanchuan bu (Department of Propaganda of the Beijing Municipal Party Committee). "Guanyu zai Beijing fasheng de fangeming shijian de shishi" (Facts about the counterrevolutionary event in Beijing). *Renmin ribao* (People's daily), June 10, 1989.

Beijing wenxue (Beijing literature), June 1989.

Butler, Judith. "Variations of Sex and Gender: Beauvoir, Wittig, and Foucault." In Seyla Benhabib and Drucilla Cornell, eds., *Feminism as Critique*. Minneapolis: University of Minnesota Press, 1988.

Cai Xiang. "Qing yu yu de duili: dangdai xiaoshuo zhong de jingshen wenhua xianxiang" (Conflicts between love and lust: a spiritual and cultural phenomenon in contemporary fiction). *Wenxue pinglun*, Mar. 1988: 36–43.

Can Xue. *Dialogues in Paradise.* Trans. Ronald R. Janssen and Jian Zhang. Evanston, Ill.: Northwestern University Press, 1989.

———. *Tuwei biaoyan* (Performance of breaking out of an encirclement). Shanghai: Shanghai wenyi chubanshi, 1990.

Cheng Depei. "Zhenmo Can Xue de meng" (The Dream That Tortures Can Xue). *Shanghai wenxue,* June 1987: 71–72.

Cheng Yongxin, ed. *Zhongguo xinchao xiaoshuo xuan* (Selections of new-wave short stories in China). Shanghai: Shanghai shehui kexueyuan chubanshe, 1989.

Chow, Rey. *Woman and Chinese Modernity.* Minneapolis: University of Minnesota Press, 1991.

———. *Writing Diaspora: Tactics of Intervention in Contemporary Cultural Studies.* Bloomington: Indiana University Press, 1993.

Chow Tse-tsung. *The May Fourth Movement: Intellectual Revolution in Modern China.* Cambridge, Mass.: Harvard University Press, 1960.

Cihai: yuci bufen. 2 vols. Shanghai: Shanghai shangwu, 1981.

Dai Jinhua. "Liegu de lingyi cepan" (On the other side of the rift valley). *Beijing wenyi* 1989, no. 6.

Dai Qing. "Chonghun zui" (Double-marriage criminals). *Nüxing ren* 1989, no. 2.

———, ed. *Xing kaifang nüzi* (Sexually liberated woman). Hong Kong: Yiwen tushu, 1988.

Decker, Margaret. "Femininity as Imprisonment: Subjectivity, Agency, and Criminality in Ai Bei's Fiction." In Lu Tonglin, ed., *Gender and Sexuality in Twentieth-Century Chinese Literature and Society.*

Delannoi, Gil. "Nations et lumières: Des philosophes de la nation avant le nationalisme." In idem and Pierre-André Taguieff, eds. *Théorie du nationalisme: Nation, nationalité, ethnicité.* Paris: Kimé, 1991.

Ding Ling. *I Myself Am a Woman.* Trans. and ed. Tani Barlow and Gary Bjorge. Boston: Beacon Press, 1989.

Dirlik, Arif. *The Origins of Chinese Communism.* New York: Oxford University Press, 1989.

Doane, Mary Anne. *Femmes Fatales: Feminism, Film Theory, Psychoanalysis.* New York: Routledge, 1991.

Dong Xiao, Huang Ziping, Li Tuo, and Li Ziyun, eds. *Zhongguo xiaoshuo yijiubaliu* (Chinese fiction, 1986). Hong Kong: Sanlian, 1988.

Eide, Elizabeth. *China's Ibsen: From Ibsen to Ibsenism.* Scandinavian Institute of Asian Studies Monograph Series, no. 55. London: Curzon Press, 1987.

Engels, Frederick. *The Origin of the Family, Private Property and the State.*

Trans. Alec West. Rev. and ed. E. B. Leacock. New York: International Publishers, 1972.

Fan Keqiang. "Xungenzhe: yuanshiqingxiang yu banyuanshizhuyi" (Root-searchers: primitive tendency and semi-primitivism). *Shanghai wenxue*, Mar. 1989: 64–69.

Feng Deying. *Kucai hua* (Bitter flowers). Beijing: Jiefangjun wenyi, 1958.

Feuerwerker, Yi-tsi. *Ding Ling's Fiction: Ideology and Narrative in Modern Chinese Literature.* Cambridge, Mass.: Harvard University Press, 1982.

Funk, Nanette, and Magda Mueller, eds. *Gender Politics and Post-Communism: Reflections from Eastern Europe and the Former Soviet Union.* New York: Routledge, 1993.

González Echevarría, Roberto. *Myth and Archive: A Theory of Latin American Narrative.* Cambridge, Eng.: Cambridge University Press, 1990.

Gu Yanwu. *Rizhilu* (Notes on daily topics). Shanghai: Shanghai guji, 1985.

Guo Xiaodong. "Muxing tuteng: zhiqing wenxue de yizhong jingshen biange" (Totem of motherhood: a spiritual variation of literature among the educated young). *Shanghai wenxue*, Jan. 1987: 90–96.

Hu Shi. "Yipusheng zhuyi" (Ibsenism). *Xin qingnian*, June 15, 1918, 489–507.

———. *Zhongguo gudian xiaoshuo yanjiu* (A study of the classical Chinese novel). Taipei: Yuanliu, 1986.

Huang Ziping and Li Tuo, eds. *Zhongguo xiaoshuo yijiubaba* (Chinese fiction, 1988). Hong Kong: Sanlian, 1989.

———. *Zhongguo xiaoshuo yijiubaqi* (Chinese fiction, 1987). Hong Kong: Sanlian Press, 1989.

Irigaray, Luce. *Amante marine de Friedrich Nietzsche.* Paris: Minuit, 1980.

———. *Je, tu, nous: Pour une culture de la différence.* Paris: Bernard Grasset, 1990.

———. *Speculum of the Other Woman.* Trans. Gillian C. Gill. Ithaca, N.Y.: Cornell University Press, 1985.

———. *This Sex Which Is Not One.* Trans. Catherine Porter. Ithaca, N.Y.: Cornell University Press, 1985.

Laclau, Ernesto. *New Reflections on the Revolution of Our Time.* London: Verso, 1990.

Laclau, Ernesto, and Chantal Mouffe. *Hegemony and Socialist Strategy: Towards a Radical Democratic Politics.* London: Verso, 1985.

Lau, Joseph, C. T. Hsia, and Leo Ou-fan Lee, trans. and eds. *Modern Chinese Stories and Novellas, 1919–1949*. New York: Columbia University Press, 1981.

Lauretis, Teresa de. *The Technologies of Gender: Essays on Theory, Film, and Fiction*. Bloomington: Indiana University Press, 1987.

Legge, James, trans. *The Chinese Classics*, Vol. 1, *Confucian Analects, The Great Learning, The Doctrine of the Mean*. Hong Kong: Hong Kong University Press, 1960.

Li Disheng, ed. *Xunzi jishi* (The *Xunzi*, with collected annotations). Taipei: Taiwan xuesheng, 1979.

Li Tuo. "Xue beng hechu" (Where did the avalanche start?). Preface to Yu Hua, *Shibasui chumen yuanxing* (To embark on a long journey at the age of eighteen). Taipei: Yuanliu, 1990.

Li Xiaojiang. *Xiawa de tansuo* (Eve's search). Zhengzhou: Henan renmin chubanshe, 1988.

Liang Bin. *Hongqi pu* (Genealogy of the red flag). Beijing: Zhongguo qingnian, 1957.

Liu Shaoqi. *Lun gongchandang ren de xiuyang* (On the cultivation of Communist party members). Beijing: Renmin chubanshe, 1962.

Liu Xie. *Wenxin diaolong* (The literary mind and the carving of dragons). Ed. and annot. Liu Yongji. Hong Kong: Zhonghua shuju, 1980.

Liu Xiaopo. "Shenmei yu chaoyue" (Aesthetics and sublimation). *Wenxue pinglun*, June 1988.

Lu Fang, ed. *Hese niaoqun* (A crowd of brown birds). Beijing: Bei shida, 1989.

Lu Tonglin. "How Do You Tell a Girl from a Boy? Uncertain Sexual Boundaries in *The Price of Frenzy*." In William Burgwinkle, Glenn Man, and Valerie Wayne, eds. *Significant Others: Gender and Literature East and West*. Manoa: University of Hawaii Press, 1993.

——. *Rose and Lotus: Narrative of Desire in France and China*. Albany: SUNY Press, 1991.

——, ed. *Gender and Sexuality in Twentieth-Century Chinese Literature and Society*. Albany: SUNY Press, 1993.

Lu Xun. *Lu Xun quanji* (Complete works of Lu Xun). 16 vols. Beijing: Renmin wenxue chubanshe, 1981.

Luo Guangbin and Yang Yi. *Hongyan* (Red rocks). Beijing: Zhongguo qingnian, 1961.

Mao Dun. "Ziran zhuyi yu Zhongguo xiandai xiaoshuo" (Naturalism and modern Chinese fiction). In *Zhongguo xin wenxue daxi* (A comprehensive anthology of new literature in China), vol. 2. Shanghai: Liangyou tushu yinshua gongsi, 1935.

Mao Zedong. *Mao Zedong xuanji* (Selected works of Mao Zedong). Beijing: Renmin chubanshe, 1969.

———. *Mao zhuxi shici* (Chairman Mao's poems). Beijing: Renmin wenxue chubanshe, 1962.

Marquez, Gabriel Garcia. *One Hundred Years of Solitude.* Trans. Gregory Rabassa. New York: Avon Books, 1970.

Meisner, Maurice. *Mao's China and After.* New York: Free Press, 1986.

Meng Yue and Dai Jinhua. *Fuchu lishi dibiao* (Emerging from the surface of history). Zhengzhou: Henan renmin chubanshe, 1989.

Meyer, Richard. "Rock Hudson's Body." In Diana Fuss, ed., *Inside/Out: Lesbian Theories, Gay Theories.* London: Routledge, 1991.

Minta, Stephen. *Garcia Marquez: Writer of Colombia.* New York: Harper and Row, 1987.

Mo Yan. *Touming de hongluobo* (Transparent red radish). Beijing: Zuojia chubanshe, 1985.

Nan'an wenshi ziliao (Historical documents of Nan'an), vol. 8. Special issue on Li Zhi. 1987.

Ouyang Xiu, ed. *Tangshu yiwen zhi* (History of the Tang: treatise on writings). Shanghai: Shangwu yinshuguan, 1936.

Peng Ruijin. *Taiwan xin wenxue yundong sishi nian* (Forty years of the new literature movement in Taiwan). Taipei: Zili wanpaoshe wenhua chubanshe, 1991.

Reiss, Tim. *Truth and Tragedy: Study in the Development of a Renaissance and Classical Discourse.* New Haven: Yale University Press, 1980.

Rosemont, Henry. *A Chinese Mirror: Moral Reflections on Political Economy and Society.* La Salle, Ill.: Open Court Publishing Company, 1991.

Salisbury, Harrison. *The New Emperors: China in the Era of Mao and Deng.* Boston: Little Brown, 1992.

Sedgwick, Eve Kosofsky. *Between Men: English Literature and Male Homosocial Desire.* New York: Columbia University Press, 1985.

Sima Xiangru. "Changmen fu" (Rhapsody on Changmen). *Guwen guanzhi* (Essence of classical prose). Beijing: Zhonghua shuju, 1959.

Spivak, Gayatri Chakravorty. "Three Women's Texts and a Critique of Imperialism." In Catherine Belsey and Jane Moore, eds., *The Feminist Reader: Essays in Gender and the Politics of Literary Criticism.* New York: Basil Blackwell, 1989.

Su Tong. *Qiqie chengqun* (Crowd of wives and concubines). Taipei: Yuanliu, 1990.

Suleiman, Susan Rubin. *Subversive Intent: Gender, Politics, and the Avant-Garde.* Cambridge, Mass.: Harvard University Press, 1990.

Tai, Jeanne, trans. and ed. *Spring Bamboo*. New York: Random House, 1989.

Tocqueville, Alexis de. *De la démocratie en Amérique*. Paris: J. Vrin, 1990.

Tu Wei-ming. *Neo-Confucian Thought in Action: Wang Yang-ming's Youth (1472–1509)*. Berkeley: University of California Press, 1976.

Vance, Eugene. "The Châtelain de Coucy: Enunciation and Story in Trouvère Lyric." In idem, *Marvelous Signals*. Lincoln: University of Nebraska Press, 1986.

Wang Xiaoming. "Bu xiangxin de he bu yuanyi xiangxin de: guanyu sanwei 'xungen' pai zuojia" (What one does not believe and what one does not want to believe: concerning the literary creation of three "root-searching writers"). *Wenxue pinglun* (Literary criticism), Mar. 1988: 23–27.

———. "Pibei de xinling" (Exhausted hearts). *Shanghai wenxue*, May 1988: 72–75.

Wang Yangming. *Chuanxi lu* (Instructions for practical living). Shanghai: Shangwu yinshuguan, 1927.

Wilhelm, Richard, trans. *The I Ching or Book of Changes*. Princeton: Princeton University Press, 1967.

Witke, Roxane. "Mao Tse-tung, Women and Suicide." In Marilyn B. Young, ed., *Women in China: Studies in Social Change and Feminism*. Ann Arbor: University of Michigan, Center for Chinese Studies, 1973.

Wolf, Margery. *Revolution Postponed*. Stanford: Stanford University Press, 1985.

Wu Liang, Zhang Ping, and Zong Renfa, eds. *Huangdan pai xiaoshuo* (Absurd fiction). Changchun: Shidai wenyi, 1988.

———. *Mohuan xianshi zhuyi xiaoshuo* (Magic realist fiction). Changchun: Shidai wenyi, 1988.

Yang Mo. *Qingchun zhige* (Song of youth). Beijing: Renmin chubanshe, 1960.

Yü Chün-fang. *The Renewal of Buddhism in China: Chu-hung and the Late Ming Synthesis*. New York: Columbia University Press, 1981.

Yu Hua. "Ouran shijian" (An accident). *Changcheng*, Jan. 1990: 32–49.

———. *Shibasui chumen yuanxing* (To embark on a long journey at the age of eighteen). Beijing: Zuojia chubanshe, 1989.

Yuan Jing. *Xin'ernü yingxiongzhuan* (New heroic biographies of sons and daughters). Beijing: Zhongguo qingnian, 1956.

Yue Ming-bao. "Gendering the Origins of Modern Chinese Fiction." In Lu Tonglin, ed., *Gender and Sexuality in Twentieth-Century Chinese Literature and Society*.

Zhang Jianye. *Li Zhi pingzhuan* (Annotated biography of Li Zhi). Fuzhou: Fujian renmin chubanshe, 1981.

Zhang Nuanxin. "Hongle gaoliang" (Reddening sorghum). *Dangdai dianying*, Jan. 1988: 55–56.

Zhang Zhizhong. *Mo Yan lun* (On Mo Yan). Beijing: Zhongguo shehui kexue yuan, 1990.

Zheng Xuan. "Shipu xu" (Preface to *Shipu*). In Mao Heng, ed., *Mao shi* (Mao's annotated edition of the *Book of Poetry*). Shandong: Youyi shushe, 1990.

Zhu Hong, trans. and ed. *The Chinese Western: An Anthology of Short Fiction*. New York: Ballantine, 1991.

Zhu Ling. "A Brave New World? On the Construction of 'Masculinity' and 'Femininity' in *The Red Sorghum Family*." In Lu Tonglin, ed., *Gender and Sexuality in Twentieth-Century Chinese Literature and Society*.

Žižek, Slavoj. "Beyond Discourse-Analysis." Appendix to Laclau, *New Reflections on the Revolution of Our Time*.

———. *For They Know Not What They Do*. London: Verso, 1991.

———. *The Sublime Object of Ideology*. London: Verso, 1989.

Character List

A Mei	阿梅
"A Mei zai yige taiyang tian li de chousi"	阿梅在一个太阳天里的愁思
"A Q zhengzhuan ewenban qian-yan"	阿Q正传俄文版前言
ai	爱
aiqing jidang	爱情激荡
Ba Jin	巴金
Bai Liping	白丽萍
baiguan	稗官
baihua xiaoshuo	白话小说
Ban Gu	班固
banlian yishu	板脸艺术
banlu	半路
Bayue de xiangcun	八月的乡村
bei fuyu le shengming he yizhi de	被赋与了生命和意志的
Beijing shiwei xuanchuanbu	北京市委宣传部
Beijing wenxue	北京文学
bi ye zhengming hu	必也正名乎
bing de guangyan	冰的光焰
bu'ai hongzhuang ai wuzhuang	不爱红装爱武装
bupo buli	不破不立
bu yiyang	不一样
Can Xue	残雪

Cao Xueqin	曹雪芹
Changcheng	长城
Chaxiang	察香
chen	沉
Chen Duxiu	陈独秀
Chen Feipu	陈飞浦
Chen He	陈河
Chen Mao	陈茂
Chen Zuoqian	陈佐千
Chencao	沉草
Cheng Depei	程德培
Cheng Yongxin	程永新
chenhe	沉河
"Chenlun"	沉沦
chensi	沉思
chiren de jiahuo	吃人的家伙
"Chonghun zui"	重婚罪
chousi	愁思
chuanqi	传奇
chuantong	传统
chuhu yiliao de yingjun nianqing	出乎意料的英俊年轻
chuiluo	垂落
chuixiao	吹箫
Chunlan	春兰
Ciren Jiemu	次仁吉姆
Cong nuli dao jiangjun	从奴隶到将军
cong yinxue li bagui wa chulai	从阴穴里把鬼挖出来
Cuihuahua	翠花花
cunliren xingxu neng lijie	村里人兴许能理解
Dagou	大狗
Dai Jinhua	戴锦华
Dai Qing	戴晴
Dalang	达朗
dao	道
daren	大人
Daxue	大学
diao	鸟
Ding Ling	丁玲
di wu dai	第五代
dixia le jige shuizhu	滴下了几个水珠
"Dongfang hong"	东方红

Duanwu jie	端午节
duhai renmin de jingshen yapian	毒害人民的精神鸦片
duyi wu'er	独一无二
fan	蕃
feng	风
Feng Deying	冯德英
Feng Menglong	冯梦龙
"Fengma zhiyao"	风马之耀
fulao xiongdi	父老兄弟
Ge Fei	格非
gei youren	给友人
geming langman zhuyi	革命浪漫主义
gexing jiefang de xianfeng	个性解放的先锋
Gu Yanwu	顾炎武
guiju	规距
"Gujin xiaoshuo xu"	古今小说序
"Guxiang"	故乡
Hanshu "Yiwen zhi"	汉书艺文志
Hao Ran	浩然
He Xinyin	何心隐
hejiu	喝酒
henyou xinji	很有心计
Hong'er	宏儿
Hong gaoliang	红高粱
Hong gaoliang jiazu	红高粱家族
Honglou meng	红楼梦
Hongqi pu	红旗谱
hong taiyang	红太阳
Hongyan	红岩
houbu daotai	候补道台
Hu Shi	胡适
huai fenzi	坏分子
Huangdan pai xiaoshuo	荒延派小说
huangman	荒蛮
huanyou kuangxiangzheng de nüren	患有狂想症的女人
huihuang	辉煌
huihuang de shuse	辉煌的曙色
hunshen doushi nazhong yanwei'er	浑身都是那种烟味儿
Ji Yun	纪昀
Jia	家

Jia Baoyu	贾宝玉
Jiang Hua	江华
Jiang Long	姜龙
Jiang Piao	江飘
Jiang Yongquan	姜永泉
Jiangjie	江姐
Jiayang Bandan	加央班丹
jiduan chouhen jiduan re'ai	极端仇恨极端热爱
jiepo ziji	解剖自己
jile yiceng huichen	积了一层灰尘
Jin Shengtan	金圣叹
jingxiang	镜象
Jin Ping Mei	金瓶梅
Jishi xiaoshuo	记实小说
"Jizai pishengzi shang de hun"	系在皮绳子上的魂
Juansheng	涓生
"Juansheng shouji"	涓生手记
Juanzi	娟子
jun dai zi er weizheng, zi jiang xixian	君待子而为政, 子将奚先
junjun, chenchen, fufu, zizi	君君, 臣臣, 父父, 子子
kaozheng	考证
ke'ai de qi'er	可爱的弃儿
kexiao	可笑
kongkong dangdang	空空荡荡
"Kuangren riji"	狂人日记
"Kuangye li"	旷野里
Kucai hua	苦菜花
kuishikuang	窥视狂
"Lan bai ranfang"	蓝白染房
Lanling Xiaoxiaosheng	兰陵笑笑生
laoye	老爷
Li Dazhao	李大钊
Li Ruihuan	李瑞环
Li Tuo	李陀
Li Xiaojiang	李小江
Li Zhi	李贽
liehuo	烈火
Liji	礼记
Lin Daojing	林道静
lingdao tongzhi zhanyu	领导同志战友

Liu Chencao	刘沉草
Liu Laoxia	刘老侠
Liu Luohan	刘罗汉
Liu Suola	刘索拉
Liu Suzi	刘素子
Liu Xiaopo	刘晓波
Liu Xie	刘勰
Liu Yanyi	刘演义
Liumeng	流氓
Lu Fang	卢方
Lu Jiachuan	卢家川
Lu Xun	鲁迅
Lu Xun jingshen	鲁迅精神
lunhui	轮回
Lunyu	论语
Luo Dafang	罗大方
"Mama de xiezi"	妈妈的鞋子
mangyuan	茫远
Mao Dun	茅盾
Mao Zedong	毛泽东
"Maodun lun"	矛盾论
maowenti	毛文体
Meishan	梅珊
meiyou guizu de shidai	没有贵族的时代
menglong	朦胧
Meng Yue	孟悦
mianfen	面粉
Mima	米玛
ming	名
Mo Yan	莫言
mohu	模糊
"*Mudan ting xu*"	牡丹亭序
Nahan	呐喊
"Nala zouhou zenyang"	娜拉走后怎样
nali shi zuo shengyi de liaozi	哪里是做生意的料子
Nan'an wenshi ziliao	南安文史资料
nanren dou buru ni	男人都不如你
nanxing xiangzheng	男性象征
neng	能
ni duiwo you shenmo yijian	你对我有什么意见
niao	鸟

shangzhong nong	上中农
shaonü	少女
Shenzong shilu	神宗实录
shifen pingchang	十分平常
shifen youmei	十分优美
shiguan	史官
shijie hui bian de meili yixie	世界会变得美丽一些
Shijing	诗经
"Shiji zhiyao"	世纪之邀
shiluan zhongqi	始乱终弃
shi qi de neixin gandao shifen wennuan	使 7 的内心感到十分温暖
"Shishi ruyan"	世事如烟
shiyan xiaoshuo	实验小说
shi yan zhi	诗言志
Shouhuo	收获
shouzu	手足
shuai	衰
shuaicao (saicao)	蓑草
shuaichen	衰沉
shuiguo	水果
"*Shuihu* dufa"	水浒读法
Shuisheng	水生
shuixing	水性
Shujing	书经
sihuo	死火
Sima Xiangru	司马相如
Songlian	颂莲
Su Tong	苏童
Sun Ganlu	孙甘露
Tabei	塔贝
taiyang tian	太阳天
Taiyang zhaozai Sanggan heshang	太阳照在桑干河上
tamen haha daxiao tamen haotao daku	它们哈哈大笑它们嚎啕大哭
tamen rangwo bani shale	他们让我把你杀了
tamen zai nainai de yanli panjie cheng she yiyang de yituan, yu hulala de shenzhan kailai	它们在奶奶的眼里盘结成蛇一样的一团又呼啦啦地伸展开来
Tang Xianzu	湯显祖
"*Tangshu* Yiwen zhi"	唐书艺文志

teshu de zaoxing lunkuo	特殊的造形轮廓
tiaopi de piaodong	挑皮的飘动
"Tongxin pian"	童心篇
Tuwei biaoyan	突围表演
wan'er bu wawa	玩儿布娃娃
Wang Shifu	王实甫
Wang Yangming	王阳明
wei nüzi yu xiaoren nan yang ye	唯女子与小人难养也
wei women suo weijing shenghuo guo de	为我们所未经生活过的
weiyi	唯一
wen	文
Wenxin diaolong	文心雕龙
wenxue geming	文学革命
wen yi zaidao	文以载道
wen yi zaidao ming qi dang ran	文以载道明其当然
women xinzhong zuihong zuihong de hong taiyang	我们心中最红最红的红太阳
wo qingqing de dui ziji shuo wo shuo jiu zheyang	我轻轻地对自己说我说就这样
wo shale ni	我杀了你
wo shuo bu qing	我说不清
wo xiang genta daqiu zenmo bata shale	我想跟他打球怎么把他杀了
"Wo zai nage shijie li de shiqing—gei youren"	我在那个世界里的事情—给友人
"Wo ziji yuanyi de meng"	我自己愿意的梦
Wu Jin	乌金
xiang	想
xiang shuiguo yiyang ganmei	象水果一样甘美
xiangtong	相通
xiang yige ren zhengzai pingjing de siqu	象一个人正在平静的死去
xiang yizhenzhen cong jiangmian shang chui guo de feng	象一阵阵从江面上吹过的风
xianzhi	先知
xiao (flute)	箫
xiao (small, petty)	小
Xiao Jun	肖军
Xiaomei	小梅
xiaoren	小人

xiaoshuo	小说
xiaoxin yiyi	小心翼翼
xiao yingxiong	小英雄
Ximen Qing	西门庆
Xin'ernü yingxiong zhuan	新儿女英雄传
Xing kaifang nüzi	性开放女子
xingku	辛苦
xingku mamu	辛苦麻木
xingku zhanzhuan	辛苦展转
xingku ziwei	辛苦恣睢
xingxu	兴许
Xin qingnian	新青年
xinren	新人
xinwenhua yundong	新文化运动
xiong	胸
"*Xixiang* dufa"	西厢读法
Xixiang ji	西厢记
"*Xixiang ji* pingdian"	西厢记评点
Xizang yinmi suiyue	西藏隐秘岁月
Xu Guangping	许广平
"Xue"	雪
xungen wenxue	寻根文学
Xunzi	荀子
"Yadang de kunhuo"	亚当的困惑
Yan Shiqu	颜师古
Yan'er	雁儿
Yang Mo	杨沫
yanggang zhiqi	阳刚之气
"Yanggang zhiqi yu wenxue piping de hao shiguang"	阳刚之气与文学批评的好时光
Yanyang tian	艳阳天
ye	野
Ye Zhaoyan	叶兆言
yeshi	野史
yeyu wenhua shenghuo	业余文化生活
yichang meili	异常美丽
yige shuzhi	一个树枝
yijian	意见
Yijing	易经
Yijiusansinian de taowan	一九三四年的逃亡
Yingsu zhijia	罂粟之家

"Yingying zhuan"	莺莺传
"Yipusheng zhuyi"	易卜生主义
yishi zhi huan	一世之患
Yu Dafu	郁达夫
Yu Hua	余华
Yu Zhan'ao	余占鳌
Yuan Zhen	元稹
yuan yaqin yi biandiao, zou chousi bu kechang	援雅琴以变调, 奏愁思不可长
Yue Fei	岳飞
Yuntao	运涛
"Zai Yan'an wenyi zuotanhui shang de jianghua"	在延安文艺座谈会上的讲话
Zaochun eryue	早春二月
zashi	杂史
Zhang Junzhao	张军钊
Zhang Nuanxi	张暖忻
Zhang Yimou	张艺谋
zhansi shachang	战死杀场
Zhaxi Dawa	扎西达娃
"Zhemo Can Xue de meng"	折磨残雪的梦
Zheng Xuan	郑玄
zhengming	正名
"Zhengming pian"	正名篇
zhenshi	真实
zhenti	真谛
"Zhenyang fenxi nongcun jieji"	怎样分析农村阶级
zheshi wei shenmo wei shenmo	这是为什么为什么
zhiqing wenxue	知青文学
Zhongguo funü	中国妇女
Zhongguo gudian xiaoshuo	中国古典小说
Zhongguo xiaoshuo shilüe	中国小说史略
Zhongguo xiaoshuo yijiubaliu	中国小说1986
Zhongguo xiaoshuo yijiubaqi	中国小说1987
Zhongguo xiaoshuo yijiubaba	中国小说1988
Zhongguo xinchao xiaoshuo xuan	中国新潮小说选
Zhongshan	钟山
Zhu Xi	朱熹
"Zhufu"	祝福
"Zhuzi wannian dinglun"	朱子晚年定论

ziji de xiangfa	自己的想法
Zijun	子君
Ziye	子夜
zongzi	粽子
zui	最
zui choulou	最丑陋
zui fengfu	最丰富
zui jiben	最基本
zui meili	最美丽
zui shengdong	最生动
zuoce	作册

Index

In this index an "f" after a number indicates a separate reference on the next page, and an "ff" indicates separate references on the next two pages. A continuous discussion over two or more pages is indicated by a span of page numbers, e.g., "57–59." *Passim* is used for a cluster of references in close but not consecutive sequence.

"Adam's Bewilderment" ("Yadang de kunhuo"), 14, 79
Ambiguity, 77
Analects (Confucius), 9
Anderson, Marston, 41
Anti-Japanese war, 52
Antonioni, Michelangelo, 78

Ba Jin, 34
Ban Gu, 10
Bataille, Georges, 176–77
Beliefs: ideological, 39, 45, 54, 100–102, 114, 163–64, 182–83; objectified, 182–83
"The Biography of Yingying" (Yuan Zhen), 47–48
Bitter Flowers (Feng Deying), 52–62 *passim*
Black magic, 136, 164

Book of Changes (*Yijing*), 93
Butler, Judith, 150

Camouflage, 82f
Can Xue: double subversion, 22, 76–77; criticism, 22, 74–79 *passim*, 100; language, 76–81 *passim*, 86, 92, 95, 99–100; marginality, 79, 101; Mother–daughter relationship, 98; art of putting on a stern facial expression (*banlian yishu*), 102–3
—works: "A Mei's Melancholy Thoughts on a Sunny Day" ("A Mei zai yige taiyang tian li de chousi"), 80–83; "Aura of Dynamic Masculinity and the Good Period of Literary Criticism" ("Yanggang zhiqi yu wenxue

Library of Congress
Cataloging-in-Publication Data

Lu, Tonglin.
Misogyny, cultural nihilism, and oppositional politics :
contemporary Chinese experimental fiction / Lu Tonglin.
p.   cm.
Includes bibliographical references and index.
ISBN 0-8047-2463-6 :   — ISBN 0-8047-2464-4 (pbk.) :
1. Chinese fiction—20th century—History and criticism.   2. Women
in literature.   I. Title.
PL2443.L8   1995
895.1'35209352042—dc20   94-22076   CIP

⊗This book is printed on acid-free paper.
It was typeset in 10/12.5 Bembo by Wilsted & Taylor.